4.18.79

BANKING TOMORROW

Managing Markets Through Planning

BANKING TOMORROW

Managing Markets Through Planning

Thomas W. Thompson, Ph.D.
Leonard L. Berry, D.B.A.
Philip H. Davidson, Ph.D.

VNR **VAN NOSTRAND REINHOLD COMPANY**
NEW YORK   CINCINNATI   ATLANTA   DALLAS   SAN FRANCISCO
LONDON   TORONTO   MELBOURNE

Van Nostrand Reinhold Company Regional Offices:
New York Cincinnati Atlanta Dallas San Francisco

Van Nostrand Reinhold Company International Offices:
London Toronto Melbourne

Library of Congress Catalog Card Number: 78-5987
ISBN : 0-442-80423-7

Manufactured in the United States of America

Published by Van Nostrand Reinhold Company
135 West 50th Street, New York, N. Y. 10020

Published simultaneously in Canada by Van Nostrand Reinhold Ltd.

15 14 13 11 10 9 8 7 6 5 4 3 2 1

Library of Congress Cataloging in Publication Data
Thompson, Thomas William, 1934–
    Banking tomorrow.

    Includes index.
    1. Bank management. 2. Banks and banking—Planning.
3. Bank marketing. I. Berry, Leonard L., 1942–
joint author. II. Davidson, Philip H., joint author.
III. Title.
HG1615.T48   658'.91'3321   78-5987
ISBN 0-442-80423-7

This book was not written in a weekend. Nor was it written in two weekends. To our wives and our children, who understood and supported our commitment to this time-comsuming project, we dedicate this book.

PREFACE

Banking Tomorrow is a how-to book on planning. It is based on our understanding of planning theory and on several years of experience in applying these principles in the real world of bank holding company operations. *It is about managing change.*

Most books on planning deal chiefly with the process: i.e., the reasons for initiating a plan, the techniques of planning, and the implementation of the plan. We covered this subject in a first book, tracing the values of planning, and then both explaining and exemplifying such essential steps as the setting of objectives and action strategies. However, our experiences caused us to write a second book—or, more precisely, to blend the first and second books together under a single title.

The subject of the second book is the application of planning techniques to the actual process by which banking's human resources, *its people*, deliver need-satisfying financial services to customers in the most efficient and profitable manner. Each element in this equation was recognized.

Blending these two books together is the unique framework or structure for strategic planning presented in Chapter 9. Neither the analysis of environmental developments or the formulation of strategic responses can be done effectively in a vacuum or on an ad hoc basis. There must be a comprehensible and relevant structure that consistently ties together environmental developments and the multitude of internal responses. This structure simultaneously must be able to cope with the full range of external circumstances as well as the full range of banking activities—from lending to operations to personnel. Without such structure, studies of the environment and strategic responses lack coordination, precision and effectiveness.

Based on the expected future of banking's environment and on banking's areas of activity, it is our contention that the appropriate structure is provided through the *markets approach to planning*. By identifying the principal markets in which banks function and developing environmental analyses and strategic plans in terms of these markets, a useful framework is created. The foundation of the principal markets approach to planning is that the marketplace is where change occurs. It is where external developments have their impact—on banks and on their customers. This approach focuses on the fundamental reality that the customer is the business. Unless a bank recognizes its customers' changing needs and how to satisfy those needs efficiently, it will not achieve acceptable levels of performance.

The three principal markets are those for customers (commercial and retail), investors and people resources. In each case it is anticipated that performing in these markets will be more competitive and more challenging in the future. Thus, accurately assessing these changes and developing efficient and effective strategies in a systematic and coordinated fashion is the key to performance. These concepts are presented in detail in Chapter 9, in between the two books. Unfortunately, there is no clearly "best" position for this Chapter in the book. We think its position between the "two books" is desirable. Others, however, may find it more valuable to read Chapter 9 after Chapter 2. That choice is left to the reader.

A critical step in the planning process calls for conducting an *environmental analysis*. The objectives, action strategies, and implementation procedures or tactics that follow are constructed on a realistic assessment of the existing socioeconomic, legislative-regulatory, competitive, and technological parameters that comprise the banking environment. Probable changes based chiefly on current, discernible trends also influence this assessment as, frankly, do more visionary projections.

In *Banking Tomorrow* we have conducted an environmental analysis. Although our reading of banking's future may not be totally accurate in all of its particulars, nonetheless it is this kind of analysis that gives real meaning to a book on planning. It shifts the focus from principles to applications, from theory to action— demonstrating that *planning is managing*.

The task of managing the results of an environmental analysis in a systematic manner led us to develop a series of action strategies applicable to bank employees and bank customers. The approach we took in doing this required a good deal of stage-setting.

A reasonable projection of where banking most likely will be tomorrow evolves from an understanding of where it is today and how it reached this point. Some readers may find that this historical perspective either contains much familiar material or that they understand the past and present quite well because they have lived through it. However, other readers will find it a necessary reference. This especially seems the case if they are readily to understand the evolution of significant alterations in banking practice (such as, NOW Accounts or greater degrees of consumerist regulation) and, of course, their longer-term implications.

A book of this size and scope imposes certain limitations. A few of them should be pointed out.

First, in applying the planning process to banking's customer markets we generally have concentrated on the application of objectives and action strategies to retail and commercial customers. Quite clear, however, is the need to consider distinctively such key operational areas as trust banking, international banking, and the widening field of bank-related activities (i.e., factoring or lease financing).

Second, we have not dwelled at any great length on EFT and the transition to a world of electronic banking; however, we have acknowledged the pervasive influence of the on-going technological revolution, as symbolized by EFT, in shaping banking's future. We are also fully aware that innovations and developments in this area are literally changing overnight. This fact is a good reason for planning and preparedness.   It also seems a good reason for emphasizing principles and trendlines and downplaying specifics.

Another limitation is that an environmental analysis necessarily will be influenced by what is happening *now* in terms of the economy, the competitive practices of nonbank institutions, and current legislative and regulatory proposals.   What this means is that our status report is geared to conditions as they were at yearend 1977.   Some issues by now will have been outdated by the passage of time or the unfolding of new priorities. But again, this only implies the importance of the planning process as a discipline for managing change.

Finally, we readily admit that we have limited our book to commercial banking.   This limitation, however, should not be taken to infer that we have overlooked other financial institutions—e.g., savings banks, savings and loan associations, insurance companies, finance companies, brokerage firms, credit unions, factoring firms, and the like.   To the contrary, we have tried to assess what these competitors are doing and planning since these actions understandably impact banking.

This contention has two dimensions.   The first is that planning principles and applications affect banks *and* their competitors; this is especially so as many of these competitors continue to acquire banklike powers and, most notably, inclusion within the payments system.   Second, any evaluation of *Banking Tomorrow* is anchored in an appreciation of the competitive environment; in other words, what the competition is up to and what it wants shapes the future.

Going one logical further step, it is evident that not all banks are alike.   Consider, for example, industry attitudes toward such fundamental issues as branching, consumerism, automation, and NOW Accounts.   Disagreements among banks segmented by size and geographic location historically have been deep-felt and divisive.

In this respect, we have taken a big bank approach—*not advocacy, but approach*—chiefly because the complexity of the planning process is best illustrated by the activities of larger organizations, particularly those involved in both banking and bank-related activities. But the principles remain the same as they flow downward, only narrowing in scope as bank size and breadth of activity diminish.

Throughout *Banking Tomorrow*, we have followed the custom of labeling banks as big, medium-sized, and small. These terms are relative. A $500 million banking organization is hardly *big* by New York City standards. In Kansas, Idaho, or West Virginia, it not only would be a big institution but a dominant one. We leave it to the reader to draw distinctions in applying planning techniques and considering action strategies. But bear in mind that they are relevant irrespective of size and other criteria. Any doubters might think long and hard about the following prediction that frequently has been made by many of today's banking observers: The future will find our present number of 14,000 commercial banks at least halved. With this in mind, we are talking of a future considered within the traditional planning horizon.

The authors owe a particular debt of gratitude to Frederick Deane, Jr., chairman and president of Bank of Virginia Company. He believed in planning and provided a "greenhouse" in which theories could be nourished into workable procedures.

We also thank two bankers who reviewed our manuscript and took the time to critique it constructively. Henry V. Berry, senior vice-president, The Arizona Bank, and Dr. R. Pierce Lumpkin, senior vice-president, Bank of Virginia Company, were the best kind of reviewers: hard but friendly critics who asked nothing less than the best performance we were capable of offering. Our appreciation also is extended to Mrs. Cynthia James, Mrs. Alice Norris, and Ms. Sandra Highberger for their help in preparing our manuscript. Finally, we owe a number of friends and colleagues a special thanks. In so many cases, it was their response as bankers and bank customers that convinced us that *planning is managing*.

Richmond, Va.   T.W.T.
L.L.B.
P.H.D.

CONTENTS

BANKING TOMORROW

Managing Markets Through Planning

1 INTRODUCTION: THE ART OF MANAGING CHANGE

INTRODUCTION

What will tomorrow be like?

How often we ask this question in our personal and business lives. And all we really can conclude is that tomorrow will be different from today. *It will have changed.*

A very safe, odds-on bet is that the pace and degree of change occurring over the emerging generation will move faster and prove more profound than during the time span recognized as our present. Experience clearly supports this contention. It shows that change tends to precipitate greater change in geometric progression. Man's continuing achievements in the conquest of space aptly illustrate this point. Less than a half century after *The Spirit of St. Louis* crossed the Atlantic Ocean nonstop, *Apollo Fifteen* astronauts reached the moon; only a few years later the first Mars probe was launched.

Futurist W. W. Simmons adds this important dimension:

The conditions which bring about significant changes in our culture, as well as the nature of change itself, have become so accelerated in the past two decades, that a person entering almost any profession today can be assured of experiencing, within his own career, as much alteration in the conditions on

1

which his business depends, as have transpired since his grand-father started out . . .

This new pace forms the framework of competition and has thereby accelerated the amount of gains accruable to timely decisions as well as the costs of bad decisions . . . *Reaction to time and anticipation have become essential to business* [italics added].[1]

However, this is only one dimension; change is a coat of many colors and delicate shadings.

What will tomorrow be like? We don't know for sure. Massachusetts Institute of Technology professor Jay Forrester is said to view it this way: "We are living in a complex, rapidly changing, unpredictable environment, in which it is virtually impossible to predict our future with any degree of certainty. We only know," he adds, "that it will not be like the past, nor will it necessarily be what we think it is going to be."[2]

However, we can recognize certain trends or patterns of development that in their combination tell us a great deal about the future, particularly as it falls within a five- or ten-year time frame.

It is very probable, for example, that the business of banking will be "revolutionized" by a nationwide electronic funds transfer system that will break down geographic restraints against branching, while simultaneously enlarging the industry's customer and product base. It is probable that existing operational distinctions among types of financial institutions will continue to blur, ultimately fading into insignificance. Moreover, it seems reasonable that better educated and informed consumers will increase their demands for clearly stated, fair rates and for more equitable treatment; in "The Age of the People" nothing less can be expected.

It therefore can be ventured that banking's "tomorrow" assuredly will be characterized by the following features:

- *more competition*, especially in the retail banking field,
- *from more competitors*, including some which today are not considered competitors, notably the retail department store chains, and they will be
- *armed with more banklike powers.*

This is a plausible enough prediction. In fact, it could have been ventured in 1950 or 1960 and proven correct. The singular difference between then and now would have been the casting of *new* competitors. In the 1950s, commercial banking's leadership worried over the dynamic growth of the savings and loan business; a decade later, the credit union movement came striding boldly into the competitive arena, and by the 1970s the worry was, "alas, the retailers are coming."

UNCERTAINTY—THE CHILD OF CHANGE

More important, the actualization of these probable trends in turn will create other uncertainties. For example, what will be the implications of more competition from more competitors armed with more banklike powers? Will they combine to alter dramatically the world of the smaller, community-oriented financial institutions? Will they serve to promote greater concentrations of economic power in private sector institutions? Will they thereby provoke public sector responses in the form of additional, perhaps unnecessarily rigid regulatory constraints? Will they foster new methodologies for acquiring funds and allocating credit? What will they mean for pricing structures? And many more questions.

We don't know the answers for sure. But we can recognize that any predictable change, since it does break from current ways of thinking about things and doing them, generates additional layers of equally predictable uncertainties.

Most discernible trends, it should be added, are external. They are associated with the environment in which financial institutions operate. In this sense, they are beyond individual or institutional control. We can understand and cope with them; we can perhaps even influence the direction they take by implementing new rules of the road in a distinctive manner. But neither as banking, nor as a segment of this powerful and vital industry, can we alone fashion them. At best, trends are sound guides to decision making.

THE PAST AS PROLOGUE

Although tomorrow will be different, it nonetheless presumes a continuation of the present. This dimension of change is known;

it is a constant based on man's past experience. The past, even where we are today, is an accumulation of attitudes, perceptions, values, and judgments. It is a perceived, commonly shared, and deep-felt understanding about things. Experience also reveals that such feelings change slowly. Equally important, they remain pervasive in influencing both the pace and degree of change. Particularly, they tend to rebel against radical departures from what is considered the norm.

One understanding of banking that already has crossed many bridges along the difficult route from past to present is the idea of *diversity*.

As the editors of *The United States Investor/Eastern Banker* observed in a Bicentennial tribute:

What is very special about the American banking system is its diversity. Unlike Canada or England, our banking system is not a small core of very large banks operating a nationwide chain of branch offices. And no central bank competes with privately owned institutions in taking deposits or granting credit.

Diversity is the fact of more than 14,000 commercial banks and their (many thousand) branch offices, most independently owned and operated, and highly responsive to the diverse communities providing their leadership. Diversity is the side-by-side existence of money center giants with billions of dollars in deposits operating in national and international markets *and* small, community-oriented banks concerned with home and car loans, loans for crops and farm machinery, and school and hospital bond issues. . . .

Another element of diversity is the relationship of commercial banks—*call it interdependence*—with thousands of allied specialized lenders and financial service institutions. The American banking system in its truest perspective involves interaction between these many and varied types of financial institutions.

And finally, diversity is the fact that commercial banks (and certain other specialized lenders) are regulated by both Federal and State authorities. . . .

In sum, diversity is the power of private, individual decision making lodged in the management and stockholders of state and national banks; no less, it is the checks and balances exercised for the public interest by governmental authorities.[3]

If diversity is the singular value characterizing the American banking system, then we should not treat lightly the implications of changes that seemingly threaten its continuity.

For that matter, we cannot assume either easy or rapid acceptance of changes departing markedly from this time-sanctified tradition. Looking back from the vantage point of today, it is evident that much, if not most, of the financial industry's hostility to innovation can be traced to instinctive fears that new, possibly even better ways of serving customers would threaten diversity and its complex, workable checks-and-balances relationship. What toqk so long building and what is so well regarded evidently must work because it is there, because it simply exists.

The fact of diversity, and its axial position in the American banking system, also points to the multiplier effect inherent in change. Such a "watershed" step as moving from regulated (Regulation Q) to free-market interest rate structures on consumer savings would visibly shatter competitive relationships between commercial banks and thrift institutions on one hand, and among commercial banks grouped by size, location, and marketplace differences on the other. In turn, this sharp break with tradition could well affect how the many and varied types of financial institutions acquire funds and allocate credit.

On a larger scale, what has evolved over many generations commonly becomes structured, and rather rigidly at that. It is society. It is class and caste. It is a system of economic, political, religious, and social institutions that become intricately interrelated. It becomes an organized bulwark blocking forces for change. It intrinsically possesses a vested interest in preserving the *status quo*, thereby preserving itself. Paradoxically, both the need to change and resistance to change become institutionalized.

This means that while the future assuredly will be different, *just how different it can afford to be takes shape as an issue of paramount importance.*

THE CONSEQUENCES OF CHANGE

These observations underscore the necessity to carefully choose what we carry with us on our journey into the future. How we make this selection, what we choose, and how we bind together many disparate parts will shape future directions and purposes. Expressed differently, any understanding of what tomorrow will be like begins with an awareness of the present—*of today, how we got here, and why*.

Finally, it must be assumed that somehow tomorrow will be better than today. Use any predictive standard, and it likely will signify improvement. People will live longer. They will eat better and enjoy finer housing. Work will be less burdensome and intellectually more satisfying. More comforts will be appreciated by more people, and they will be served faster and more conveniently.

Actually, it may not turn out that way, but instinctively we comprehend that tomorrow always will be bigger and better. It must be. This is the touch-stone of progress. People are instinctively optimistic in contemplating their ability to better their situation. Both individually and collectively, this optimism is the energy of civilization. This is also the "why" of change, its essential value. This is the distinctive element that allows change to occur and gain maximum societal acceptance.

Of course, not all changes in the way we live, work, play, and think actually prove to be better. The expectation that they will be better is what counts. This expectation is the glow at the end of a long tunnel that continually beckons humanity forward.

Assuredly, we chiefly look for the good in things that change. Not infrequently, as a result, we blind ourselves to adverse implications or, at the very least, underestimate the impact of change.

Harvard University sociologist Daniel Bell in *The Cultural Contradictions of Capitalism*, a seminal, "must-read" treatise for environmental analysts, touches on this point in a significant manner:

Modern culture is defined by extraordinary freedom to ransack the world storehouse and to encourage any and every style it comes upon. Such freedom comes from the fact that the axial principle of modern culture is the expression and remaking of the "self" in order to achieve self-realization and self-fulfillment. And in its search, there is a denial of any limits or boundaries to experience . . .

Accordingly, the cultural, if not the moral justification of capitalism has become hedonism, the idea of pleasure as a way of life.[5]

If self-fulfillment and the seeking of personal pleasure become the supreme expectations associated with change, then, as we move toward tomorrow, Bell suggests that we well may ponder the disposition of such older values as loyalty to others, to the state, and to business institutions; familial relationships; and even the concept of thrift.

Where resources are prodigal, or individuals accept a high degree of inequality as normal or just . . . consumption can be accommodated.

But when everyone in a society joins in the demand for more, expecting this as a matter of right, and resources are limited (more by cost than by quantity), then one begins to see the basis for the tension between the demands in the polity and the limitations set by the economy . . .

We find institutionalized expectations of economic growth and a rising standard of living; these have been converted, in the current change of cultural values, into a sense of entitlements. What we have today is *a revolution of rising entitlements*.[6]

A number of easily perceived benefits can be anticipated from this revolution: ample housing, incomes equalization, job and post-retirement security, cradle-to-grave health benefits, an optimal education experience, and a minimization of discriminatory practices related to race or sex. Moreover, in an age of "rising entitlements," the judgmental standard necessarily must be egalitarianism: Equality and its rewards (pleasure, self-fulfillment, etc.) must be provided to all people, not merely those individuals who pursue and achieve it. Certain social and economic costs could be over-looked or ignored.

Alternatively, Bell feels that there are other costs and problems that stem from the ongoing push for egalitarianism.

The ultimate problem presented by the revolution of rising entitlements is not that it will cost a lot of money—although it will certainly do that. What is potentially more dangerous is the threat that the revolution presents to our political system. It threatens to overload the system, to confront it with far more grievances than legislators and judges know how to cope with. What makes this threat especially devastating is the absence, thus far, of any agreed-upon rules for settling the differences between all the contending interest groups.[7]

It is possible that other "threats" posed by this revolution (for example, the subordination of the work ethic) will eventually prove to be more "devastating" in their impact on society. But this is a secondary issue. Far more basic is the perception that *more is a right*, and that this concept will navigate the course of change.

Paradoxically, just as people generally equate change with progress, they nonetheless fear and dislike it, particularly in its initial appearance. When the commercial banking industry introduced automated teller machines (and before that, the credit card), it encountered a major headache in encouraging customers to use a machine *the first time*. Thereafter, customer concern, though not necessarily operational problems, tended to diminish.

ACCOMMODATING CHANGE

Thus far, we have seen that a number of forces, even clearly conflicting forces, are at work in shaping what tomorrow will be like. Technological innovation, along with an optimism that insists tomorrow somehow will be better, confronts existing structural rigidities nourished by tradition, not to mention deep-felt fears of the unknown. Nonetheless, we instinctively realize that tomorrow will be different and that the coming of change tends to accelerate while simultaneously spinning ever-widening, overlapping circles.

We also have seen that the actualization of one or another distinct change creates a set of new uncertainties, demanding a variety of responses to cope with them. *Change may be accommodated, but only by other changes.*

Finally, it has been suggested that change is not an event that can be marked precisely. It is not a particular development nor an innovation. Rather, it is a continuing process that again and again triggers actions and reactions. Quantum leaps, the historical watersheds, are indeed rare. Even so, we commonly tend to think in terms of the climactic and insist that what's ahead will be profoundly different. We exaggerate our own expectations of the future; therefore, we are shocked to discover in later years how little those times differed from today. But even in exaggeration there lingers an essential truth. It is reflected in the following polarizations.

BANKING'S TOMORROW

Between the Poles, or at the Extremes?

What will banking's tomorrow be like? Will it follow the polarized scenarios described here, as many believe it will, or will compromise and rationalization foster a middle-ground approach that preserves a great deal of the past and maximizes competitive equality and institutional distinctiveness?

A Characterization of Tomorrow: Which Will It Be?

1. A cashless society in which money matters are processed nearly instantaneously through national and international networks of electronic machines? *or*

1. A less-check society depending on machines to facilitate routine financial transactions, while fostering new opportunities for personal bankers to better serve human needs and wants?

2. The further erosion of *or* 2. The revitalization and free-market forces by a triumph of competitive "galloping socialism" enterprise because it spurred ever-forward by works best in satisfying Big Government, Big individual and societal Labor, and Big Business? needs?

3. An era of institutional *or* 3. The coexistence of side-bigness in which only by-side trends toward supergiants can thrive by bigness and smallness, putting it all together? toward integration and specialization, toward consolidation and inde-pendence?

4. *Or is there a middle ground?*

Some bank managements making decisions and setting priorities in the early 1970s perceived that tomorrow would evolve as a less-check, less-cash world of electronic financial transactions. In time, money machines operated by fraud-proof plastic identification cards would "replace" tellers. The time span before this change would occur was, as it still is, a much debated issue. But through hundreds of thousands of machines located in supermarkets, drug stores, factories, office buildings, and transportation terminals, most if not literally all basic consumer financial transactions would be processed instantaneously. Some wondered, "Why money at all?" It is the transfer of financial data that is relevant. Why a plurality of checking, savings, and loan accounts? Just one account would do fine, with a bank paying interest for surplus funds and charging interest where the balance was negative. Others said, "Why even banks?" In other words, a bank would only be a storehouse for financial records and a place to meet with corporate clients and the trust department's "rich old ladies in tennis sneakers."

Other bank managements predicted that tomorrow naturally must incur a further erosion of free-market forces. It was rea-soned that the private enterprise system would have surrendered what little remained of its independence and innovative spirit to a debilitating, stultifying, and increasingly meddlesome bureaucracy that was slave only to the self-seeking representatives of labor and the addled advocates of consumerism. What was banking? Not judgment, but compliance. Not making loans, but filling in and filing forms.

And some managements believed deeply that tomorrow belonged to a race of supergiants: colossal, multi-national conglomerates providing every conceivable form of financial service and responsive only to the other titans of business, labor, and government. Or, the supergiants would be a handful of nationwide banking institutions, headquartered on Wall Street, with thousands of far-flung electronic and bricks-and-mortar branch offices. And certainly, these supergiants would be "department stores of finance," having integrated traditional bank and nonbank activities. Today's holding company movement would have achieved fruition by becoming redundant.

But to other bank managements, tomorrow would be quite different indeed. Their view of the future was more optimistic. The electronic age, while admittedly standardizing routine financial transactions, concurrently would foster new and improved opportunities for servicing customer needs and wants. These opportunities, while relying heavily on technological support, nevertheless would be anchored by continually active personal contact relationships. Markets, whether viewed as consumers, business or government customers, or further segmented by such measures as earning capacity and investment potential, would be served by better skilled, better educated, and more resourceful cadres of *personal bankers*. These would be men and women who frequently went calling on targeted customers; they no longer waited for them behind richly veneered desks or glassed-in teller cages.

Some bank and financial institution managers also sensed that tomorrow would see a revitalization of the free-market system, with State and Federal governments actually encouraging the gradual but orderly breakdown of long-standing restraints born of another time and place. A competitive enterprise system again would prove the most workable and effective response to changed societal needs. It would redemonstrate its efficacy as the most viable mechanism, if not the most just and satisfying in human terms, for allocating financial and material resources. Capitalism would not be defeated by an "age of rising entitlements"; rather, it alone could make it achievable.

And finally, there were financial institution managements committed to a belief that smallness and specialization held a clearly defined place in the world of tomorrow. These managements anticipated lifestyle alterations and new cultural impulses that placed extraordinary value on quality of service or product and its personalization: *make it good and make it especially for me*. They also perceived a future in which a sense of community was even more intense than in the past, where *belonging* in an otherwise impersonal environment had come to mean so much more: *I want to be; I want to belong; I don't want to be a digit*.

By implication, these alternative scenarios possess different bottom lines in terms of institutional and managerial performance. They mandate far different results with respect to corporate earnings and shareholder profitability; the allocation of credit and investment capital; the hiring and promotion of people; the building and furnishing of bricks-and-mortar offices; the designing of product and service promotional schemes; and even the wooing of customer allegiance. They demand, in fact, different goals and strategies.

For all of this, the various scenarios have one thing in common. These sets of alternative views recognize that tomorrow—at some undetermined point in time—will be greatly different from today. In all probability the degree of change rests at a point between the two poles, although even this expectation is not a certainty since largely uncontrollable external events could well swing the pendulum of change far wider. In any event, the common element is change. It is the known on which we build tomorrow. It is the unavoidable that clearly threatens the unwary.

COPING WITH CHANGE THROUGH PLANNING

What will tomorrow be like? It will not be like the past. It may not be what we believe it will or should be. *It can, however, more closely approximate what we want it to be by endeavoring now to establish realistic objectives and devise effective policies, strategies, and tactics that in their combination and interaction will fulfill these objectives.*

The process of establishing and fulfilling reasonable objectives is the subject of this book. Emphasis is on the structured, though flexible management of change. It involves understanding enough about the present to chart the future and enough about that probable tomorrow to devise plans that will (1) maximize projectable opportunities; (2) minimize the adverse impact of prospective challenges; (3) maintain a viable competitive posture that will deal with both opportunities and challenges; and (4) optimize profitability.

The desire to optimize profits is the reason why a financial institution should bother with planning. But the point must be made at the outset that profitability takes more than one form. It is a fair return on stockholder investment and a risk premium for uncertainty. It is a measure of managerial performance. Indirectly, it is an indicator monitoring the satisfaction of customer, employee, community, and societal needs.

It is enterprise, the art of baking a bigger pie that gives all members of society a larger slice. Finally, profitability is the touchstone of survival: It alone assures a future for you and your institution; it alone substantiates the institution's underlying values.

Peter Drucker, the architect of modern corporate management and for so many, the apostle of decision making through planning, has argued that "We must stop talking of profit as a reward. It is a cost. There are no rewards; only the costs of yesterday and tomorrow."[8] Profitability stems from our performance in handling these costs, including both the dollar costs of doing business each day and the social costs implicit in this activity. Increasingly, especially because the nature of change has been accelerating, distinctions between these costs have blurred; no longer distinct, they are entwined in the planning process. Profitability is the result of pencil-sharp cost analysis; it is what can be expected *if you have done all your homework.*

The thesis of *Banking Tomorrow: Managing Markets Through Planning* is that profitability is optimized by designing effective responses to the fact of change, and then applying them in a reasonable and systematic manner.

Its logical corollary is that planning forces decision making now, as well as on the road ahead. The planning process identifies alternative courses of action and then mandates a reasonable choice. *Not* planning also is a decision. The difference is simple enough. Planning allows choice in determining actions and reactions; it explores the parameters of possibility. Planning is to contemplate the many changes creating tomorrow and to commit to appropriate responses in a positive manner.

And there is the terribly pragmatic dimension to planning raised by Dr. Maurice Mann, former Federal Reserve official, bank executive, and savings and loan industry regulator:

> Have banks *in toto* really thought through the far-reaching consequences of bank planning? For example, how far are we from a single credit card that would be nationally, or even universally accepted . . . Not very far when you think about it. We have the hardware and the software to achieve this goal . . . perhaps within a decade. But who will be in charge of the use of an all-purpose form of instant credit? Who, for that matter, will control it? Or issue it?
>
> This is not a question of philosophy, or of bank regulation of supervision. This is a matter which lies at the heart of what bank planning is all about.[9]

This book is dedicated to the thoughtful financial institution executive. It is about banking, but it cannot avoid also being about this industry's present and future competitors, since surely what appropriately characterizes the future is the primary fact of more competition from more competitors armed with more banklike powers. Equally, it is about all kinds of banks: large and small; city, suburban and rural; and those that seek or would fight change. It is about tomorrow and how some of us get there.

STRUCTURE OF THE BOOK

In the several chapters comprising Unit One, the fundamental values and concepts of planning are introduced. Systematic, strategic, long-range planning is defined. We look at what it is, as well as what it is not. The concern of this unit then focuses on the several steps involved in preparing for planning and organizing procedures to carry out this task on a structured, continual, and effective basis.

Finally, this unit deals with the everyday "nuts and bolts" that make planning happen—the external or environmental analysis; comprehension of existing internal strengths and weaknesses; design of an organizational purpose and objectives given these evaluations; and then the initiation of action strategies and the implementation of procedures for effecting them.

Unit Two—The Yesterday, Today, and Tomorrow of Banking— is the authors' analysis of the external environment in which banks operate. It is predictive of things to come, though based primarily on currently discernible trends and the developments underlying them. This environmental analysis begins with an understanding of where we are today. The evaluation, of course, requires comprehension of where we have been and how we have reached the present. From this foundation, we build for tomorrow.

The central theme of Unit Two is that financial institution managers can predict what most likely will occur over a reasonable period of time. This fact necessitates the creation of organizational responses that focus on the disciplined allocation of human and financial resources through compatible manned and machine delivery systems that satisfy customer needs and wants at a profit. This concept of planning is developed more fully in the next unit.

The single chapter in Unit Three maintains that the *marketplace* is the object of change. This assertion clarifies the natural link between planning and marketing. Planning focuses on what the organization reasonably needs to do in preparing for the future and how this vital task can be carried out. Marketing becomes the plan in action; it is a philosophy of doing business that permeates the entire organization and gives *thrust* to purpose and direction.

The *marketplace* then is defined as three principal markets:

1. the *customers* served by financial organizations, which then are characterized as *retail* or consumer customers and *commercial* customers

2. the *people resources* utilized by financial institution managements to serve customers; these are employees, including
   managers, who either sell or support the selling of financial
   products and services
3. the market for investors; they are the sources of capital, the
   base of the business of banking

Unit Three concludes by evaluating existing and projected
delivery systems, particularly computer-based technologies, by
which financial resources and related services are delivered to
customers.

The final Unit in this book develops further the thesis that the
markets for customers, people resources, and investors are the
object of change through a consideration of a series of action
strategies conceived to improve organizational performance in
these markets as tomorrow's intensely competitive environment
unfolds.

This approach indicates how planning really works as a practical
management tool for accomplishing predetermined, though always
flexible, objectives.   The objectives delineated in the several
chapters comprising this Unit have been selected arbitrarily by the
authors. We believe they are reasonable, and, moreover, applicable
to most larger financial organizations. They may not be *yours*,
however.   Even so, they probably will be in competition with
yours and merit attention for this reason.

Finally, it should be understood that these suggested action
strategies just won't work for *all* banks or their competitors. Once
again, however, this realization reaches to the heart of the planning process.   Its purpose is determining objectives and setting
action strategies that work best for you.

We turn now to the critical first step in this process: *the reasons
for making a commitment to planning*.

FOOTNOTES

1. Remarks by W. W. Simmons, president, Applied Futures, Inc., at the Bank
   Marketing Association Annual Conference, Las Vegas, NV, October, 1975.
2. Cited at the Carter H. Golembe Associates Executive Seminar: *Long*

Range Planning in an Uncertain Environment—An Examination of Technique and Results, Washington, DC, May 29–31, 1974.

3. *People, Progress, Prosperity: 200 Years of American Banking,* United States Investor/Eastern Banker, October 6, 1975.

4. Daniel Bell, *The Cultural Contradictions of Capitalism* (New York: Basic Books, 1976), p. 13f.

5. Ibid., p. 23.

6. Daniel Bell, "The Revolution of Rising Entitlements," *Fortune,* April, 1975, p. 103, Time, Inc., New York.

7. Ibid., p. 104.

8. John J. Tarrant, *Drucker: The Man Who Invented The Corporate Society,* (Boston: 1976).

9. Remarks by Maurice Mann, at the Carter H. Golembe Associates Executive Seminar: *Long-Range Planning for Banks,* Washington, DC, May 29–31, 1974.

UNIT ONE: PLANNING: MANAGING THE FUTURE

2 EXTERNAL CHANGE, MANAGEMENT, AND STRATEGIC PLANNING

INTRODUCTION

The reality of change is very much upon us in the business of banking. We can fully expect that the patterns and magnitude of change in economic activity, in regulatory and competitive structures, and in electronic technology that have emerged over the last decade will continue through the next decade. The broad thrust of much of the expected change is foreseeable; only the timing and details are unknown.

Any financial institution that intends to achieve high-level performance in the future must learn to anticipate change and to develop appropriate responses well in advance. This approach is more likely to be successful if (1) applied on a regular, consistent, rational, comprehensive, and coordinated basis or (2) a formal, long-range, strategic planning process is implemented. Strategic planning is not only a process for managing change, it also is a management technique for improving decision making and thus the overall performance of management.

The benefits of planning and the costs of not doing so represent the bottom line of planning. Without planning, management reacts to change only belatedly or practices the notably ineffective "management by crisis." With planning, the management process is systematic and controlled, thus better able to cope with change.

The purpose of this chapter is to introduce the basic concepts and procedures of planning. How does planning relate to management? What are the steps of planning? In general terms, how is a plan developed? This chapter also describes the benefits of planning. Can its costs be justified? How does planning affect performance?

The answers to these questions are addressed first by discussing planning as a management tool. Next, the steps of planning are briefly noted, with detailed discussion saved for Chapters Three and Four. Then, the values of planning are presented, as well as some examples indicating the prospective costs of not planning. Finally, a definition of planning is offered. Instead of beginning the discussion with a definition, its presentation is delayed until after the complex characteristics of planning have been examined.

PLANNING AS A MANAGEMENT TOOL

Managing and planning cannot be separated. Essentially, they are one and the same. Management is the formulation and implementation of a series of decisions, each of which addresses some specific end and the means to achieve it.[1] Regardless of how the decision-making process works or the magnitude of the decisions, the combination of decisions that a manager makes, in effect, constitutes his or her plan. The totality of a manager's decisions define where he/she wants the organization to go and how he/she wants it to get there. These are the two basic planning questions. Thus, even the day-to-day decisions of managers produce a plan.

Any combination of decisions can, at one extreme, be implicit, informal, unstructured, and subject to frequent change. Or, it can be formal, long-range, and strategic. Either way, the type of planning depends on management's approach to decision making.

Informal and Unstructured Decisions

Decisions can be made under a variety of circumstances with respect to the availability of information and the extent of structure or guidelines. Informal and unstructured decisions are made with minimal background information or with little knowledge about their future implications. For example, in financial institutions the subsequent impact of a decision will be considerably less clear if there has not been an examination of expected trends in economic and financial activity, regulatory and competitive structures, or electronic technology. In the 1960s many banks purchased early generation computers, soon discovering that their equipment was obsolete. Some examination of prospective developments in this field probably would have avoided such problems.

Similarly, without a consistent framework or set of policy guidelines, decisions are unstructured. Even if guidelines have been formulated, they need to be updated frequently to avoid unstructured decision making. Most banks, at least at their outset, may have had some objectives and broad policies in mind, but until the last few years, it was a rare organization that updated them to reflect changing circumstances. Until the mid-1950s, for example, large segments of the banking industry continued to ignore the emerging retail market. Meanwhile, the thrift institutions were making tremendous inroads that took banks another decade to recapture.

Although *ad hoc* decision making sometimes is unavoidable, it is usually undesirable. Decisions made in the darkness of ignorance rarely produce results superior to those made in the light of knowledge and guidance of structure. Perhaps there was a time when banking was sufficiently simple, constant, and predictable so that casual decision making and planning were adequate; however, in a world of far more rapid change (economic fluctuations, regulatory adjustments, and shifting competitive forces), decision making and planning need to be systematic to ensure satisfactory performance.

Formal and Structured Decisions

At the other end of the spectrum, when decision making is explicit and structured, then planning is formal and strategic. As a result, it is likely to entail a careful look at the world of tomorrow, the establishing of objectives and goals, and the formulation of policy guidelines and action strategies. Although these steps are systematic, a framework is required that relates them to the real world. As we shall see in later discussions (Chapters 7 and 8), the most likely characteristic of the banking business in the years ahead will be markedly increased competition, particularly in the retail area. Because competition occurs in the marketplace, banks and similar financial institutions will need to have a clear understanding of their markets and how to perform in them. Thus, banking's principal markets are proposed as the most relevant framework for planning (Chapter 9). In this sense, the term "markets" refers not only to traditional retail and commercial customers (Chapters 10 and 11), but also to markets for people resources (Chapter 12) and for the financial resources provided by investors (Chapter 13).

Inducing Management to Plan

A structured approach to planning inevitably produces superior results, although not necessarily in the short run. Because of this lack of immediate results, there tends to be some resistance by management in adopting a formal planning program.

Managers are willing, however, to devote the necessary resources to a formal planning process if they view it as an extension and refinement of existing activities. Since managers tend to be goal-oriented, formal planning can take advantage of this human characteristic by inducing the manager to address the two basic planning questions of where are we going and how are we going to get there? In formal planning, the answers to the first questions establish the purpose, objectives, and goals. (See glossary on pages 36–37 for the definitions of these and other terms that will be used in this book.) Answering the second question provides policy guidelines, action strategies, and implementation programs.

Effective managers also tend to be future-oriented. They are inclined to have some sense of what tomorrow will be like. Planning responds to this inclination since it is predicated on the belief that the future can be improved through active intervention in the present.   By using the planning process to examine the future impact of alternative decisions, performance can be enhanced.

Who Formulates Plans?

Planning is not the sole responsibility of any particular level of management. Each has its own responsibilities and tasks. As a rule, top management has the broadest role in planning with each succeeding lower level of management having a more specific one.

For example, planning is a vehicle that enables top management to discharge one of its major responsibilities—setting the overall course of the organization, not just for the present, but also for well into the future. This task can be executed through the component of planning known as the purpose or mission. Formulating a purpose only in light of contemporary circumstances is not sufficient, however, since it is unlikely to be relevant at a later time in a rapidly changing world. For business organization to remain strong and productive over time, formal, long-range, strategic planning must be the guiding philosophy and dominant management style.   The success of planning hinges on management commitment to this belief.

Lower levels of management function more effectively with the benefit of a solid commitment to planning by top management that includes a carefully developed purpose and objective. With this foundation, senior and middle management then can address the responsibilities of setting goals and creating strategies and programs for achieving them. Thus, the responsibilities of varying levels of management define the tasks of planning, which in turn constitute the planning process.

THE PLANNING PROCESS

The planning process can be divided into the following major steps:

Management commitment
Environmental analysis
Internal analysis
Purpose or mission

Objectives
Goals
Policies and guidelines
Action strategies
Implementation programs
Monitoring

These steps are illustrated in Figure 2.1, the Planning Pyramid, which shows how planning proceeds in a building-block fashion from a broad foundation and background elements on up to specific activities such as the implementation programs. When all of these steps have been executed the result is the plan.

After *management commitment* is established, an *environmental analysis* should be conducted to identify probable future trends among critical external forces (socioeconomic, legislative-regulatory, and technological). The term "environment" is used in planning to refer to those developments that are external and over which an organization has little or no control. A well-designed and implemented environmental study not only identifies critical future trends but also examines their impact on the organization; it will even suggest various responses.

The complement of the external analysis is the *internal analysis*. By determining current strengths and weaknesses, management can better formulate appropriate future courses of action.

No organization can function effectively without a *purpose* or *mission*, which broadly states the nature of its business. Even if the chief executive chooses not to share his or her thinking on the subject with subordinates, nevertheless a purpose exists and the business has direction. More often, the purpose is explicit and widely known. Most important is that management not be afraid to ask with some frequency, "what is our business? why are we here? what are we trying to accomplish?"

The next step is to develop *objectives*, which give the purpose sharper focus. Largely the responsibility of top management, objectives should be prepared in greater detail and be more specific than the purpose. Even so, they usually are conceptual and qualitative as opposed to quantitative.

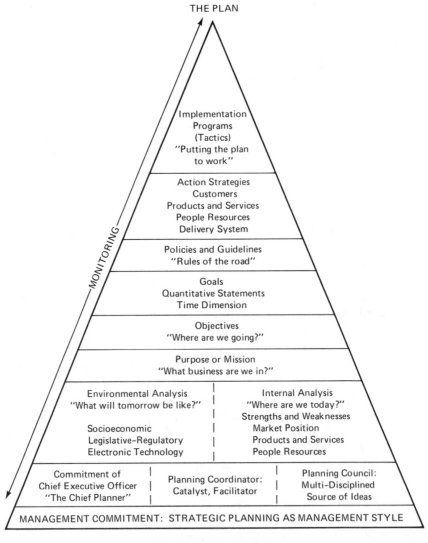

THE PLANNING PYRAMID

Figure 2.1.   The Planning Pyramid.

Taking the process of establishing where the organization is going to a specific conclusion are the *goals*. They delineate the objectives by setting quantitative standards of performance for a specified time period. Goals must be neither too easy to attain nor virtually unattainable.

Policies and guidelines provide the rules of the road. Financial institutions not only must adhere to extensive governmental regulations, but they also should have clear policies and guidelines for managing risk and maintaining liquidity and solvency. Typically, policies and guidelines are set by top or senior management and altered only infrequently.

After the organization has established "where it is going," the second major task of planning is figuring out "how to get there." The initial step in this process is to formulate action strategies, which show how the organization is to move away from its current situation (within the limits of the policy guidelines) to achieve its objectives and goals. They state, for example, whether an organization intends to emphasize retail operations or commercial operations, to what extent electronic devices will be used to interface with consumers, or what kinds of commercial customers will be sought.

Unless strategies are converted into action through detailed *implementation programs* (sometimes referred to as tactics) that assign responsibility for specific tasks, then the planning gap will remain. Implementation programs, which call for accountability from a given individual, should be closely tied to specific strategies in order that the interrelationships among the different components are clear.

Once the plan is in operation, the *monitoring* process must be undertaken. Monitoring, which is shown on Figure 2.1 along the lefthand side, utilizes the plan as a standard of performance. Although top management assumes the basic responsibility for monitoring progress, it delegates responsibility for individual components (objectives, goals, etc.) to those levels of management substantially involved in their determination and execution. Evaluation of performance as well as of the validity of the plan itself sets the stage for further rounds in the planning cycle.

Implementing the Planning Steps

For the most part, especially in the first experience with planning, these steps should be implemented in the order outlined in the Planning Pyramid. On the other hand, in reality planning is a continuous process and it may be difficult to designate a clear beginning point. Circumstances vary considerably from one financial institution to another, precluding any absolute statements about the order and content of the planning process. Accordingly the process offered in this book should be adapted to suit the idiosyncracies of individual institutions. To a considerable degree, the process we will be discussing has been developed and altered to accommodate depository financial institutions. But even within these bounds, a given institution needs to decide which steps to emphasize, which steps to underplay, who should be responsible for different steps, and how each step is to be implemented and monitored. Flexibility in determining just how the process is to work for a given institution is one of the basic characteristics of strategic planning that helps maximize its many benefits.

The next section discusses the benefits or values of planning and how it contributes to improving overall performance.

BENEFITS OF PLANNING

Formal, long-range, strategic planning requires a major commitment of resources, especially of management time. Thus, it is reasonable to expect that management will want to examine benefits carefully as compared with costs. A benefit-cost analysis of formal planning is complicated because, although the costs can be readily identified and measured, the benefits are difficult to quantify. Moreover, they tend to accrue over an extended period. It is a contradiction in terms for planning to be profitable immediately.

The Costs of Not Planning

There are at least two methods for evaluating planning that readily justify costs. One approach is to consider the costs of not planning. Over the years, banks and the banking industry have made their share of mistakes. Did they really think through or do much planning for policies such as:

- the mass mailing of credit cards,
- diversification through the holding company movement, or
- the formation, financing, and lending policies of real estate investment trusts (REITs)?

More currently, how much planning is being done by individual banks for the emerging world of EFTS and their participation?

Even if some planning is done, it must be part of a comprehensive coordinated system. Too often the retail marketing staff develops new products independently from the operations staff. The result is that implementation is frequently delayed, costs escalate, market share is lost or quality of service is so poor that customers are dissatisfied. Once again the costs of not having a properly structured planning process are evident.

The Problems of Not Having a Purpose and Objectives

An organization without a plan, with only a vague notion of where it is going is like a ship without a rudder.[2] It tends to go around in circles without proceeding to a specific destination. There is nothing to harness, control, and guide the energy of the wind caught in the sails. Similarly, a bank may have a sound deposit base with attractive lending opportunities, but without a plan, mediocrity probably will be its fate. Inevitably, management will be unable to decide with any consistency such basic questions as retail versus commercial, people resource allocation, or purchased funds versus core deposits. If a bank does not have clearly defined objectives and goals, any course of action is acceptable, and many lead to dead ends.

One of the best examples of a large organization that for some time lacked well-defined objectives was the Chrysler Corporation.[3] Without them, Chrysler management was never certain of its particular place in the automobile market. As a result, goals and strategies fluctuated widely for years, and the public was not exactly sure what Chrysler represented. Moreover, lacking clear objectives, Chrysler, which traditionally had emphasized engineering, found that it was the engineers formulating strategies, even for marketing. Marketing, however, is not the task of engineers; chances that they will establish effective marketing strategies are limited (evidenced in the public's indifference to that engineering marvel, the push-button automatic transmission).

As the era of electronic funds transfer unfolds, banks that permit their computer specialists, in effect, to establish the bank's marketing strategies probably will not have delivery systems that effectively serve customer needs. Planning that includes objectives, goals, and strategies devised in all areas of the organization by different levels of managers does not permit any one group to dominate. In fact, planning will result in greater coordination among a variety of functional areas.

Limiting Fluctuations in Earnings

Randomly selecting courses of action without a plan is likely to produce wide fluctuations in earnings. Sometimes an *ad hoc* choice of action is correct and earnings improve sharply. Just as frequently, perhaps more often, an incorrect choice is made and earnings suffer. Excessive fluctuations in earnings leave the investment community unsettled.[4] Earnings must increase consistently and produce an attractive annual compound growth rate to satisfy investors. Strategic planning helps to minimize the bad decisions that lead to reduced or stagnant earnings.

The importance of stability in bank earnings is evident in the experience of the 1960s and 1970s. During much of that period, the investment community had the idea that banking, because of the bank holding company movement, was a growth and glamour industry. This kind of thinking evaporated with the recession of 1974–75 and the concomitant deterioration in bank earnings performance. Now that the glamour has been tarnished, investors are looking for earnings stability and few surprises.

The Values of Planning

A more positive approach to evaluating planning is to consider its values, which are explicit, clear, and numerous. They can be discussed in the following terms:

- how future performance is affected by current decisions;
- how the structure provided by planning improves the total decision-making process.

Planning is Inherently Concerned With the Future

We have seen how management constantly is faced with decisions that have most of their impact in the future. Planning is valuable because it can improve the quality of those decisions since it is inherently concerned with the future.[5] Each of the components of the planning process, from the environmental analysis through the implementation programs, is designed to answer two future oriented questions: where are we going and how are we going to get there?

Since planning is actively concerned with the future, it helps management anticipate the future and develop responses that will produce an optimum fit between the organization and its environment. Merely reacting to events as they unfold is not sufficient in a world of rapid change. After NOW accounts have been introduced nationwide or after Regulation Q has been lifted is too late to begin planning action strategies. By then, those banks that anticipated such changes will have made their plans; they will be ready to swing into action at the sound of the bell, thereby gaining a competitive edge.

Another important value is that planning minimizes the apparently natural propensity to be blinded by this year's, or even this quarter's, earnings without considering the long-run implications—the classic *earnings now* syndrome. With its inherent emphasis on the future implications of any current decision, planning focuses on the trade-offs between performance today and tomorrow. Knowing the trade-offs, management will be able to make sound decisions that ensure stable earnings both now and later.

Since it is not possible to forecast exactly when and how major changes will occur, alternative possible scenarios and contingency plans for action can be developed. For example, the countless ramifications of removing Regulation Q are not readily apparent. But by examining the possibilities and setting forth alternative responses, management has a much better understanding of the issue and how to begin positioning itself. In sum, when strategic planning is used, management has much more information in making decisions today that affect performance tomorrow.

Moreover, emphasis on future developments forces managers to focus on the ways that tomorrow will be different from today. The value of such a forward focus is that plans tend to be based on expectations about the future as opposed to extrapolations of past experience. In a world of change, simple projections of past experience often are not valid indications of the course of future events. Over the past twenty five years, for example, banking has gone from indifference to a love affair with retail activities and now seems to be refocusing on the commercial area. Understanding past trends and shifts can be helpful; building on them is vital, but living in the past can be destructive.

The Structure of Planning Improves Decision Making

Planning is beneficial to performance because the structure provided by the planning process contributes to and improves the execution of management responsibilities. The components of a continual planning process establish a framework for decision making that is regular, consistent, rational, comprehensive, and coordinated. Once the process is under way, the specific elements of the plan serve as points of reference for decision making.

Regular and Consistent. With planning, various decisions become more regular because the ongoing rotation through the steps of planning keeps raising questions that require decisions. One key question that has to be answered in each round of planning for example, regards management succession and subordinate career development. These are management responsibilities that easily are shifted into the background because they are difficult tasks and only rarely appear pressing. But the planning process automatically forces decisions about the disposition of people resources. Questions about branch size and location can be decided consistently from case to case within an existing package of objectives, strategies, and guidelines for retail banking.

Rational. The planning framework also leads to decision making that is rational, impersonal, and less political. With decisions made on the basis of established standards and guidelines that are recognized throughout the organization, personalities play a reduced role. The reasons for a decision are clear and less shrouded in corporate politics. It becomes easier for top management to say no and to place certain projects low on the priorities list without appearing merely to be favoring one department or individual over another.

Comprehensive and Coordinated. The structure of planning causes decisions to be comprehensive and coordinated. Since the structure of planning demands that a given decision be evaluated with respect to existing objectives, goals, guidelines, and strategies, it is less likely that a decision about retail banking would be made that conflicts with commercial activities. Too much decision making is done in relative isolation. In many instances this is because proper communication channels are not established, general inertia prevails, or individual departments act as independent empires threatening constructive interdepartmental relationships. But with the specifics of a plan committed to writing and readily accessible, the chances of conflict, complication, and duplication are reduced.

Forces Decision Making. The planning structure identifies certain decisions that need to be made and ensures that they are made. In the case of one bank, it moved along for years with a well-defined retail effort, while its commercial effort was vague (although not unproductive). Management recognized the eventual need for better definition of goals and strategies in the commercial area, but did not know how to go about it. Accordingly, they tended to avoided making *any* decisions. Once the planning process moved into high gear, however, management was forced either to define the commercial effort or short-circuit the plan. They chose the former route. The bank made substantial changes in the commercial area that benefited overall performance, increased short-term profitability, and moved the company in the direction of desired longer-term objectives.

Importance of Flexibility. Continually changing external circumstances, which in many cases are unpredictable, require a high degree of flexibility. Often it is felt that the formulation and implementation of a specific plan reduces flexibility. Thus, planning is shunned in favor of "hanging loose." A given plan may be temporary and frequently changed, but a properly structured planning process and decision-making framework give management a tool for analyzing and accomodating even the least predictable change. For example, some external event, such as the legalizing of NOW accounts on a national basis, may force an organization to alter its retail strategies. When New England banks and thrifts were confronted with NOW accounts, it was much easier for those organizations with existing planning functions to make the necessary alterations because they had an established framework for making decisions. Also, a process for formulating strategies was in place so that the strategy to be altered was clearly defined, widely understood, and comprehensible in the broad scheme of operations. Moreover, the remainder of the plan that did not need to be changed served as an effective guide for determining the new strategy and for measuring its effectiveness.

Without a planning process, responses to external events are generated on an *ad hoc* basis or essentially plucked out of the air. Trying to achieve flexibility through noncommitment to a plan usually leads to time-consuming foundering instead of productive action and performance. A bank can become over-flexible—moving back and forth, never really forging ahead. Flexibility can become a response to fads and fancies, and a bank can lose sight of fundamental purposes.

A Standard of Performance.   Through the monitoring process in particular, but also through the overall structure, planning assists in setting up controls that assure effective and immediate checks and balances.   By assigning responsibility and tracking performance, monitoring makes evident whether or not specific tasks are being executed.   Budgeting also satisfies this control criterion, but not to the same extent, since it is concerned almost entirely with financial results.   Monitoring performance through all of the elements of the plan focuses on the full scope of management tasks, many of which cannot be evaluated by looking at year-end financial statements.   How much progress was made in developing new commercial accounts?   Were specific career development programs implemented?

Risk Management.   Finally, because the structure established by planning causes decision making to be more regular, consistent, rational, comprehensive, and coordinated, risk management is improved.   Sometimes it is said that planning reduces risk.   Perhaps, in an indirect sense, that is the effect.   In reality, however, *most risks encountered in the course of doing business are external and cannot be altered.*   Risks are determined by the nature of the business (banking versus retailing versus manufacturing) and the kind of environment (regulated, competitive) in which the business functions.   Management may assume or avoid these risks in varying degrees depending on its ability to withstand losses, among other things.

Strategic planning enhances management's ability to cope with risk because of the numerous values (future orientation, structure) that it provides.[6]   Other things being equal, an organization practicing strategic planning will be better prepared to identify the risk characteristics of various courses of action and then pursue those that provide a reasonable expectation of generating greater earnings.   An example of being able to take risks is anticipatory planning to meet future developments such as NOW accounts, ATMs, etc.   Those institutions having a better understanding of future trends are better prepared; therefore, they can implement bolder, riskier strategies in order to increase profitable market share.

Other examples stem from the structure of planning that provides more stable earnings behavior and thus permits the organization to make an occasional higher risk or to acquire a business with greater earnings fluctuations. In a sense, planning helps to identify and to permit taking *the right kind of risks.*

Few of these values of planning can be instantly translated into bottom line results. Nevertheless, their overall constructive impact on the organization is evident.

PLANNING DEFINED

As we have seen, planning can range from the extremely casual to the highly formal. Assuredly, the latter has considerably more potential as a management tool, especially for coping with change. Now that planning has been examined from several different angles, a definition can be offered:

> Formal, long-range, strategic planning is a management technique for determining where the organization is going and how it will get there through regular, consistent, rational, comprehensive, and coordinated decision making that commits resources to action.

What Planning Is Not

Through the years a variety of notions about planning have emerged. Most are misleading, some simply incorrect. Unfortunately, many of these perceptions have become rather widespread.

Not Forecasting. Frequently, planning is confused with forecasting. Although forecasting future environmental conditions is a necessary and important *component* of planning, it is not planning. Forecasting merely sets the stage. Planning goes further by stating how the organization intends to perform in the world of tomorrow. Planning is structuring an active response as opposed to delineating a set of future circumstances. It is doing something about predictions.

Not Budgeting.   Another area of confusion is the relationship between planning and budgeting. The building of projected financial statements (called budgeting for one year and financial forecasting when longer periods are involved) is related to planning, but is not a substitute.

The annual projecting of financial statements a year ahead essentially establishes the financial results that management feels are achievable. Budgeting itself does not address such tasks as purpose, objectives, or strategies. In fact, these tasks should be completed well in advance of budgeting, since they provide the conceptual framework and guidelines within which a realistic budget can be built. Planning is a larger, more comprehensive, and less quantitative responsibility than budgeting or financial forecasting.

2047925

Not Capital Rationing.   After strategic planning has been operating for a few years, sometimes much of the process is devoted to rationing and allocating limited capital (and even people!) resources among a plethora of competing demands from various sectors of the organization. Although establishing priorities among potential projects is a legitimate and valuable function of planning, the entire process cannot deteriorate into a matter of refereeing competing claims. If it does, the broader tasks of planning will be submerged in a clash of politics and personalities. Planning should foster cooperation, not encourage divisiveness.

Not a Panacea.   Finally, planning is not a panacea for an ailing firm. Although planning is a tool that can be used to help improve weakened or deteriorating conditions, ultimately it is the *quality* of the decisions made within the planning process that determines the level of performance.

CONCLUSION

Managing is planning. Decisions made as part of the management process are likely to be superior if they are explicit and structured and the product of a formal, long-range, strategic planning process. In a world of rapid change, the costs of not planning—loss of market share, internal inefficiencies, fluctuations in earnings—are all too evident.   The benefits of strategic planning are that it is inherently concerned with the future and that it provides a framework for regular, consistent, rational, comprehensive, and coordinated decision making.

In theory and on paper these concepts appear promising, But the real test is in their implementation and application.   For a financial institution to realize the benefits of strategic planning in coping with the changing world of tomorrow, the process must be installed and put to work.   *How* is the subject of the next two chapters.

GLOSSARY

The following definitions of frequently used planning terms are by no means universal. Both in concept and in practice, the specific application of these terms varies a great deal. For consistency and comprehension, throughout this book these terms will be used as defined herein.

Formal, Long-range Strategic Planning	A management technique to determine where the organization is going and how it will get there through regular, consistent, rational, comprehensive, and coordinated decision making that commits resources to action.
Plan	The document that contains all of the components of the planning process.
Purpose or Mission	The component of the planning process that explains why the organization exists and in broad terms what it intends to accomplish.
Objectives	The component of the planning process that explains conceptually and qualitatively where the organization intends to go. Objectives usually are stated in broad terms and are not designated as being achievable within specific time periods.
Goals	The component of the planning process that explains in clear well-defined, specific (often

	quantified) terminology where the organization intends to go. Usually goals are regarded as intermediate steps in achieving objectives and thus are stated on an annual basis.
Policy Guidelines	The component of the planning process that establishes the ground rules within which the action strategies will be formulated. They designate certain activities that will be undertaken, other activities that will not be engaged in, and in some cases to what extent certain activities will be undertaken.
Action Strategies	The component of the planning process that explains in broad terms how the organization intends to achieve its objectives and goals.
Implementation Programs or Tactics	The component of the planning process that explains how action strategies will be carried out in terms of responsibility and timing. Sometimes this step in planning is referred to as tactics.
Planning Coordinator	The individual responsible for structuring the planning process, inducing managers to execute their appropriate tasks in the planning process, completing the process in a timely fashion, and ensuring that the plan is used as a standard for performance. Although sometimes referred to as the planner, this term is erroneous since only managers can develop plans.

FOOTNOTES

1. George A. Steiner, *Top Management Planning* (New York: Macmillan, 1969), p. 322.
2. Harold Koontz, "Making Stategic Planning Work," *Business Horizons*, April 1976, p. 37.
3. Peter Vanderwichen, "What's Really Wrong at Chrysler," *Fortune*, May 1975, pp. 176, 178.
4. Jack C. Rothwell, "Concepts and Tools for Bank Planning," a Speech at Executive Seminar of Carter H. Golembe and Associates, Inc., November 12, 1970, Dallas, TX, p. 1.
5. Steiner, p. 6.
6. Ibid., p. 18.

3 ORGANIZING AND PREPARING FOR PLANNING

INTRODUCTION

Successful application of strategic planning as a management tool depends not only on understanding why strategic planning is valuable but also on how it works and how to do it. Coping with the changing world of tomorrow was outlined in Chapter One. Strategic planning to meet these changes was explained in Chapter Two. Chapters Three and Four discuss how to organize and how to implement a planning process in a financial institution. The discussion is divided into two parts: Chapter Three focuses on organizing for planning and developing valuable background information; Chapter Four focuses on implementing the planning process on a step-by-step basis.

It should be noted, however, that no single planning process has universal applicability, even among financial institutions. Each institution has a unique character, reflecting its primary business, size, structure, management, and market. With a little insight and creativity, approaches that generally have been shown to be effective can be adapted to fit most depository institutions. We all are different; we know this, but do our customers?

The explanation of the planning process follows the Planning Pyramid diagram in Figure 3.1. Its shape shows how planning

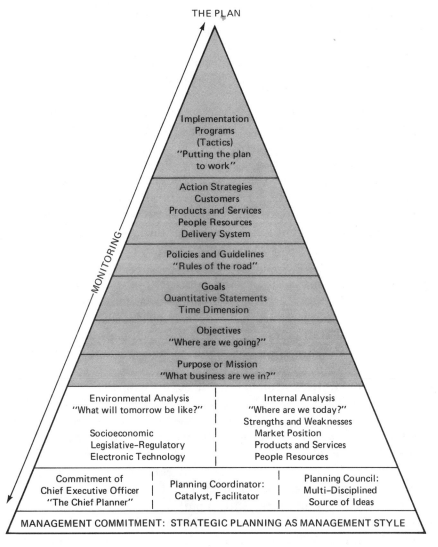

THE PLANNING PYRAMID

Figure 3.1.   The Planning Pyramid.

evolves from management commitment, moving through the various steps, eventually to produce the planning document—the plan.

MANAGEMENT COMMITMENT AND THE CHIEF EXECUTIVE OFFICER

The foundation of planning is the active commitment of management to formal, long-range, strategic planning as a management style for decision making. Commitment to coming up with a plan is insufficient; a proper commitment must be to planning as a decision making process or managerial technique. It is not developing a plan as the product of several months or years work, but being responsive to each step and integrating specific goals and programs into the continuing process of decision making. It is, in effect, keeping longer-term objectives and strategies in mind while actually making immediate, shorter-term decisions.

Accordingly, management commitment appears on the Planning Pyramid in Figure 3.1 as its fundamental element. Without the support of management, planning can only be an abstract project of an isolated staff group. With the support of management, however, the expected values of planning (most importantly, improved performance) may be realized.

The commitment of management begins with the specific commitment of the chief executive officer. He/she is the overall leader of the organization; by definition and without exception, the CEO is the chief planner. This role is shown on the second layer of the Planning Pyramid. The extent to which the CEO commits to and actively participates in the planning process sets the tone for broad management commitment to and participation in planning throughout the organization. If the CEO manifests his or her commitment through enthusiastic and constructive participation, other levels of management will sense it and perform accordingly. If not, the entire process will flounder.

Commitment by the chief executive is demonstrated by actual execution of certain tasks:

- establishing the fundamental direction or purpose;

- deriving a set of objectives to clarify the purpose and make it more specific;
- reviewing and evaluating other parts of the plan;
- and monitoring its implementation.

Only through aggressive execution of these tasks can the CEO build credibility as the chief planner. The ultimate test of how the CEO regards planning is whether his or her decision making adheres to the structure of formal, long-range, strategic planning. In other words, does the plan deteriorate into unilateral, *ad hoc* decisions regardless of the existence of planning structures? If it does, verbal and written exhortations urging subordinates to plan will never persuade them that the CEO really means it.

Persuading Management to Plan

Often a commitment to planning and the execution of planning tasks can be gained from the CEO and other levels of management through the inclination of such individuals to be highly motivated and strongly goal-oriented. This inclination can be transformed into a strategic planning program by showing how planning first delineates goals and, more importantly, how it then develops programs for *achieving* them. In essence, the best way to gain management's commitment is by demonstrating the value of planning in a direct, practical approach. When the CEO asks, "what can planning do for the bank and for me?" he/she must be shown how planning can help both the bank and the CEO achieve their goals, as well as help to avoid major problems that short-circuit goals. A direct, practical approach might show how planning would have avoided making an unprofitable acquisition, prematurely over-commiting to electronic-age "bells and whistles," or being sued by the Equal Employment Opportunity Commission for affirmative action violations. Once the CEO understands what planning can do for him or her, the CEO will have a vested interest and will be more likely to make the proper kind of commitment.

Although commitment by lower management is perhaps assured by a firm top management position, its participation in planning will be more effective if each level of management understands its tasks in the planning process. Too often, executive-level managers are so busy "putting out brush fires" they have no time to plan. Without question, making decisions about goals and strategies *is* difficult. And most managers have not had exposure to planning as they rose through the ranks. Instead, most of their experience has been gained in day-to-day problem solving—personnel problems, bad loans, customer complaints, etc. Shifting to making decisions that require thought, vision, and creativity simply may prove too demanding without sufficient education and training. Management development programs should teach young managers that as they move up the corporate ladder, their scope of activity, responsibility, and decision making becomes broader and broader; that senior managers establish objectives and goals, not short-term strategies and implementation programs. Executive managers make executive decisions, which require breadth of vision and creative thinking.

Avoidance of Planning Oversell

Once management commitment has been gained, it should not be jeopardized by promising more from the initial cycles of planning than realistically can be delivered. If top management feels that precious resources have gone into a program that is supposed to cure all of the bank's problems instantaneously, disappointment is inevitable. As a result, commitment is likely to be withdrawn or at least reduced, leaving planning without a foundation.

Another pitfall is "overplanning" in the early stages. The measure of successful planning is decisions actually made and programs implemented. Grandiose planning studies, massive statistical analyses, and sophisticated audio-visual presentations only detract from planning during the first or second cycle. These accoutrements can be valuable later on, but only when the fundamentals of planning are widely understood and implemented.

Using management commitment as the foundation, a valuable planning process can be built. Its architect is the planning coordinator.

PLANNING COORDINATOR AND PLANNING COUNCIL

Assisting the chief executive officer as the chief planner is the planning coordinator. Except in the smallest organizations, a planning coordinator is necessary to ensure the implementation of a successful strategic planning program. Because the structure and format of the planning process are so important, they warrant the full-time attention of a knowledgeable planning officer. On the other hand, the coordinator is not responsible for the content of the plan. Decisions regarding desired levels of profitability, the quality and mix of the loan portfolio, or the purchase of automated teller machines must *not* be made by the planning coordinator. These are decisions for line and staff management. Only those members of the management team with properly designated responsibility and authority should make these decisions.

Top management determines profitability goals, not the planning coordinator. The head of the commercial division establishes loan policy, not the planning coordinator. The head of the marketing division decides on the thrust and content of advertising strategies, not the planning coordinator.

Activities of the Planning Coordinator

The role should be viewed as that of catalyst. The coordinator makes things happen, but does not substantively participate in their actualization. His or her activities might include devising a proper framework and setting the appropriate circumstances in which top management can make quality decisions about profitability. What does it mean to devise a framework or set appropriate circumstances?

First, the planning coordinator should have a thorough understanding of the basic concepts of planning and the numerous steps in the process. Reading and studying the extensive written information on the subject is important as well as attending planning conferences and talking to experienced planners.

Second, a detailed schedule of responsibilities and timing for the various steps needs to be formulated.

Third, a combination education and selling program should be presented to the levels of management that will have identifiable responsibilities and tasks. This program should emphasize the values of strategic planning to the organization and its managers.

Fourth, each manager participating in the planning process should be shown specific responsibilities and how these coordinate with the responsibilities and tasks of others.

When completed, these four preliminary steps develop the appropriate framework for getting down to the business of formal, strategic planning.

As the planning process proceeds, the tasks of the coordinator become increasingly varied. He/she quickly becomes general overseer of the process—prodding managers to complete their individual parts of the plan, making sure that schedules are followed, reviewing plans for structural accuracy and completeness, and answering all kinds of questions. More specialized responsibilities include assisting managers in preparing presentations of their plans to top management or listening to managers complain about the perceived burdens of planning, but persuading them to complete their plans on time anyway. In a morning meeting the planning coordinator might have to comprehend the organization from the broad perspective of top management and then by mid-afternoon have the perspective of a line manager responsible for the retail branching network. In summary, the planning coordinator must execute multifaceted responsibilities and tasks.

Selecting the Planning Coordinator

Who in today's typical financial institution is a likely candidate for coordinator? Unfortunately, there is no straightforward answer to this question. Such variables as the size and structure of the organization, its prior experience with planning, and the skills and attitudes of several key members of the management team must be considered.

Choosing a Coordinator in Smaller Institutions

In smaller banks and thrift institutions, planning generally is not a complex and time-consuming process, especially on a continuing basis. For the most part, the CEO can function effectively as the planning coordinator. Initially, outside assistance from a consultant or upstream correspondent bank is useful in structuring the process and conducting environmental and internal analyses. From this base, the CEO can work with the other members of the management team to formulate objectives and strategies. When the contents of the plan need to be reviewed and updated, the CEO can function as planning coordinator to lead this same group through the necessary tasks, again relying on outside assistance where appropriate.

Choosing a Coordinator in Larger Institutions

In medium to large organizations, including banks, bank holding companies, and thrifts, a specific individual usually will be designated as planning coordinator. The assignment may vary from a part-time responsibility to a full-time responsibility, including a sizeable staff. Because the CEO always retains the responsibility of chief planner, it is advisable that the planning coordinator not be too far removed from the CEO in the organizational structure. Frequently in a medium-sized or even in a larger organization, the planning coordinator reports directly to the CEO. In much larger organizations, understandably, the coordinator may be a step removed from the CEO or even two, but never more than that. Usually, there is a greater inclination to manage by planning in the larger organizations because the top level people tend to have stronger backgrounds as professional managers than as specialists. Moreover, management by committee is a common practice among the largest organizations, which means that there probably is a planning committee that includes the CEO.

Most of the largest financial institutions have practiced formal, strategic planning for several years. They have built large staffs of professional planners; commonly, they rotate promising young managers through the planning department as part of career path development. On the planning staff are futurists, economists, financial analysts, and full-time observers of the legislative-regulatory scene and the world of electronic technology. The head of the controller's department in such an organization is a professional accountant.

Among those financial institutions that are neither small nor huge, planning only recently has come into vogue. Thus, in many of the nation's banks and thrifts, there are few established practices with respect to the planning process and its coordinator. Initially, at least, planning responsibilities probably will be assigned to an individual with other responsibilities. Likely candidates are the controller or chief financial officer, the marketing or personnel executive, the corporate secretary, or the economist. The choice among these possible candidates should be based on the presence of those characteristics desirable in a planning coordinator.[1]

A planning coordinator should possess *knowledge* of many areas such as economics, finance, accounting, marketing, organizational behavior, management, and political science. It is necessary to be a generalist. Although past experience in specific banking activities also would be valuable, a competent generalist can usually acquire such knowledge easier than a specialist can be broadened into a generalist.

Valuable *skills* include problem solving, good interpersonal relations, and consulting ability. The coordinator should be able to identify problems accurately and pose alternative solutions to assist line managers in making major strategic decisions. A great deal of time is spent with line managers and much of that interaction involves interpersonal skills such as leading, communicating, understanding, persuading, prodding, negotiating, and selling. Consulting skills include the ability to influence people over whom one has no authority, with the primary mission being to help them do a better job.

Finally, the *personal attributes* of a successful planner are judgment, an ability to tolerate ambiguity and uncertainty, a breadth of experience, a broad exposure and outlook, integrity, imagination, and creativity.

Without a doubt, any individual possessing all of these characteristics would be a candidate for sainthood, or at the very least, chief executive officer. As we have said before: Managing is planning. Although it is unlikely that most organizations will have an individual who satisfies all of these criteria, they nevertheless provide a valuable guide to selecting a planning coordinator.

The Planning Council

Some organizations form planning councils or committees. These groups should not be viewed as a substitute for the CEO as chief planner or for the planning coordinator. Rather, a planning council functions as an independent body to accomplish tasks such as:

- facilitating the process of reviewing, examining, and evaluating plans and performance;
- generating ideas for new business directions and action strategies.

In the largest financial institutions where management by committee is common, the planning council should be structured as a senior management group. Its position in smaller-sized financial institutions will be determined by general management philosophy with respect to committees and planning.

The typical planning council should have multi-disciplined, senior-level representation from a cross section of banking activities. Just as with the planning coordinator, however, there are no areas within the organization that are necessarily better suited than others or that should be represented automatically. Much depends on the capabilities of a given individual, including a disposition toward systematic planning efforts. The council needs to have a balance between line and staff people, but all should understand the concepts of planning and be practitioners of planning as a management style. Of course, in an organization with a strong planning program and council, inexperienced managers or those skeptical of planning can be placed on the council for a learning experience.

With the right combination of members, the council can be used effectively for "brainstorming" or "think tank" sessions. Developing novel (and it is hoped, sound) approaches to coping with imminent changes in the world of banking is an especially appropriate task. A two-day session away from the office might be stimulated by an open-ended presentation given by one or more external resource person(s) on the changing world of tomorrow.[2]   Subsequent planning council discussion might focus first on the impact of projected environmental changes on the organization and second on possible strategic responses.

If the council is assigned specific tasks and expected to produce useful results, it can be a constructive addition to the planning process. Without direction, however, it becomes another bureaucratic barrier to corporate efficiency or a bull-session for airing gripes or pushing pet projects.

STRUCTURING THE PLANNING PROCESS

At this stage, the planning coordinator must make some fundamental decisions about the planning process. Most importantly, a structure for working through each of the steps must be developed and then approved by management. Without a structure, a plan is comprised only of lists of objectives, goals, strategies, and programs that may or may not be related. Consistency among the components of planning is important for at least two reasons. First, if the components of the plan are not consistent with one another, then the plan will be changed frequently and there will be no systematic effort toward implementing it. Planning will become an activity and not an action. Second, the planning process needs to be consistent from one cycle to the next in order to produce such planning values as flexibility, regular decision making, and internal coordination.

The structure that eventually is devised also must reflect the realities of the organization and the environment in which it functions. Thus, setting the structure prior to conducting the environmental and internal analysis could well result in having to alter the structure. For this reason, our recommended planning framework is discussed in detail in Chapter Nine, after the environmental analysis of Chapters Seven and Eight.

Planning Steps and the Structure of the Organization

There are at least six distinguishable steps in the planning process that will be performed at four basic organization levels. (Small independent banks have such a simple structure that they probably only have a single organizational level.) This complex interaction between planning and the organization can be simplified through the use of the matrix in Figure 3.2. Down the left-hand side are shown the steps in the planning process. Across the top are several organizational levels as follows:

- corporate   the total organization or top management
- group   major business areas such as domestic banking, international banking, trust, bank-related activities
- unit   separate operating affiliates of subsidiaries such as individual banks or individual bank-related companies
- staff   major staff divisions such as personnel, marketing, or operations

Although this structure is representative of a rather complex financial institution such as a multi-bank holding company, it can readily be simplified to suit alternative structures by eliminating excess levels.

The shaded boxes indicate that a particular planning step is not performed by the corresponding organization level. For example, there is no need for the staff divisions to develop their own purpose as it will be incorporated into their objectives. The numbers indicate the order in which the planning steps should be undertaken by various organizational levels. In some cases the same number is in more than one box, which may mean, as with group, unit, and staff internal analyses, that more than one step should be executed coincidentally. It may also mean that more than one level should be working on a given step simultaneously.

Planning and Timing Considerations

Inevitably, questions arise regarding the length of the planning period, the frequency for going through each cycle, and the time schedule for this process.

The traditional length of the planning period is seen as five years. Half a decade seems long enough to accomplish broad ob-

	Corporate	Group	Unit	Staff
Purpose	1	/////	/////	/////
Environmental Analysis	2	2	2	2
Internal Analysis	3	3	3	3
Objectives	4	5	/////	/////
Goals	6	7	9	11
Strategies	/////	8	10	11
Implementation Programs	/////	12	12	12

Figure 3.2. The Planning Process.

jectives, but short enough for environmental conditions to be fore-casted with a reasonable degree of accuracy. More recently, as the pace of change has accelerated, a three-year planning horizon has appeared to be a more manageable length of time. The most appropriate answer is what best suits the organization, and this qualification is affected chiefly by a number of intangibles: how fast responsive decisions can be made and efficiently implemented; the competitive quality of an organization's primary marketplace; the organization's perceived and desired marketplace positioning; and, above all, an appreciation of internal strengths and weaknesses.

The planning process should not be attempted more frequently than annually. Serious arguments based on time and resource commitments maintain that the total process only should be executed every other year, with revisions and updates made in the intervening years.   Again, each institution must make its own decision regarding frequency. The relevant criteria appear to be:

- the extent to which formal strategic planning integrates with overall management style;
- the rapidity and extent of change in environmental conditions;
- and the resource costs (dollars and people-time) of the process.

After the first cycle is completed, the planning process should take no more than three to six months, preferably the former. The most opportune time is during the first half of the year; there are fewer conflicts with other traditional activities such as budgeting, summer vacations, or November–December holidays.   Conduct planning simultaneously with budgeting only under extreme circumstances.   Although the two activities are not in conflict, the "this year" orientation of budgeting can detract from longer-sighted analysis.

ENVIRONMENTAL ANALYSIS

Referring back to the Planning Pyramid in Figure 3.1, it can be seen that following management commitment to planning, the next layer of activity is a comprehensive analysis of external and internal conditions.   The external analysis specifically is referred to as the environmental analysis and it will be discussed in this section with the internal analysis explained separately in the next section.

Environmental analyses examine future trends in the world in which the financial institution operates.   The accelerating pace of change in socioeconomic conditions, regulatory and competitive structures, and electronic technology is a major theme of this book.   The significance of change was introduced in Chapter One while the details of past changes and the prospects for future change are discussed in Unit Two.   At this stage, we will focus our attention on the mechanics for conducting an environmental analysis.

Conducting an Environmental Analysis

There are two broad approaches to forecasting and evaluating external change. Many small banks and thrift institutions do not have staff members qualified to examine such technical areas as economic forecasting or electronic technology. Thus, one approach is to obtain such information either from paid consultants or larger upstream correspondents.

Larger banks are more likely to employ an economist, a legislative liaison, and technology specialists, individuals who can perform formal environmental studies. If so, the first step is for the planning coordinator to sit down with each of these people and explain what needs to be done. A forecast of major developments in each environment should be made year by year for three to five years, and in the aggregate for another three to five years. Each development should be assigned a probability factor that is to be monitored continually (this process will be explained in another section).

Socioeconomic Environment

An analysis of this area should address broad social, political, and economic questions in terms of their impact on the operations and performance of the bank and on customer groups. Some questions to consider might be:

- what are people demanding from government? what is the future of consumerism? human rights? what kinds of business regulation will be forthcoming?
- how much larger (or less) a proportion of total economic activity will the public sector become? what existing private economic activities will be made public?
- how will the energy issue be resolved? what is the future of OPEC? what role will concerns for environmentalism and quality of life play in shaping national energy policies? what are the prospects for mass transportation?
- what will be the long-term results of the woman's liberation

movement?   how will minorities and low income groups respond to rising economic and social status?

Although definitive answers to these questions are essentially unavailable, no organization can afford to be ignorant of major developments in these fields.   The larger the organization, the greater the potential impact of the socioeconomic environment. In fact, in the smallest organizations the impact may be minimal except for a few landmark events.

More specific analysis of future economic activity might be made in terms of the business cycle. Where in the cycle will the economy be in each of the next few years? How wide will be the inevitable fluctuations in economic activity?   Will short-term interest rates peak at eight percent or twelve percent? What major structural shifts will occur in the mix of American industry? Most importantly, forecasts should stress how future developments will affect the organization.

For example, the textile industry is located chiefly in the Southeast with the heaviest degree of concentration in the Carolinas.   In recent years, the viability of this key industry has been eroded by the imports of cheaper foreign goods. Will the erosion continue?   What steps can be taken to halt it?   Are they taking form?   Are they likely to?   Assuming a somewhat negative response, what does continued erosion imply for textile industry profitability, jobs, bank financing arrangements, and so on.

The same questioning can be applied to other key industries and consumer groups.   In the latter case, society presently faces a population bulge in the 25–35 year-old age group—the "baby boom" of the late 1940s and 1950s come of age. Will they tend to be heavy savers or heavy borrowers compared to preceding generations? Will they tend to be home-buyers or apartment-renters?

Legislative-Regulatory Environment

Environmental studies also assess prospective legislative changes, regulatory developments, and potential shifts in competitive relationships.   In many respects, this area will be the most critical for banks and thrift institutions over the next few years with such probable developments as the spreading of NOW accounts, the further liberalization of branch restrictions, and the possible easing of Regulation Q. Other legislative developments having a major impact are likely to occur in the areas of consumerism and equal credit and employment opportunity.

Although the timing of actions by Congress and regulatory agencies often are difficult to forecast, each must be monitored closely. In addition, state legislation affecting financial institutions will be subject to major change. Indeed, as suggested in Chapter Eight, the leading edge of change in the late 1960s to mid-1970s was at the state level. Important examples have been enlarged thrift industry powers, liberal approaches with respect to the implementation of electronic banking systems, experiments in flexible rate residential mortgage lending, and NOW accounts.

Electronic Technology Environment

Another critical area for environmental analysis is electronic technology and its potential impact on data transfer and customer interface. Automated clearing houses along with consumer devices such as automated tellermachines (ATM) and point of sale terminals (POS) have been in use for some time. But exactly where these developments will be in another five years and, for example, the implications for capital investment remain hazy. Projections regarding this environment especially need to focus on:

- the continuing and rapidly changing state of electronic technology, both in terms of hardware and software developments;
- its impact on auxiliary equipment;
- the level of customer acceptance—generally and with respect to specific EFT devices;
- governmental policy;
- and expected costs.

Thus, in addition to the computer research specialists, marketing researchers also need to be involved. Hardware developments will be important, but sound EFT policies can be formulated only if we understand if, when, and how the public will accept the implied massive changes—and only if we are aware of prospective government involvement in shaping and administering EFT developments. In this sense, it is realistic to ponder whether in the long run the public or private sector will call the shots as the electronic banking era unfolds. Are we building a public utility or a new branching form?

A carefully developed series of forecasts regarding *likely* external developments needs to be coupled with a detailed examination of how they will impact specific operations and overall performance. At this stage, interface between the "blue-sky thinkers" and key line and staff managers in areas such as retail, commercial, operations, personnel, and finance is required. This process applies to organizations of all sizes, although in small banks, it may be only a matter of reading, digesting, and debating studies obtained from correspondents or consultants.

Managers should gain an understanding of what is expected to occur and then translate expectations into likely impacts on their areas of primary responsibility. For example, a retail manager must understand what the future holds for automated teller machines. Then he/she must analyze their likely impact on customer interface, on-line systems capability, and existing bricks-and-mortar branches. These steps occur well before responses are formulated.

During the initial cycle of a planning process, the environmental analysis usually is performed with one massive effort right at the beginning. It is an exciting introduction to planning and is an effective means for convincing managers of the need for strategic planning. It shocks them into awareness. When they are exposed to some of the significant, unsettling, probable changes comprising the world of tomorrow (indeed, often the world of today!), they realize that existing operations and attitudes need to be reevaluated. For example, "women in banking" no longer are coming; they appear to be arriving.

An Ongoing Environmental Analysis

After the planning process has moved into its second or third cycle, the environmental analysis becomes an ongoing procedure.

The outlook for various external developments is updated frequently. Small institutions that contract out their environmental analysis will want to make provisions for receiving updates on a timely basis. Larger institutions conducting their own studies should assign individuals to monitor events in their respective areas. This step is important because the most difficult element to forecast is timing. Although many observers know that another recession, or nationwide NOW accounts, or a less-check society appear inevitable, very few if any can offer an accurate approximation of when such events will occur much in advance. Only by regularly monitoring key economic variables or telltale legislative maneuvering can reasonable forecasts be made.

A simple and moderately expensive approach to monitoring environmental developments is to subscribe to the publications of various trade associations.[3]   Other sources of information might be the various regulatory agencies.[4]   Somewhat more expensive, but also more valuable sources of information are the various survey and consulting organizations.[5]

Within the monitoring process a system can be developed for indicating when a bank should *prepare* for the actualization of some specific event. For example, the removal or modification of Regulation Q seems highly probable within the planning horizon. But exactly when is virtually unpredictable as of planning year one. Thus, this event might be assigned a probability factor of .9 as transpiring within the next five to seven years, but only .1 for the next year. Careful monitoring of legislative activity eventually may raise the short-term probability to .75 for the ensuing eighteen months. This might serve as a triggering level for developing contingency plans for performing in a "world without Q." A similar process could be installed with respect to many other likely external events possessing critical implications for organization activity.

At first glance, an environmental analysis might appear to be a mind-boggling assignment. But a little investigation will reveal more sources of information than one might suspect. Moreover, it is the assessment of potential impact that is even more important, and this process need not be conducted in detail until change is fairly certain. Admittedly, managing change is difficult, but inevitably it is a key to success.

INTERNAL ANALYSIS

If a knowledge of likely future events is critical to developing a plan, so is a basic understanding of what and where the organization is today. Realistic goals and effective strategies require familiarity with existing conditions. For example, formulating a strategy in the commercial area that heavily depends on loan officers possessing sophisticated selling skills is pointless if most of them essentially are "back office" credit analysts. An internal analysis is designed to reveal strengths and weaknesses about the organization, its market position, and its competitive relationship.

Conducting an Internal Analysis

Preparation of a Financial History

The first step in conducting an internal analysis is to work up a financial performance history of the organization. Balance sheets and income statements for at least the prior five years should be spread with a determination of key growth rates and ratios. This information should be discussed and evaluated by management. Its examination ought to focus on strengths and weaknesses of specific aspects of this performance.

Because bankers long have been accustomed to working with the financial side of their organizations, they probably are quite familiar with these data, especially for the most current year. They may not, however, be as aware of various trends revealed by five years of data. Shifts in the composition of income and expenses that were neither deliberate nor desirable may become evident. A substantial rise in the proportion of people costs might appear only over a five-year comparison. Similarly, it would show if there has been a shift in the sources of income between commercial and retail activities.

Comparisons with industry data or competitors also may be made to identify areas of strength or weakness. Although no two organizations necessarily should have the same structure and perform the same, nevertheless, what others are doing provides a rough starting point for evaluating internal activities.

Examination of Existing Plans

Although an organization may not previously have engaged in strategic planning and may not have set explicit objectives and strategies, there is bound to be some implicit understanding of where the organization is going and how it intends to get there. However undeveloped and fuzzy such objectives and strategies may be, they need to be uncovered and articulated so that there is a reasonably clear picture of existing circumstances. The new policies and strategies that are departures from existing practice must be recognized as such. Otherwise, effecting change will be even more difficult.

Identifying current objectives and strategies is the responsibility of the planning coordinator. Interviews with several members of the management team at various levels should provide the necessary information. Among these individuals, however, there may not be complete agreement, especially in the objectives area. Resolving such disputes with pinpoint accuracy is time-consuming and unnecessary. Achieving general agreement about existing policies, strategies, and programs is more important because they keep the organization functioning on a short-term basis. This step in planning should not be allowed to become protracted and drawn out. Going forward with tomorrow's action plans is more productive.

Assessment of Market and Competitive Position

Although evaluation of the market and competitive position is not strictly an internal task, it is more appropriately conducted here. The environmental analysis, while concentrating on external factors, is completely future-oriented. The internal analysis, however, deals with existing circumstances, and particularly *primary* strengths and weaknesses.

Market and competitive position needs to be determined from the point of view of the organization and the point of view of the market. To measure the former, the best approach is to question employees. Details will vary depending on the size of an organization. Smaller institutions may have an advantage because top management is more familiar with the organization and can perform its own analysis. In some ways they may be too familiar, but that bias can be offset by seeking the counsel of an outsider, possibly even a perceptive director. Arrangements also might be made to use a marketing or personnel executive from an upstream correspondent. Another possibility might be to use the business school faculty at a local university.

Evaluating the organization from the viewpoint of the market, especially in smaller institutions, may best be handled informally and directly. Conversations with existing customers and a correspondent banker knowledgeable about the institution and its market probably will provide sufficient information regarding market and competitive position.

Another effective technique for determining market and competitive information, which may be used by both small and large institutions, is a professionally designed questionnaire to survey employees and market participants. The questionnaires for these two groups should be analogous so that comparisons can be drawn between employee and customer perceptions.

Different questionnaires need to be used for different areas of activity such as retail, commercial, trust, or bank-related. Questions should address the following concerns:

- the perceived images of the organization and its competitors;
- types of existing customers by socio-economic status or industry as appropriate;
- quality of products and services;
- quality of service delivery;
- location and convenience factors;
- and any other information deemed valuable.

Employees surveyed should be representative. Market participants surveyed should be a statistically reliable sample of all types of customers and noncustomers in the institution's identified market(s).

CONCLUSION

Organizing and preparing for planning are critical preliminary steps that cannot be shortchanged. The strength of the management commitment constitutes the foundation upon which the entire process is built. Understanding the proper roles of the planning coordinator and council is an important determinant of the eventual success of planning.

In a world of rapid change, future developments in the various operating environments need to be projected and carefully examined before specific plans can be formulated. Similarly, existing strengths and weaknesses need to be identified through an internal analysis.

After these preliminary steps have been completed, management then addresses the two fundamental issues of planning:

- where are we going?
- how are we going to get there?

FOOTNOTES

1. Much of this material is derived from a working paper on this subject prepared by Robert L. Joss, vice-president, Wells Fargo Bank, N.A., in 1975 for the American Bankers Association Corporate Executive Planning Committee.
2. Refer to discussion in Chapter 7.
3. Possibilities include state bankers associations, American Bankers Association, U.S. Savings League, Independent Bankers Association, Conference of State Bank Supervisors, Bank Marketing Association, Bank Administration Institute, etc.
4. The major regulatory agencies are Comptroller of the Currency, Federal Reserve system, Federal Deposit Insurance Corporation, Federal Home Loan Bank Board, Federal Savings and Loan Insurance Corporation.
5. The best known are Booz-Allen and Hamilton, Inc., Yankelovich, and Golembe Associates.

4 IMPLEMENTING THE PLANNING PROCESS

INTRODUCTION

This chapter continues the discussion of the previous chapter on how to prepare for and implement the planning process. With the preliminary steps behind us, we now can look at how to develop the purpose, objectives, and goals—*where the organization intends to go*. The ensuing planning steps—policies and guidelines, action strategies, and implementation programs—establish *how the organization intends to get there*. In the remainder of the chapter, various types of plans and the monitoring process are described.

PURPOSE OR MISSION

The essence of formulating the purpose or mission is answering questions such as why are we in business? What business are we in? What are we trying to accomplish? Without reference to the results of the environmental study, casual answers to these fundamental questions might include the following: the business of banking; taking deposits and making loans; and to maximize profitability. But as any environmental study will reveal, the prospective elimination of Regulation Q, the expanding impact of consumerism, fluctuations in the business cycle, or expanded thrift institution powers, greatly complicate the answers to these questions. Thus, in the Planning Pyramid (reproduced as Figure 4.1) the purpose appears in the level just above the environmental and internal analyses.

Top management writes the purpose; they must—it goes with the job. However, it is the task of the planning coordinator to ensure that the basic decisions involved in determining purpose or mission are made with adequate information and in the proper manner. Top management should understand how significantly the purpose affects the tone of other planning decisions regarding objectives, goals, and strategies. The degree of specificity, inspiration, or aggressiveness revealed in the mission will vary among different organizations.

One approach is to begin with an informal presentation to top management. At this time the major implications raised by the environmental study can be elucidated. For example, most observers expect that future banking will be more competitive, with more competitors pursuing customers more aggressively. Recognizing such changes, the purpose might state that the organization's business is providing a broad array of financial services as opposed to simply banking services.

Next, the planning coordinator should orchestrate a discussion among the members of the top management team in which they express their views about the purpose or mission of the organization. Prior to such a session, the coordinator will provide appropriate background materials. Examples of purposes set by other banks can be a useful guide. Sometimes it helps top management to comprehend the parameters of its task by reviewing basic information about the management of organizations in other business fields. In this respect, the work of Peter Drucker is most applicable.[1] From this discussion, the coordinator can develop draft language for a statement of purpose. This then is reviewed, evaluated, and finalized by top management.

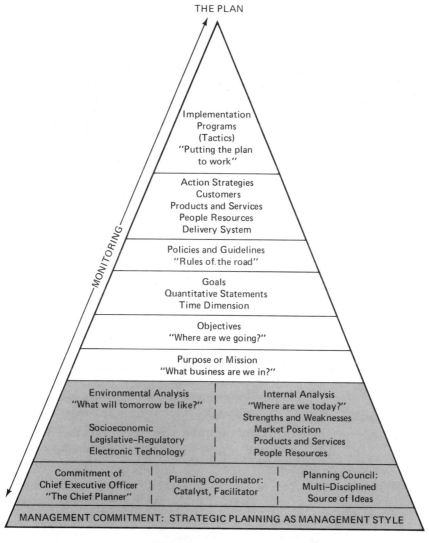

THE PLAN

Implementation
Programs
(Tactics)
"Putting the plan
to work"

Action Strategies
Customers
Products and Services
People Resources
Delivery System

Policies and Guidelines
"Rules of the road"

Goals
Quantitative Statements
Time Dimension

Objectives
"Where are we going?"

Purpose or Mission
"What business are we in?"

MONITORING

Environmental Analysis
"What will tomorrow be like?"

Socioeconomic
Legislative-Regulatory
Electronic Technology

Internal Analysis
"Where are we today?"
Strengths and Weaknesses
Market Position
Products and Services
People Resources

Commitment of
Chief Executive Officer
"The Chief Planner"

Planning Coordinator:
Catalyst, Facilitator

Planning Council:
Multi-Disciplined
Source of Ideas

MANAGEMENT COMMITMENT: STRATEGIC PLANNING AS MANAGEMENT STYLE

THE PLANNING PYRAMID

Figure 4.1. The Planning Pyramid.

Example of Statement of Purpose

... to earn substantial profits for its stockholders. But this aim is entirely compatible with, and indeed, can be achieved only by satisfaction, to the fullest extent possible, of the needs of customers, employees, and the public. Those needs can be satisfied only if the company markets in aggressive fashion a broad array of financial services in selected state, regional, national, and world markets.

Since it is important that top management demonstrates to lower level managers a long-range view of events and an understanding of how the bits and pieces fit together, formalizing and communicating the organization's purpose has critical implications for managerial and staff morale. If management indicates it *knows* where it is going, people at lower levels more easily can discern how they fit into the scheme of things to be.

OBJECTIVES

The next distinguishable step in the planning process is the formulation of objectives. They are in the pyramid tier just above the purpose. By adding specificity to the purpose, the objectives provide a better answer to the question "where are we going?" Formulating these objectives for the entire organization is primarily the responsibility of top management. However, the chief officers of the other organizational levels shown in Figure 3.2 will have major responsibility for setting objectives at their levels. As opposed to the purpose, senior managers also should contribute in setting objectives. The extent of their role depends upon the style of top management and their relationship with top management. The planning coordinator must be sensitive to such considerations, orchestrating the formulation of the objectives accordingly.

Stimulating Management Thinking

Objectives tend to develop as broad, qualitative statements without reference to a specific time dimension. Bank managers, however, are not accustomed to thinking in these conceptual terms;

usually they are action-oriented. To inspire conceptual thinking, a brainstorming session can be valuable, especially if held outside the normal office routine. Maybe one day in a hotel suite will be sufficient; perhaps a full weekend away might prove necessary. One successful approach involved a three-day weekend at a resort during which working sessions and relaxation were mixed. No spouses. No phones. No secretaries. No subordinates. No brush fires to distract anyone—just the business of creative planning.

The responsibility of the coordinator is to structure such sessions and to prepare each participant through exposure to the environmental analysis, the purpose, and the planning framework. Other background materials might include sample objectives of other organizations. Another means of stimulating discussion could be a controversial speech or position paper on a major topic. A little "now-shock" can enhance interest in a "future shock" environment. In addition, the participants should be asked to prepare some draft objectives. Perhaps a structural outline, similar to the one shown in Exhibit 4.1 (page 66) would help them order their thinking. (The format of this outline reflects our recommended planning structure, which focuses on the principal markets in which a financial institution must perform.)

After the objectives have been finalized, they should be circulated, along with a summary of the environmental analysis and the purpose, among the various levels of management that will participate in the ensuing steps of the planning process. Providing management with such information not only is critical to the success of their planning efforts, but also fulfills the important communications function.

Examples of Objectives

... fastest profitable growth in selected geographic/product markets ...

... achieve profitability superior to that of major competitors ...

... obtain the highest possible rating for debt securities ...

... equal opportunity via affirmative action will be the rule ...

... establish a reputation as a first-class wholesale banking organization ...

Exhibit 4.1
Planning Structure

I. Overall
   A. Earnings
   B. Image
   C. Growth
   D. Financial Strength

II. Customers Market
   A. Markets
   B. Relationships
   C. Products and Services

III. People Resources Market
   A. Needs, by Type and Number
   B. Nature of Employment Opportunities
   C. Management, Training, and Development

IV. Investors Market
   A. Quantity of Capital
   B. Debt/Equity Mix
   C. Accessibility to the Market

V. Delivery System
   A. Elements
   B. Interaction Among Elements
   C. Cost Control

GOALS

Not all of the elements in the planning process should be executed top down. At some point, lower levels of management need to participate so that planning assumes a bottom-up character. Where the top-down and bottom-up efforts meet cannot be determined independently from the individual characteristics of each organization. In general, however, these divisions of responsibility interface in the formulation of the goals. Both top management and lower levels of management should participate in goal setting.

Goals, which appear on the Planning Pyramid just above objectives, are more specific than the objectives in several important ways:

- goals are quantitative
- goals have a definite time dimension

- goals apply to functional areas or divisions as well as to the total organization

The Definitive Nature of Goals

The strength of strategic planning is that thinking, judgment, and concepts are emphasized. It is much more than a financial forecast or multi-year budget. However, as long as there has been considerable thinking in the formulation of the purpose and objectives, numbers can be introduced without jeopardizing the program. Numbers are useful as a standard for measuring performance and as a specific management guide for devising strategies and implementation programs.

In banking, the use of numbers is commonplace and cannot be avoided. In fact, many bankers tend to be uncomfortable when removed from a precise, quantified world. This attitude underscores the need for emphasizing the qualitative and strategic components of planning such as the purpose, objectives, and strategies. For the same reason, the formulation of goals in quantitative terms must not be permitted to rule or dominate planning.

With respect to time considerations, goals should be set on an annual basis for each year in the planning period. In this sense, goals become intermediate steps in achieving objectives. Equally, they help activate interest in formulating strategies; annual goals as numbers become a tangible trail to pursue.

Setting Goals

Procedures for setting goals are dependent on the size and structure of the organization. For a small bank or thrift institution, the entire organization constitutes a single operating unit. Thus, there will be only one set of goals. The most complex banking organizations—such as diversified multi-bank holding companies that operate in regional, national, even international markets—usually will have multiple operating units. Each unit should have its own separate set of goals following the principal markets approach in Exhibit 4.1.

Top management contributes to setting goals by communicating performance expectations to the heads of the operating units. These expectations will be determined by objectives for the total organization, projected environmental circumstances (especially economic and financial activity), and an assessment of the unit's ability to perform in its specific market.

Setting goals from the bottom up is a more substantive and detailed procedure. Direct inputs for the unit manager to consider are the environmental study, the purpose and objectives, the top-down goals, and the internal analysis. All of these inputs combine to establish upper bounds for the goals except the internal analysis, which is more likely to have a restraining effect. For example, one objective may be to become the leading wholesale bank in a designated market. Based upon this objective, the inclination is to set goals for rapid growth in commercial loan outstandings. But a careful review of the internal analysis might indicate serious weaknesses in the adequacy of commercial lending personnel, either in terms of numbers, skill levels, or both. Thus, loan growth goals will be tempered by the limitations imposed by existing people resources.

Setting goals must involve more than the head of each unit. The managers of functional areas or divisions such as retail, commercial, or operations should be assigned to work with their key people in developing goals for their areas. Every goal has a quantitative and qualitative dimension. The quantitative may be expressed in absolute dollars or as a percentage growth rate. The qualitative dimension, which clearly is the more important, is an explanation of why the specific quantitative component was chosen in terms of the following:

- historical performance;
- market position and circumstances;
- the results of preceding steps in the planning process;
- and other factors deemed relevant.

Especially during the first cycle of planning, developing goals is a time-consuming procedure involving considerable research, discussion, and evaluation. Revising existing goals in ensuing planning cycles to accommodate changing circumstances requires less work. The initial investment in time is justifiable because it reveals much valuable information about the organization in terms of existing resources and aspirations.

The mechanics of setting quantitative goals raises a number of difficult issues. On the one hand, it is unproductive and distracting for the planning effort to become bogged down in fine tuning a set of financial statement items. On the other hand, any set of numbers that is not internally valid (e.g., the sum of the growth rates of various asset categories does not equal the total asset growth rate) will not be credible. In a small organization, the controller usually can smooth over any inconsistencies after each functional area submits its goal. Many larger banks have computerized financial statement models that can perform this function. It is important, however, that the work of those individuals producing goals be separated from the accounting process. If not, goal setting easily can deteriorate into a data-massaging activity, or at worst, playing with numbers until they prove what you want them to—valid or not.

After a draft of the goals for each unit has been submitted, they need to be reviewed and evaluated by top management based on these criteria:

- as consistent with the overall objectives;
- as intermediate steps to achieving objectives;
- as consistent with other unit's goals.

At some stage, goals are negotiated between top management and unit heads. Thorough and realistic discussions are necessary. Without negotiation, it is unlikely that clear understanding or agreement will emerge.

Examples of Goals

. . . annual percentage growth rates for earnings, total assets, various asset and deposit categories . . .

. . . ratios of fixed expenses such as total people costs and total delivery system costs to total assets . . .

explanations of why these specific goals were chosen.

One final note of warning. Avoid being mesmerized by goals and turning them into absolutes. A one percent return on assets is a goal. It is not a commandment to be followed at all costs, especially not at the expense of risky, high yielding credits that otherwise would not be made. Goals are set to induce systematic habits of good judgment, not to foster recklessness.

POLICIES AND GUIDELINES

In conducting the activities of any business enterprise there are certain rules of the road that must be observed. For a regulated industry such as banking, and one that is so much in the public spotlight, the rules of the road are of even greater importance. Essential determinants of policies and guidelines are legislative and regulatory statutes, public concerns regarding safety and liquidity as well as fairness and disclosure, and management attitudes regarding organizational relationships with regulators and the public.

In recent years, banks and other financial institutions have had to deal with such regulatory agencies as the Securities and Exchange Commission, the Federal Trade Commission, the Federal Reserve, the Comptroller of the Currency, the Federal Deposit Insurance Corporation, and various state banking commissions. The SEC currently is concerned about the lack of disclosure to investors of critical loan information, and the FTC has been scrutinizing banking's responsiveness to a variety of consumerist issues.

Difficult economic and financial circumstances have made both the public and bank management wary about such basic matters as solvency and liquidity. The possibility that the availability of purchased funds—large denomination certificates of deposit, repurchase agreements, Federal funds, etc.—would dry up for any one bank was very real in mid-1974. It actually happened to a few unfortunate institutions!

On the other side of the ledger, asset quality, especially real estate loans, also was deteriorating in 1974. Some bank managements finally realized that during the early 1970s they had permitted long-standing loan quality policies to slide or to be abused in favor of greater profits.[2] Risk was simply assumed, not carefully managed. But then, the early 1970s was a rose-colored world. It was hard to make a mistake. Things kept going up, and few bothered to recall that at some point things eventually turn down.

The business of banking, therefore, demands that there be careful management of risk. This is especially the case when factors such as the following are considered:

- the major portion of available funds comes from depositors, which is substantively different from selling securities to investors, the existence of Federal deposit insurance notwithstanding;
- the likelihood of loan repayment is dependent upon variables as difficult to predict as credit quality, economic conditions, and business risk in a variety of industries.

Policies and guidelines set the standards for risk management as well as for complying with relevant statutory requirements. Within the context of the planning process they establish the lateral boundaries for projected activities.

For the most part, policies and guidelines should be ascribed in general terms by top management with specific points developed by lower levels of management. For example, top management might outline the desired overall quality of the loan portfolio. The commercial people then develop technical details commensurate with the overall guidelines for top management review. Policies and guidelines are stated for each of the market areas in which objectives and goals are devised, as shown in Exhibit 4.1.

By way of practical illustration, here are a few of the new rules of the road that the public interest, acting through Congress, state legislatures, and the regulatory authorities, had laid down or were proposing by the mid-1970s:

- There can be no discrimination due to race, creed, ethnic origin, sex, or marital status—especially at the loan desk and in the personnel office.
- The savings and loan business is *too* closely related to banking to be a "proper incident thereto."

ACTION STRATEGIES

The fundamental strength of the planning process lies in the development of strategies that commit resources to action. Detailed studies and inspirational goals are admirable, informative, and necessary; however, they are not sufficient to result in actual performance. A planning process that does not focus on means for achieving goals will turn out to be little more than an exercise in frustration for all involved, if not a waste of time. To complete planning, there must be action and there must be performance. Simply put, what has gone before is preparatory, a rehearsal. Now the show must go on.

Closing the Planning Gap

Referring to Exhibit 4.2, the interior of the diagram is labeled "the planning gap." That area is bounded by the objectives and goals at the top, the internal analysis at the bottom, and the policies and guidelines on the sides. This area defines what must be done and within what limits in order to move from where we

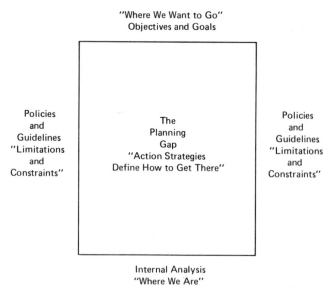

Exhibit 4.2. The Planning Gap.

are today to where we want to be tomorrow. The activities of the planning process thus far have delineated this gap. However, filling it in involves the design of action strategies and their implementation programs.

As a highly competitive, closely regulated industry, with homogeneous products, the objectives and goals for most financial institutions of comparable size in a given market are bound to be similar. Meaningful distinctions are based on how they perform— this means which strategies are employed and how well they are implemented. We have no desire to belabor an obvious point. However, many observers—including the authors—believe that *institutional distinctiveness* will be the name of the game as a more competitive environment and an electronic era unfolds. Action strategies successfully implemented are the cornerstone of distinctiveness. They make it happen.

Devising Strategies

Strategies should be devised on a functional basis, or in terms of the major functional areas of activity in financial institutions. For small banks, these areas are retail and commercial, though there also might be a trust operation. Separate strategies should be developed to achieve goals for retail banking, for commercial or wholesale banking, and for trust banking. Within each of these broad categories, specific strategies should be defined for performing in the principal market areas:

- customer segments;
- product and service lines (loans, deposits, etc.);
- utilization of people resources; and
- delivery systems.

Each strategy describes and integrates the customers to be sought, the products and services to be used, the people resources required, and the delivery system to be used.

This same general approach to devising strategies also applies to larger institutions having more complex structures. In a diversified multi-bank holding company, each separate unit should develop sets of strategies. An affiliate bank can handle strategies in the same fashion as a small independent bank (see above outline). However, a bank-related subsidiary, such as an equipment leasing operation, only needs to formulate commercial strategies since it has no retail customers.

In either case, the elements of a properly developed strategy would include the following: a specification for asset portfolio composition by desired customer and product characteristics; a detailed personnel structure of the organization showing types and numbers of people; the delivery system elements such as size and scope of backroom operations; and the customer contact facility network (buildings and electronic devices). The value of this strategy is that it is market-oriented; lends itself to the creation of innovative, distinctive implementation programs; and is easily monitored.

Examples of Strategies
Commercial or Wholesale Banking

Customers
> . . . only total relationships with whom we can reasonably expect to become their primary or secondary bank . . .

> . . . the composition of the loan portfolio will emphasize medium- to large-sized businesses of strong to moderate credit quality . . .

Products/Services
> . . . a broad array of credit arrangements and financial services will be offered . . .

> . . . revolving credits and intermediate-term loans will be heavily promoted . . .

People Resources
> . . . the types of individuals and the number of each . . .

> . . . an organization chart . . .

> . . . education and training will include courses in . . .

Delivery Systems
> . . . commercial lending capability will be emphasized in these locations . . .

> . . . a systematic call program will be used to develop prospects and existing customers . . .

Strategies for Staff Divisions

One major facet of a bank's internal activities that has not been discussed are the staff and support functions such as marketing, finance, personnel, data processing, and others. Since these functions serve the needs of the operating areas in a responsive or supportive way, they cannot complete their planning until the goals and strategies of the line functions are known.

In setting a framework for staff division planning, these units ought to view the line divisions as their customers and their functional responsibilities—marketing, personnel, etc.—as their products. Staff strategies for customers, products, and services should focus on responding to the relevant needs of the line divisions. Under the categories of people resources and delivery system, staff strategies should describe people requirements to implement customer and product strategies and strategies for interacting with the line divisions.

An example may help to clarify. Suppose that the commercial division in the bank wants to upgrade its officer call program. The commercial division is a line function that has expressed a *need*. It largely must be satisfied by several staff and support divisions. Sensitive to the needs of their customers, the following internal units offer support:

- the marketing staff conducts background market research to identify financial needs of businesses and what they expect from calling officers;
- the personnel staff develops a product knowledge/selling skills training program for commercial calling officers;
- and the data-processing support group designs a management information system that records and stores call data and effects an efficient retrieval system for continuing use.

These activities exemplify the customer and product strategies of these various staff and support divisions. Accompanying strategies must address, for example, the people resources required by the personnel division to develop and conduct such a training program. Moreover, strategies for delivering the program must be described.

Procedures for Devising Strategies

The responsibility for devising strategies falls to the heads of the functional areas and their key subordinates. The chief commercial officer is responsible for commercial strategies, the chief retail officer is responsible for retail strategies, and so forth.

The first task of the planning coordinator is to be certain that the division heads are familiar with and understand the objectives and goals relevant to their areas. Usually this task requires considerable one-to-one discussion. Next, the division heads need to be shown how to identify the nature and magnitude of the planning gap for their areas. It needs to be specified in terms of customers, products/services, people resources, and delivery systems.

The third step for the coordinator is to hold discussion sessions attended by the key people in the division. Possibly a few staff people also could be invited to produce ideas for strategies. In these sessions the coordinator encourages extensive debate regarding the merits of alternative strategies. Perhaps, the issue might be turned over to the relevant staff division for more careful study. Actual choices, however, must be made by the line people who will implement the strategy—someone else's choice is unlikely to be successful.

Finally, the entire package of strategies needs to be carefully reviewed. The review process has several components. First, the planning coordinator should examine the strategies to see if they conform to the designated structure, include all of the necessary elements, and satisfy other mechanical requirements. Second, the strategies must be evaluated to determine whether they constitute a coordinated and integrated package of business activities and whether they are deemed appropriate and acceptable. Top management has ultimate responsibility in both cases, but may delegate a preliminary examination to the planning council. This initial use of a planning council is often the procedure in the larger and more complex financial institutions in which the review task probably is too great a burden for top management. With its multi-disciplined representation, the planning council is particularly qualified to test for coordination among various strategies.

Eventually, however, top management must give its well considered approval. The buck must stop here, and a decision made.

IMPLEMENTATION PROGRAMS

If objectives and goals provide the inspiration, and strategies provide the strength, then implementation programs are the linchpin that holds the entire process together. Action strategies make it happen, and the implementation programs (sometimes called tactics) become the actual event. They ensure execution of the strategies by assigning responsibility and designating timing for committing resources to action.

Implementation programs initially should be developed in conjunction with the strategies. They are more believable when the details of how they will be put into action are known. Thus, as the strategies are developed, assignment of responsibility and timing should be made.

As an example, the earlier illustration of improving the call program as a commercial strategy can be expanded. If one component was to develop a training program, the head of the commercial division should assign one of his officers to work with the personnel staff on this program. Together they would devise implementation tactics that might include the following:

- development of the training program/content;
- assignment of specific individuals to go through the program; and
- setting a specific time schedule.

Implementation programs will differ greatly from institution to institution; they will reflect the personalities, managerial styles, and organizational characteristics of each institution. The point we would leave you with is that the planning trail ultimately must lead to action and each institution will have to adapt broad planning techniques to suit its own needs in order to move planning off the drawing board and out into the market place. The well-designed and properly executed planning process will create an atmosphere that mandates implementation. It should bring about an imperative, a demand for decisions and action.

MONITORING

To complete the planning cycle, there must be a mechanism for monitoring performance against the standards set by objectives, goals, strategies, and implementation programs. Strategic planning can only become a prevailing management style (as well it should) if the CEO evaluates management performance in terms of the plan. A hierarchy for monitoring is evident from the components of planning and the levels of management responsible for them:

- the stockholders and directors hold top management responsible for fulfilling the purpose and the broadest objectives;
- top management holds senior management responsible for achieving certain objectives and goals;
- senior management holds the division heads responsible for attaining specific goals and designing strategies;
- and the division heads hold key subordinates responsible for executing implementation programs.

The role of the planning coordinator is not to make judgments about whether the plan is being implemented successfully. Rather, he/she must make sure that each layer of management, beginning at the top, monitors the performance of its subordinates in terms of the plan. The coordinator must ensure that the strategic planing process is part of management's style. In other words, all decisions should be made within the context of the process; if they are not, the coordinator *must make sure this fact is understood.*

Evaluating performance in light of the purpose and objectives is highly subjective and not very meaningful over short periods of time. Only after two or more years can top management look back and decide to what extent the purpose has been fulfilled or the objectives accomplished.

The other components of planning are more precise, have specific time frames, and can be evaluated more systematically. An X percent increase in primary commercial accounts or an X percent increase in consumer savings deposits within two years either is achieved or it isn't. Commercial officer calls are happening or they are not. Training programs are taking place or they are not. These are tangibles that can be monitored both in terms of quantity and quality. Weaknesses can be rectified and inaction resolved.

The ease and value of the monitoring process depend on the structure of the goals, strategies, and implementation programs. These elements must use a common structure, and they must be consistent. The strategies have to be related to the goals and the implementation programs have to be related to the strategies. If the monitoring process reveals that a given goal is not being achieved, the only way to explain why not is to be able to examine the strategies and implementation programs devised to achieve the goal. By being able to trace through the elements of the plan systematically, much of the burden of the monitoring process is reduced to a mechanical task.

The substantive aspect of monitoring is management's responsibility for evaluating and rewarding performance. At the outset, the chief executive officer must make it clear that management will be held responsible for the execution of the plan. Substantial resources cannot be committed to its development only to have the plan shelved and forgotten. Evaluation of management responsibility for executing the plan occurs in the monitoring process.

The reward mechanism may only be loosely tied to fulfilling the plan or it may be directly tied in a sophisticated, quantitative fashion. The choice depends upon the individual organization. Usually smaller institutions find it unnecessary to establish complex methods while larger organizations find it more equitable to do so.

The monitoring process also is valuable because it provides an explicit linkage from one planning cycle to the next. The planning document is finite, but the planning process is continuous. In an environment of rapid change, revising goals and updating strategies are ongoing activities. The monitoring process provides the stimulus for keeping the various steps current. It identifies what needs to be done in the next round to improve on the prior round.

THE PLANNING DOCUMENT

The immediate tangible result of planning is a document usually referred to as "the plan." Inevitably, the planning process produces reams of paper ranging from abstract background and feasibility studies to "nuts and bolts" implementation programs. Because many people have invested so much time in generating all of this paper, the usual inclination is to reproduce it in a large, fancy, and formal document. If possible, however, this temptation should be resisted in favor of an informal and flexible approach— the loose-leaf notebook approach. Moreover, the smaller the document, the more manageable.

Informality is important because people should not have the impression that the planning document is the most important product of planning. Rather, the process itself—the thinking, creativity, choosing among alternatives, dealing with the futurity of current decisions—is the most important part of planning. Moreover, the process is dynamic and ongoing like the world with which it is designed to cope.

Flexibility also is important. As the process continues, the contents of the plan must change to accommodate the inevitable surprises. With a simple loose-leaf notebook, pages or entire sections easily can be removed and replaced.

If the document is not informal, flexible, and of moderate size, it will be shelved away. As a result, its valuable applications probably will not be realized. The plan itself is instrumental in monitoring its actual implementation and success. Objectives and strategies that have been written down and made known within the organization typically carry a stronger commitment and provide a ready standard for evaluating performance.

The planning document, when distributed among top and senior management, helps one division to know and understand what another division is doing. It provides a handy reference to a retail manager who is about to make a decision that either will influence or be influenced by commercial activities.

In summary, do not permit the planning document to be cast in bronze. Keep it informal and flexible to reflect the dynamics of the real world. The proper commitment is to planning as a management style, not to a stagnant pile of papers.

OTHER PLANNING ACTIVITIES

Not all of the planning activities that many financial institutions need to undertake can be directly included in the overall, regular planning process. Of necessity, acquisition plans, short-run or special project plans, and contingency plans should be developed apart from regular planning activities. These plans involve programs that are not the direct and specific responsibility of any single planning unit.

An acquisition plan, for example, requires input from several disciplines (finance, legal, marketing, etc.) and possibly from external sources. Often, a special multi-disciplined task force is created to draw up such a plan. In fact, historically, many financial institutions have confined their planning activities to the acquisitions area. For that reason such a task force may have been in existence prior to adopting an overall planning program. If so, the danger that the acquisition plan will not be properly integrated with the overall plan is considerable. The responsibility for assuring integration rests with top management. They must examine both plans to be certain that a projected schedule of acquisitions falls within the standards and guidelines established by objectives and action strategies.

In light of rapidly changing environmental circumstances, contingency planning is becoming increasingly important for financial institutions. For example, although projected changes in banking regulation (such as paying interest on demand deposits) usually are anticipated well in advance, precise timing is not. Thus, a contingency or "if-when" plan should be developed outlining the institution's responses. As expected changes become more probable, contingency plans should be updated to reflect changing circumstances. Again, contingency planning requires a multi-discipline approach that, while separate, cannot be totally independent from the content of the overall plan.

All of these specialized planning programs are the prerogative and ultimate responsibility of top management. Nevertheless, other members of the management team should suggest the need for such efforts to top management when the occasion requires.

CONCLUSION

Once the proper foundation for planning has been laid, actual decisions can be made regarding the content of the purpose, the objectives, the goals, the policies and guidelines, the action strategies, and the implementation programs. Careful attention to each of these steps will cause strategic planning to become the dominant management style. Actual performance will reflect intention rather than situational response. The entire management team will understand the direction and activities of the organization, which will contribute to their fulfillment.

This chapter has emphasized the how-to of these planning steps. It has explained which levels of management are responsible for each step and what procedures are involved in accomplishing each step. Having a firm grasp of the procedures is an important prerequisite to launching an organization into the process.

We now turn our attention to a combination internal and external analysis in Chapters Five through Eight. A discussion of major developments on the banking scene over the last quarter-century sets the stage for a series of predictions and analyses of future changes in the industry.

FOOTNOTES

1. Peter F. Drucker, *Management: Practices, Tasks and Responsibilities* (New York: Harper & Row, 1974), Chapters I–VIII.
2. The pressure for profits stemmed in part from the emergence of the bank holding company as a vehicle for rapid growth, which required access to the capital markets and thus rapid growth in earnings. In no time, holding company management became fixated on quarter-to-quarter earnings gains at the expense of long-run judgment and prudence.

UNIT TWO: THE YESTERDAY, TODAY AND TOMORROW OF BANKING

5 BANKING DISCOVERS PEOPLE: THE POSTWAR YEARS

INTRODUCTION

The planning framework requires that we build on where we are today. This means careful and honest appraisal of a financial organization's resources, including people resources, its existing customer base, and the means it employs to deliver products and services. Moreover, the organization must comprehend its position in the marketplace, both as a distinctive, individual financial institution operating in a particular geographic area, and as a member of a larger family of commercial banks, mutual savings banks, savings and loan associations, credit unions, finance companies, whatever. The organization then must view this positioning in terms of such critical characteristics as its ability to:

- utilize branch offices
- engage in diversified bank-related activities through a holding company mode
- provide services through electronic money machines and point-of-sale transaction terminals

In addition, any realistic appraisal of where we are today should recognize the pervasive impact of the external environment in shaping and reshaping organizational objectives, action strategies, and the implementation programs for achieving them. The external environment in a simplified, yet still important sense can be viewed as *the customer*. It is people and their intricate complex of attitudes and expectations. Understanding the external environment, therefore, involves preparing realistic answers to questions such as these:

- what does the customer as consumer, saver, borrower, investor—even as employee—want and need?
- why does the customer feel this way? Are perceived desires deep-rooted and meaningful or faddish?
- what does the customer think of us, expect from us, demand from us—if indeed, he or she bothers to think of us at all in a distinctive manner?
- is the customer concerned, possibly even angered, by an organization's interrelationships with other customers? Does the home-buyer or small business entrepreneur believe that he or she is denied a fair shake or a just share? Does the environmentalist abhor a bank's financing of nuclear energy development? Does a black or a woman customer presume an institution's predilection to enslave them as second class citizens?

When all is said and done, the competitive response as an industry or as an individual financial institution is triggered largely by changing customer wants and needs, most of which, in turn, are determined by socio-economic, political, and technological changes that cause people to think and act differently. Where we have been and are today, therefore, is influenced immeasurably by customer patterns for buying, spending, and saving: *The management of money is banking's business.*

PEOPLE: THE NEW CUSTOMER

It is commonly acknowledged that during the first decade following the devastation of the Depression and World War II, the commercial banking industry turned to people, to the retail market, for a growing, rapidly expanding share of its business. Because of a traditional orientation toward corporate customers, this thrust was capsulized by the convenient though misleading notion that banking, like Rip Van Winkle, had awakened from a long slumber to discover that ordinary people could make good customers: They would supply more funds than they borrowed; they would promptly pay their debts; and they would earn a bank an acceptable profit.

Banking did in fact discover people. It did go after their savings and credit needs in an explosive manner. It did respond energetically to new marketplace imperatives. And over time, banking did turn itself inside out with respect to the products and services it offered and, just as significant, the methods for delivering them. So strong was this response in the retail field that it came to be seen as a symbolic, watershed event—a Druckerian "discontinuity." Contemporary commentators labeled it as a retail revolution.

In the larger scheme of things, this development really was more of an evolutionary step than a revolution. It did not signal a radical departure from the past. The postwar discovery of people was not an innovation, although the emerging procedures for reaching customers and responding effectively to their needs and wants did mandate escalating levels of innovation as time passed. Nor, did retail banking precipitate a dramatic shift away from business lending. To the contrary, an excess of consumer deposits over consumer borrowings funded an expansion of both business and governmental lending.

Retail banking was evolutionary in still another sense. Its foundations had been laid prior to the Great Depression; indeed, a number of today's largest banking organizations are descended from the Morris Plan movement launched early in this century. Moreover, the nation's always substantial number of independent country and community banks historically had been greatly concerned with serving consumers in their particular, though limited marketplaces. Then, too, an interest in acquiring a substantial share of consumer income was much in evidence during the years prior to the Depression, especially as money center banks acted in a dual capacity as depositories and agents for speculative investment.

But if the fact was not revolutionary, the extent was. From the 1950s on, banking reached out to the retail market in a big way and on a broad front: through extensive branching; through the "plastic branch," the credit card; by employing the consumer certificate of deposit; by paying ever-rising rates for savings; and by utilizing the holding company structure to overcome restraints on geographic expansion and product development.

These changes also *appeared* revolutionary because they signi- fied a demarcation between yesterday and today: between a time of pens and adding machines *and* the computer age; between a time of unit banking *and* branch banking and the holding com- pany; and between a time of largely domestic banking *and* an age of multi-national leaders.   It is the results rather than the re- sponses that came to be seen as a discontinuity, as evidence that change had taken place and that somehow things were greatly different.

Later in this unit, we will analyze the internal and external forces that combined to precipitate banking's responses and their characterization as "discovering people."   First, however, it is appropriate to add up the results. These facts and figures attest to commercial banking's postwar performance.   They serve as an impressive prologue to any consideration of the future. Equally, they certify the efforts of the planning executive by indicating what is possible. What has been achieved after all reasonably argues for what is achievable.

A TRILLION DOLLAR INDUSTRY

Number and Type of Bank Offices

As shown in Table 5.1, there were 14,164 commercial banks in operation in 1950, and they administered 4,945 branch offices. By year-end 1975, the number of banks was virtually unchanged, totaling 14,654. However, the number of branches had increased *sixfold* to 30,262, a reckoning which excludes electronic facilities. Branch offices operated by savings and loan associations, commer- cial banking's principal competitors in the retail market, numbered 601 in 1955; in the same year there were 6,071 Federal and State- chartered associations in operation. By 1974, the number of asso-

Table 5.1. Number and Type of Commercial Bank Offices: 1950-1975.

	1950	1960	1970	1975	Change
Banks	14,164	13,484	13,686	14,654	+ 490
Branches	4,945	10,619	21,644	30,262	+25,317
Total Offices	19,109	24,103	35,330	44,916	+25,807
Unit Banks	13,246	11,391	9,874	9,114	− 4,132
Banks Operating Branches	1,404	2,594	4,305	5,540	+ 4,136

Source: *Annual Reports*, Federal Deposit Insurance Corporation, Washington, D.C.

ciations had declined to 5,071, while the number of branches they administered had increased to 8,775—or twice the growth rate achieved by banks.[1]

Over this quarter-century, the absolute number of operating commercial banks dipped slightly, then recovered in recent years to record a modest overall increase of three percent. These data are somewhat misleading, however. For one thing, many banks each year were merged as branches into multi-office systems. Between 1964 and 1974, the number of insured banks ceasing operation each year ranged from a low of 97 to a high of 165; in most instances, cessations were attributable to mergers, with many becoming branches of other banks. New bank formations during this decade ranged from a low of 92 in 1968 to a high of 408 in 1974.

Most significant, there was a clear tendency for both new bank formations and branch openings to be clustered in metropolitan suburban areas surrounding city centers and in emerging population centers in the high-growth states of the Southeast, Southwest, and Far West. What this means is that banking was following the movement of people and industry, *provided* state codes accommodated this movement. In unit-banking states where expansion was constrained by legal prohibitions against branching, new bank formations were required to accommodate population shifts; not surprisingly, therefore, the preponderance of new banks chartered since the 1950s tended to be located in the one-third of all states that prohibited outright or severely restricted branching. It is noteworthy that laws dealing with savings and loan branch expansion tended to be generally more liberal, and helps account for a continued decline in the number of operating associations between 1955 and 1974.

This explanation does not detract from the central point that during the past quarter-century there occurred a veritable explosion in the number of retail customer facilities. Indeed, their rate of growth far surpassed population increases or even changes in the proportionate number of people moving from city centers or established rural communities to suburbia.

Keeping pace with this explosion was an alteration in the type and style of banking offices. In purpose and decor, these facilities came to represent a conscious attempt to relate in a positive fashion with the customer groups they served: For example, iron-barred teller cages were replaced with open counters; sofas appeared near the new-account desk. People insisted on "friendlier" banks and banks wanted their business. Similarly, the type of banking office changed because alternative means were devised to accomodate the retail customer as well as a bank's commercial clientele. One alternative was the credit card or "plastic branch." Another was the consumer finance company affiliate of a bank holding company or, with respect to commercial customers, a loan production office in a distant city or a holding company's factoring affiliate. By the 1970s, consequently, a regional or money-center banking organization might administer this representative *branching* network (see page 89).

The Bank Holding Company Movement

Toward the end of the 1960s, and then more quickly following enactment of the 1970 Bank Holding Company Act Amendments, there occurred a dramatic increase in the number of diversified, multi-bank organizations as well as one-bank holding companies. This expansion is depicted in Table 5.2; data do not include the number and resources of the bank-related units of one-bank or multi-bank organizations. Nor do they embrace the activities of exempted (unregistered) one-bank companies and their bank-related operations, most of which tend to be smaller rural banks

Chart 5.1

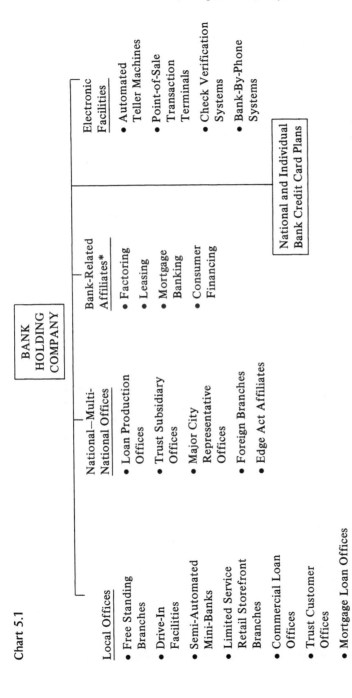

BANK HOLDING COMPANY

Local Offices
- Free Standing Branches
- Drive-In Facilities
- Semi-Automated Mini-Banks
- Limited Service Retail Storefront Branches
- Commercial Loan Offices
- Trust Customer Offices
- Mortgage Loan Offices
- Investment and Money Management Offices

National–Multi-National Offices
- Loan Production Offices
- Trust Subsidiary Offices
- Major City Representative Offices
- Foreign Branches
- Edge Act Affiliates

Bank-Related Affiliates*
- Factoring
- Leasing
- Mortgage Banking
- Consumer Financing

Electronic Facilities
- Automated Teller Machines
- Point-of-Sale Transaction Terminals
- Check Verification Systems
- Bank-By-Phone Systems

National and Individual Bank Credit Card Plans

*The Bank Holding Company Act Amendments of 1970 as interpreted by the Federal Reserve Board initially authorized 16 activities to be 'closely related to banking' and therefore permissible under Section 4(c)8 of the Act.

Table 5.2. Number and Deposits of Registered Bank Holding Companies:
1956-1975.

	1956	1965	1970	1975
Number of Registered Bank holding Companies	53	53	121	1,821
Number of Affiliated Insured Commercial Banks	428	468	895	3,674
Branches	783	1,486	3,260	18,382
Total Offices	1,211	1,954	4,155	22,056
Total Offices as a Percent of all Insured Bank Offices	(5.8%)	(6.7%)	(11.8%)	(49.4%)
Total Deposits ($-Bil.)	$14.8	$27.5	$78.0	$528.0
Total Deposits as a Percent of all Insured Bank Deposits	(7.5%)	(8.3%)	(16.2%)	(67.1%)

Source: *Bank Holding Companies Today*, The Association of Registered Bank Holding
Companies, Washington, D.C., November, 1976.

administering a wide range of community-centered agricultural
and commercial activities. Trust department offices and financial
resources also are excluded.

Structurally, commercial banking consolidated through mergers,
de novo branching, and affiliate acquisitions. It then enlarged its
operational base through bank-related activities assuring further
geographic and product extension. To be sure, not all or even a
majority of the nation's banks elected to move in this direction.
However, many did, most of them larger, urban-centered organizations. More important, the holding company mode came to
radicalize notions about bigness, concentration of economic
power, and competitive parity.

Where the Money Came From

Table 5.3 focuses on the growth in business and personal deposits
in commercial banks between 1950 and 1975. It highlights several
key developments.

During the first decade, between 1950 and 1960, total deposits
increased by some $60 billion, or by nearly 50 percent. During
the next decade, however, the total increased by $207.3 billion

Table 5.3. Growth in Business and Personal Deposits In Insured Commercial
Banks: 1950-1975.

$ = Millions Year	Total Deposits	Demand Deposits	Pct. of Total Deposits	Time and Savings Deposits	Pct. of Total Deposits
1950	$127,480	$ 89,993	70.6%	$ 34,583	27.1%
1955	158,145	108,366	68.5	45,891	29.0
1960	188,016	116,606	62.0	66,834	35.6
1965	275,205	139,078	50.5	130,195	47.7
1970	395,247	181,987	46.0	204,963	51.9
1975	647,889	246,559	38.1	389,781	60.2
Percent Increase 1950-75:	408.2%	174.0%	....	1027.1%	....

Source: *Annual Reports*, Federal Deposit Insurance Corporation, Washington, D.C.

or 110.2 percent. Between 1970 and 1975, deposits rose by
$209.4 billion, or 53.0 percent. This in-flow is indeed impressive.

There was a change in where this money came from and, implicitly, what it cost and the consequences for earnings and credit
allocation policies. In 1950, 70 percent of total deposits were
held in demand accounts that did not bear explicit interest. By
1960, this ratio had declined to 62 percent, and by 1975 was only
38 percent. The proportion of interest-earning time and savings deposits rose accordingly, as did the price (interest and acquisition expenses) paid for those funds. Therefore, banking during this
period thus was attracting *more money*, but also *more costly
money*.

Most of this increase came in the form of time and savings
deposits, which during the quarter-century rose by over one
thousand percent, or six times as fast as checkbook money.
Savings funds came almost entirely from consumers. Federal
Reserve Board data indicate that between 1960 and 1973 nearly
three out of every four dollars added to time deposits each year
also came from consumers.[2]

Interrelated, from the late 1950s on, corporate treasurers
commonly began drawing down commercial bank balances. These

"disintermediated" funds tended to be invested in higher yielding money market instruments. The introduction of negotiable, high-denomination CDs and later the marketing of holding company debt issues was designed, at least in part, to counter this trend. Even so, the overall or cumulative effect was to markedly increase bank holdings of more costly funds.

As shown in Tables 5.3 and 5.5, the greatest proportionate growth in time and savings deposits or over-the-counter savings occurred between 1960 and 1975. During this period, deposits increased 483 percent. By comparison, savings and loan share accounts and other deposits increased 360 percent; mutual savings bank deposits rose 202 percent; and credit union share accounts gained 560 percent. Commercial banking thus was increasing share-of-market at the expense of savings and loans and mutuals, the principal competitors. In the preceding decade, banking only kept pace with mutuals and had surrendered market share to both savings and loans and credit unions.

A More Costly Dollar

Explanations for this turn-around are found in developments such as commercial banking's aggressive branching policies, the introduction and marketing of the corporate and consumer certificate of deposits, and certainly the credit card movement. But more important, commercial banks became *competitive* in what they paid for people's savings. As depicted in Table 5.4, the average yield on commercial bank time and savings deposits (IPC) in 1950 was one-half of the amount paid by mutuals and just one-third of the amount offered to savings and loan customers. By 1960, this gap had narrowed to approximately a single percentage point, and ten years later the differential virtually disappeared.

Studies conducted by the Federal Reserve Board reveal these tendencies among different classes of commercial banks:

- smaller commercial banks commonly pay higher rates of interest on savings. In 1975, the average rate paid by banks with deposits of less than $10 million was 5.76 percent; banks

Table 5.4. Average Annual Yields on Selected Types of Investments.

Year	Commercial Bank Time and Savings Deposits	Savings and Loan Association Deposit Accounts	Mutual Savings Bank Deposit Accounts	United States Government Bonds
1950	0.94%	2.52%	1.84%	2.32%
1955	1.38	2.94	2.64	2.84
1960	2.56	3.86	3.47	4.01
1965	3.69	4.23	4.11	4.21
1970	4.95	5.06	5.01	6.59
1975*	5.90	6.22	5.89	6.98

*Preliminary
Sources: *Annual Reports*, Federal Deposit Insurance Corporation, Washington, D.C.;
Savings and Loan Fact Book, United States League of Savings Associations,
Chicago, 1976, p. 15.

holding deposits in excess of $500 million paid rates averaging
5.49 percent.
- commercial banks located in Standard Metropolitan Statistical
  Areas, regardless of deposit size, usually offered customers
  lower rates than banks located in a rural environment.
- with respect to time deposits, the opposite tendency prevailed.
  Larger banks offered higher rates, as did banks, regardless of
  size, located in an urban environment.[3]

It should be clear from this analysis that commercial banking
must be viewed in terms of its diverse parts rather than as a whole.

Table 5.5. Over-the-Counter Savings: Changes in Market Share: 1950–1974

Percent of Savings* Held By	1950	1955	1960	1965	1970	1974
Commercial Banks	50.0%	42.3%	39.4%	43.2%	46.9%	49.4%
Savings and Loan Associations	20.1	29.5	36.4	36.5	33.3	33.3
Mutual Savings Banks	28.7	25.9	21.3	17.3	16.3	13.5
Credit Unions	1.2	2.3	2.9	3.0	3.5	3.8

*Commercial bank time and savings deposits of individuals, partnerships and corpora-
tions; savings and loan association share accounts and other deposits; mutual savings
bank regular and special savings accounts; and credit union shares and members' deposits.
Source: *1976 Savings and Loan Fact Book*, p. 14.

This point will acquire added significance as we assess such post-war developments as the liberalization of state branching laws and the holding company movement. In both instances, distinctions among different types of commercial banks played a prominent role in shaping the direction taken by these developments, certainly as much as differences between banks and other financial institutions.

Table 5.5 reemphasizes much of the foregoing. Between 1950 and 1960, commercial banking's share of "over-the-counter" savings, when contrasted with the proportion held by thrift institutions, declined from 50 percent to less than 40 percent. Between 1960 and 1974, however, this loss was recovered.

The Cost of Competition

One consequence of a more competitive posture in reaching out to acquire a larger share of consumer deposits was to increase banking's overall cost of funds.

This increase was occasioned not only by the direct cost of higher rates paid for deposits (and the proportionately slower growth of checking account balances) but also by steady gains in deposit acquisition expenses. For one thing, there was the cost of establishing branches and a corresponding enlargement of the industry's work force. Then, too, banks began to advertise and in other ways promote consumer-oriented programs, especially deposit-gathering activities. Finally, banks began incurring large expenditures—*people and machines*—for computer-based, back-room support considered critical in coping with the higher volume of consumer business. Data are not available to detail the cost to alter support operations to accommodate the industry's frontal assaults in the retail market. It is no secret, however, that just one expense—the development of the bank credit card—was, perhaps to understate the matter, exorbitant. Credit card operations still were viewed as "loss leaders" by many banking organizations in the 1970s; in fact, very few organizations would admit to recovering research and development costs. This awareness became a factor in explaining industry hesitancy to experiment aggressively with electronic banking systems.

Table 5.6 indicates that interest paid on time and savings deposits as a percentage of operating expenses skyrocketed over the past quarter-century. Responses to the fact of increasingly expensive funds resulted in major alterations on the asset side of the ledger.

Before assessing these alterations, it should be explained that banking concurrently focused increased attention on bottom-line performance, whether interpreted as spread management, earnings per share, or price-earnings multiples. Commercial bankers traditionally equated performance with growth in footings—i.e., with just how big their "shop" was and was becoming. Footings commonly meant annual increases in total assets or total deposits; marketing department footings, by way of contrast, translated as advertising lineage or television time spots. By the late 1960s, however, attention shifted from the balance sheet to income statement performance—from size to earnings.

The holding company movement, chiefly because it involved closer dealings in a *customer* capacity with money and equity markets, contributed substantially to this altered way of thinking. In any case, by the 1970s institutional performance usually

Table 5.6. Interest Paid on Time and Savings Deposits (IPC) as a Percentage of Total Operating Expenses in Insured Commercial Banks: 1950–1974.

Year	Interest Costs Per $100 of Expenses
1950	$ 8.7
1955	10.6
1960	16.6
1965	30.2
1970	34.2
1974	40.9

Source: *Annual Reports*, Federal Deposit Insurance Corporation, Washington, D.C.

was measured by annual changes (upward, it was hoped) in per share earnings, stock prices, degree of leverage, and loan portfolio mix and quality. The holding company movement was not the only force working to occasion this attitudinal change. Just as important, probably even more so, was how, where, and why banking altered its funds allocation patterns.

Loan and Investment Practices

Table 5.7 depicts both the sharp increase in the dollar amounts of credit extended and its proportionate growth as a percentage of total assets. Given alternative methods of funds allocation, it is understandable that there was a commensurate increase in *risk*: that is, in making loans at the expense of a safer investment in government-guaranteed securities. Commercial banking's loan-to-deposit ratio increased from 33.7 percent in 1950 to 51.1 percent in 1960, and to 64.5 percent by 1975. It likewise follows that risk exposure and outright losses accompanied the substantial increase in the proportion of loans outstanding. From 1960 through 1968, for example, net loan losses as a percentage of total capital accounts ranged below one percent; between 1968 and 1973, this loss ratio ranged between $1\frac{1}{2}$–2 percent annually; however, in 1974 and 1975, it moved sharply upwards as the severe recession of that period deepened. In 1975, the industry's loss ratio exceeded 4 percent, reflecting both prevailing economic conditions and high loan-to-deposit ratios.

As indicated in Table 5.7, commercial banks during the postwar years allowed holdings of cash assets and United States government obligations (with their relatively low yields during much of this period) to run down. Conversely, the loan portfolio expanded, rising from 31 percent of total assets in 1950 to 46 percent by 1960, and to 57 percent by 1975. Holdings of state and local obligations and other securities also increased sharply. Their tax free status made real yields attractive. Of equal importance in accounting for their growth were the needs of communities and state authorities to finance developments linked to demographic shifts—e.g., the move from urban centers to suburbia that meant

Table 5.7. Principal Assets and Liabilities of All Commercial Banks: 1950-1975.

Assets	1950	1955	1960	1965	($-Millions) 1970	1975	1950-75 Percent Change
Total Assets	$168,932	$210,734	$257,552	$377,264	$576,242	$965,198	+471.4%
Cash Assets	40,289	46,838	52,150	60,899	93,463	133,614	+231.6
As a Percent of Total Assets	(24%)	(22%)	(20%)	(16%)	(16%)	(14%)	
United States Government Obligations	62,027	61,592	61,003	59,547	61,742	118,527	+91.1
As a Percent of Total Assets	(37%)	(29%)	(24%)	(16%)	(11%)	(12%)	
State and Local Government Obligations and Other Securities	12,399	16,688	20,864	44,855	86,118	111,094	+796.0
As a Percent of Total Assets	(7%)	(8%)	(8%)	(12%)	(15%)	(11%)	
Loans and Discounts	52,249	82,601	117,642	201,658	313,334	546,452	+945.9
As a Percent of Total Assets	(31%)	(39%)	(46%)	(53%)	(54%)	(57%)	
Liabilities							
Total Deposits	155,265	192,254	229,843	332,436	480,940	786,532	+406.6
Demand Deposits	104,723	126,896	139,324	166,305	217,273	323,617	+209.0
Time Deposits	36,503	48,715	71,461	146,697	231,084	462,915	+1168.2
Total Capital Accounts	11,590	15,300	20,986	30,272	42,958	69,125	+496.4
As a Percent of Total	(6.9%)	(7.3%)	(8.1%)	(8.0%)	(7.4%)	(7.2%)	

Source: *FDIC Annual Reports*

schools, hospitals, sewage systems, power resources, roads and highways, and shopping centers.

Table 5.8 illustrates that banking after 1950 generally reduced the proportion of loans to business (commercial and industrial loans) and its holdings of lower-yielding mortgages on residential properties, which tended to be pegged to regulated ceilings. Conversely, banks increased the proportionate amount of credit to individuals and on real property not secured by residential property, such as shopping centers where home loan rate ceilings did not apply.

The extent of this activity is brought into clearer focus by data in Table 5.7 showing that between 1950 and 1975 total loans increased 946 percent as contrasted with deposit growth of 407 percent—a growth rate *twice* as steep. Both in absolute and proportional amounts, banking was placing more funds into rate sensitive, higher yielding, shorter maturity, and somewhat riskier credits. This was a process largely necessitated by a greater volume of more costly deposits and their higher acquisition expenses. Accordingly, banks became aware of and began to *manage the spread*.

Using somewhat different data for the 1960–1970 period,[4] the foregoing comments might be summarized as follows:

- *Individuals* were net providers of $107 billion since they supplied $171 billion in time and demand deposits and borrowed only $64 billion.
- *Business* borrowed $117 billion from the system, while increasing its demand deposits by only $4 billion. It did supply about $28 billion in time deposits, but on balance was a net user of some $85 billion.
- *State and local governments* became more involved with the banking system, providing about $26 billion to the system—an amount almost equal to that provided by the business segments—while using some $47 billion.
- *The Federal Government* became a less significant customer.

The fact that the business segment during the 1960s borrowed far more than it placed in the banking system does not detract

Table 5.8. Where Banks Put Their Money: Major Loan Categories—1950-1975.

Loan Category	1950	1955	1960	1965	1970	($ = Billions) 1975	Increase
Total Loans	$53.2	$84.4	$102.5	$204.7	$300.4	$507.2	953.3%
Commercial and Industrial Loans	22.0	33.4	45.4	71.9	113.4	179.0	713.6
As a Percent of Total Loans	(41.3%)	(39.5%)	(36.0%)	(35.1%)	(37.7%)	(35.3%)	
Loans on Residential Real Estate Property	10.4	15.9	20.4	32.4	45.6	76.4	634.6%
As a Percent of Total Loans	(19.5%)	(18.9%)	(16.9%)	(15.8%)	(15.2%)	(15.1%)	
Loans on Real Estate Secured By Other Properties	2.3	3.8	6.8	14.4	23.3	46.2	1908.6%
As a Percent of Total Loans	(4.3%)	(4.5%)	(5.6%)	(7.0%)	(7.8%)	(9.1%)	
Loans to Individuals	10.2	17.3	26.5	45.7	66.3	106.7	946.1%
As a Percent of Total Loans	(19.2%)	(20.5%)	(22.0%)	(22.3%)	(22.1%)	(22.0%)	

Source: *Annual Reports*, Federal Deposit Insurance Corporation, Washington, D.C.

Table 5.9. Consumer Instalment Debt Outstanding, by Class of Holder: 1950–1975.

	1950	1955	1960	1965	1970	($ = Billions) 1975	Increase
Total Debt Outstanding Held by Financial Institutions	$14.7	$28.9	$43.0	$70.9	$102.1	$162.2	1003.4%
Commercial Banks	11.8	24.4	36.7	61.1	88.2	144.2	1122.0%
Credit Unions	5.8	10.6	16.7	29.0	45.4	78.7	1256.9%
Finance Companies	.6	1.7	3.9	7.3	13.0	25.3	4116.7%
	5.3	11.8	15.4	23.9	27.7	36.7	592.4%
Miscellaneous Lenders* Held by All Retail Outlets	.1	.3	.6	1.0	2.1	3.5	3400.0%
	2.9	4.5	6.3	9.8	13.9	18.0	520.7%
Percent of Financial Institution Total Held By Commercial Banks: Market Share	(49.1%)	(43.4%)	(45.5%)	(47.5%)	(51.5%)	(54.6%)	

*Includes mutual savings banks and savings & loan associations.
Source: *Federal Reserve Bulletin*, Board of Governors, Federal Reserve System, Washington, D.C.

from data presented in Table 5.8. Reflected is not how much individuals or business customers added to the system, but what they used compared to other lending categories. Expressed differently, individuals added seven of every ten deposit dollars to the system; they used only one of every three deposited dollars, leaving a sizeable excess for the use of business and government customers. Banking's discovery of people in many respects involved chiefly a heightened awareness of this ratio and its implications. Consequently, the in-gathering of consumer savings emerged as a key performance yardstick. Table 5.9 adds a significant competitive dimension to this performance.

It will be seen that commercial banking's share of the consumer lending business, including credit card activity, rose from a low of 43 percent of all instalment debt supplied by financial institutions in 1955 to 55 percent within two decades. Moreover, the 1257 percent increase in bank instalment debt greatly outstripped overall bank loan and deposit growth.

CONCLUSION

These are just a few of the indicators depicting banking's response to postwar changes in the marketplace. The numbers are impressive as we have seen. But while these facts and figures are significant in and of themselves, they understandably are even more pertinent in terms of cause-effect relationships.

It can be said, for example, that both turning to people as depositors and borrowers and the general tendency toward volume lending caused commercial banking to extend the parameters of its business. It sought diversification, equally in terms of product extension and geographic expansion. One consequence was the holding company movement, through which commercial bankers sought to circumvent what many believed were largely artificial barriers erected in another time and place to control a vastly different type of business.

Not surprisingly, this trend provoked both a series of competitive responses designed to constrain holding a company growth *and*, concurrently, other actions designed to optimize the enlargement of banking and thrift institution powers (in the interest of competitive parity).

It also can be said, accurately enough, that the volume of activity—the numbers in terms of loans and deposits—associated with a turning to people, to the retail market, compelled the need for and intensified use of technology. Required was a least expensive, accurate, efficient, and convenient method for handling greater volumes of human transactions. The effect became computerized transaction handlers and, interrelated, the rise of the credit card. The effect also became the industry's entry into the emerging world of electronic banking.

As we will learn in the next chapter of Unit Two, these changes principally were compelled by a range of diverse, yet interconnected *external* or environmental forces that initially whetted banking's appetite to serve the retail market, and then excited a dramatic growth in this area. Among these were the following:

1. *the competitive gains* of other types of financial institutions;
2. *consumer lifestyle changes*;
3. higher overall levels of *educational achievement*; and,
4. the perceptions and expectations nourished by the *Postwar Economic Boom*.

FOOTNOTES

1. *Savings and Loan Fact Book* (Chicago: United States League of Savings Associations, 1976).
2. Cited in Wray O. Candilis, ed., *The Future of Commercial Banking* (New York: Praeger Publishers, 1975), p. 149.
3. *Federal Reserve Bulletin* (Washington, DC: Board of Governors of the Federal Reserve System, July, 1976), pp. 567–573.
4. See notes 1 and 2.

6 BANKING DISCOVERS PEOPLE: CAUSE AND EFFECT

INTRODUCTION

This tracing of commercial bank asset growth (Chart 6.1) arbitrarily divides the postwar period into distinct, although understandably overlapping eras:

- first, a time of *recovery and adjustment* from the war and the depression which preceeded it;
- second, banking's *discovery of people* and its deliberate emphasis on the retail market as a primary source for funds and a profitable area of funds allocation; and
- third, the *holding company era*, although if we were drawing this chart in 1980 we might also include the electronic banking era which began taking recognizable form and structure by the mid-1970s.

Our concern in this chapter is with the second and third phases. Depicted are major developments characterizing each. Just as the phases overlap, so do the characteristics. Moreover, not all banks made a transition from one phase to the other. What this division therefore represents is an effort to define the philosophy and practice that appeared preeminent in each phase. Though arbitrary, it serves several important purposes.

First, it provides a time frame that allows the reader to dis-

Chart 6.1

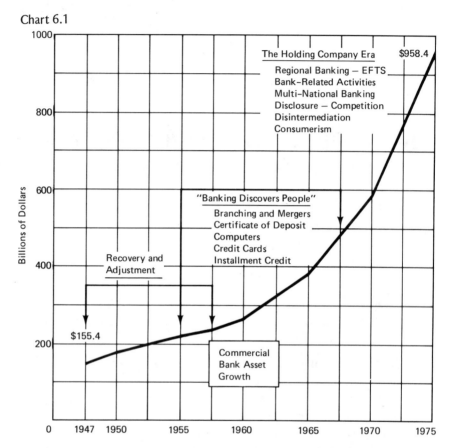

tinguish major cause-effect relationships, while simultaneously placing them within a continuum. It also demarcates breaks with the past that excited sudden leaps forward, that sense of something new and different plotted against a sharply rising growth curve.

Retail banking, of course, was not a new development. Mutual savings banks discovered people as savers a century and a half earlier.[1] State-chartered commercial banks, which virtually had been taxed out of existence by Civil War legislation, combined agricultural lending, mortgage lending, and deposit banking in forging a dynamic renaissance.[2] And in the first decades of the 20th century, Arthur J. Morris demonstrated the efficacy of his bold plan to incorporate urban wage-earners into the American credit system.   What occurred in the 1950s was that retail banking emerged as a powerful *new* thrust that excited, challenged, and even divided the industry because of the responses it evoked.

A resulting competitive imbalance prompted the need for new direction from Federal and state authorities, including "regulators" like the Justice Department that previously followed a "hands off" policy in dealing with banks.   The industry literally was stunned when in 1963 the Supreme Court supported the Justice Department contention that antitrust provisions applied to bank mergers, and by implication to the holding company acquisitions which subsequently followed.[3]

The holding company movement itself was not a new development.   For example, Chase Manhattan Bank, the nation's third largest, originated early in the 19th century as a subsidiary of a New York City water works combine.   Holding companies, moreover, were much in vogue during the 1920s.   But in the late 1960s, and especially after enactment of the 1970 Amendments, this movement took shape as a *new* and powerful thrust forward that compounded existing excitement, challenge, and schism, while simultaneously irritating prevailing competitive relationships.   In this sense, the holding company movement exacerbated problems caused by banking's forceful entry into the retail market.   Further, it mandated a reappraisal of regulatory philosophy, a consequence of which was the interposition of the Securities Exchange Commission with its eagle-eyed scrutiny of industry disclosure practices.

The trend line of bank asset growth depicted in Chart 6.1 not only is continuous, but steeper.   And properly so, since cause-effect relationships and their results build on each other.   Serving the retail customer in always bigger and (presumably) better ways precipitated an array of innovations that spurred duplication and fostered additional inventiveness.

No less, serving the retail customer tended to place nonbank competitors at a perceived disadvantage, thereby necessitating their strong thrust to restore equality, if not actually recapture an edge.   The holding company movement and now the surge toward an electronic mode have had the same impact.   For example, both the smaller independent banks and the thrift industry sought to constrain holding company expansion, and the thrifts cited banking's geographic expansion and product extension as evidence supporting their right to obtain greater powers. With respect to electronic banking, the thrifts stressed the implications inherent in this emerging future to rationalize their case for funds transfer (checking account) powers.

Banking's "discovery of people" affected consumers in a multitude of ways. One was to make them generally wiser and more demanding of fair rates and fair treatment. Truth-in-lending, savings and advertising resulted because of real and perceived abuses brought to light because of heightened consumer sophistication.

Lastly, striving to better serve the retail market and to increase a bank's share at another's expense triggered governmental actions designed to protect consumers on one hand (i.e., Truth-in-Lending) *and* to assure an orderly marketplace on the other. It enlarged the role of government.

RETAIL BANKING

As we have seen, commercial banking turned to consumers in their dual role as depositors and borrowers for a greater share of its business. Branch banking, mergers, the credit card, the POS transaction terminal, the automated teller machine, and the storefront office emerged as better vehicles for reaching people. A widening array of loan and deposit instruments were introduced, frequently with a flourish of bells and whistles, advertising broadsides, radio jingles, and premium ticklers. These flourishes helped attract customers and satisfy them in a distinctive manner. That is, banking tailored or segmented its products and services, including packaging techniques, in order to optimize sales and maximize profitability.

The banking industry especially emphasized its unique full-service capacity, arguing that only commercial banks could do it all for business and people. This claim was anchored in the industry's funds transfer monopoly, a general rather than specialized array of consumer lending powers, and long-standing preeminence of the commercial lending field. In truth, banks were full-service institutions; however, rates paid and charged customers did not always represent the best deal in town. Then, too, banks were selective in building their customer base; poorly served, if at all, was the marginal consumer or business customer, a fact which opened the door to competitor challenges.

This description, of course, looks at the whole and not at the components banding it together or, alternatively, creating irritants threatening a cohesive functioning. One irritant, for example, was banking's practice of discriminating against working women at the loan desk. Federal legislation enacted in the 1970s sought to obviate discrimination on the grounds of sex, race, and ethnic origins; but it was not eliminated entirely as evidenced by the formation of banks for women and an increase in the number of law suits charging sex and race bias. Other irritants stemmed from difficulties that arose in correcting "computer mistakes," investigating credit-worthiness, and from overly aggressive collection practices on consumer loans.

THE MARKETING DISCIPLINE

A unifying component was the coming forward of the *marketing discipline*. At some point—a good watershed is the publication of Harvard professor Theodore Levitt's classic *Marketing Myopia*—progressive industry leadership discovered that banking was selling a *product*. They found that money and financial service was little different from soap, cars, cereals, or TV sets. Money was a product that had to be developed, researched, costed, priced, publicized, advertised, sold, and then monitored. It had to be made appealing, distinctive, and competitive. It had to be offered in a convenient manner. *It had to be marketed.*[4]

A critical element in this process became the training and motivation of bank employees: Our people needed a better understanding of what they were selling and why. This requirement grew in importance as banking's product mix became more diverse, as product lines expanded, as consumers evidenced more sophistication in their financial judgments, as the competitive struggle to increase market share intensified, and as the industry employed research techniques to obtain a better handle on customer likes and dislikes. Most important, the banking sales force began to specialize and professionalize. The idea of selling, moreover, expanded conceptually to embrace senior credit officers, branch administrators, even tellers and back-room support staff. *Selling became everyone's job.*

Another dimension of the marketing discipline involved the technique of selling—the manner in which banks delivered products and services and, equally important, acquired the liabilities and capital that supported growth and expansion. The delivery process not only emphasized mechanisms such as branching and a plastic card mass-mailed or selectively mailed to millions, but also *perceptions* about bank-customer relationships. Accordingly, the retail revolution required that banking be concerned about its image: what it stood for; what people believed it stood for; how it treated people, including its own employees; how the public expected to be treated; what set an individual bank, multi-office organization, or the industry apart from the competition; and whether the public even appreciated these distinctions.

Furthermore, people were not just customers in the sense of savers and borrowers. They also became the media, opinion-makers, the academic community, women and minorities striving for real equality at the employment office and the loan desk, bank stock analysts and brokers, and people as investors in bank debt and equity. Collectively, people became the public interest whose point of view visibly was represented by private and public advocates, the Naders on one hand and the government on the other.

This concern for *image* possessed an inherent duality. Real and perceived attitudes about how banks treated the public occasioned such consequences of the retail banking revolution as fair billing and fair credit reporting measures, antired-lining legislation, RESPA codes, and so on. Likewise, it also fostered arguments demanding that banks and other financial institutions exhibit tangible evidence of improved corporate citizenship. This same perspective also explains why glossy annual reports and media parties, not to mention presentations to financial analysts, has come to occupy considerable management time and energy in recent years.

Banking had come full turn. It realized it was *selling* a *product* and that selling necessitated a multi-disciplined *marketing approach*. It learned that *image* implied important things about the product and the seller. Further, image had many dimensions: profitability and earnings performance; bigness and the belief that it fostered managerial excellence; progressiveness, especially in terms of corporate citizenship and antibias policies; and candor in media relationships.

FORCES FOR CHANGE

For the most part, product innovation, service improvement, and the emergence of the marketing discipline can be viewed as internal responses to changes in banking's operating environment. They signify what the industry did to enlarge its retail banking base and, pleased with the results, to further expand it. The holding company era in a very real sense continued and enlarged upon this trend. Before evaluating this movement, we first need to consider that range of diverse, yet interconnected *external forces for change* that initially whetted banking's appetite to serve the retail market, and then occasioned a dramatic growth in this area. These external elements can be grouped into four categories: competition, lifestyle changes, mass education, and the postwar economic boom.

Seeking the Edge

Competition from nonbank institutions, particularly the thrifts, directed attention to the profit potential inherent in the retail market. At least their successes did. The thrift industry embarked on a road of phenomenal growth in the decade following World War II. They tapped an affluent, home-wanting, car-buying, credit-demanding retail market that was materially oriented. Moreover, people wanted things now and proved willing to pay top dollar. Commercial banking responded to thrift industry achievements with a vengeance. In turn, the thrifts and other nonbank competitors reacted by demanding more banklike powers, notably a full range of consumer credit tools, credit cards, and an end to banking's funds transfer monopoly. In a slow, piecemeal fashion, these objectives inevitably began to be attained in the mid-1960s, although even today they are far from being realized by all nonbank competitors. But a beginning was made, and the process still continues. These gains served to further stimulate banking's determination to maintain an edge.

The Affluent American

Lifestyle changes greatly influenced thrift industry growth and subsequent competitive responses. Most important among these changes was the movement of people to suburbia in an age of relative affluence. This migration evoked an unparalleled demand for home ownership and the things that went with it:

- cars and appliances
- schools, hospitals, roads, and sewers
- municipal bond issues in unprecedented amounts
- innovation in the form of television that brought city life to the suburbs and exurbs, and simultaneously created and reinforced new cultural values, many emphasizing a highly materialistic mode
- retail stores and other providers of consumer goods and services followed customers from the central cities and gave birth to both the shopping center explosion and the clustering of self-sustaining satellite cities and towns
- service corporations and manufacturing firms—in essence, jobs—joined this movement away from the central cities
- suburban mobility broke patterns of neighborhood and community; people traveled by planes and interstate highways; they vacationed at beach or mountain property; and when they retired, Social Security and pensions combined with new attitudes to encourage them to follow the warm sun, thus opening new frontiers of settlement.

Homes, cars, schools and hospitals, roads and interstates, shopping centers, new industries to serve a suburban living style—

all of this and more represented a demand for credit, for consumer and business credit and for state, municipal, and Federal financing. Financial institutions followed this movement of people, homes, and jobs. They met the need for credit by establishing more and more convenient offices and through the credit card and other forms of instalment debt. Commercial banks floated billions of dollars in municipal debt, indeed far more than any other financial intermediary. However, credit extensions only could be as great as an institution's ability to generate deposits, capital, and other liabilities; therefore, banks and their competitors turned to people for their checkbook money, savings, and investment dollars.

The Knowledge Explosion

The many changes brought about by the rise of suburbia also affected American notions regarding *education.* The GI Bill sent tens of thousands to colleges and universities, individuals who might not have otherwise pursued this course and the career opportunities it opened. When these students became parents, they demanded the same opportunity for their "baby boom" offspring. Mass education, especially higher education, consequently became a critical element of the American dream. Whether it qualitatively advanced scholarship, wisdom, justice, liberalism— any of the commonly perceived values of education—is debatable. What can be accepted without reservation, however, is that more people *believed* they were wiser and more sophisticated.

This awareness had important cause-effect impacts on banking. Education led to a greater earning power, a shorter work week, and, simultaneously, it helped reinforce a materialistic (some call it hedonistic) itch for things now: boats, homes, vacations, travel, whatever, *and the credit to make it happen.*[5] Education also seemed to foster higher levels of economic sophistication (though perhaps not as high as many assume!). It took form in patterns of investment, one of which was "people's capitalism"—the consumer's increased involvement in the capital market. Another pattern became a penchant for coins, art, stamps, antiques and other collectibles.

No less significant, perceived consumer sophistication led to demands for better treatment at the loan desk, shopping for the tailored financial package, and an insistence on competitive rates of interest. The rational customer supported consumerism for protection against the unscrupulous and the discriminating; the same customer, as a more perceptive voter, encouraged government to protect these rights. Education, moreover, provided the foundation for a movement in support of equal rights for America's women and minorities; this included equality in banking and at the loan desk.

Finally, education altered banker attitudes about the business of banking and dealing with customers. Elitist traditions were broken down; many of the practices stemming from a Depression-spawned paranoia were mocked. Education fostered greater career mobility within banking, thus weakening tendencies toward parochialism and institutional isolationism. It lent an aura of acceptance to the work of the rising number of technicians joining the industry's labor force—i.e., the marketing specialist, computer programmer, etc.—the nonbanker who after all *was* a banker. Education touched subtly but significantly the questioning of what the banking business is all about; inherently, this questioning became customer-oriented. It forced attention away from what was best for the bank to what best served the needs and wants of that better educated and more perceptive customer.

The Upslope of Prosperity

Competition, lifestyle changes and educational advances were nourished by the *postwar economic boom.* They were conditioned by it; they were, in fact, made possible by the recovery from the Depression and World War II. They remain immeasurably influenced by inflationary or recessionary pressures that challenge the perceived continuum of growth and economic well-being. Reversing this equation, competition, lifestyle changes, and education helped nourish the spreading belief that *all* are entitled to participate equally, if not maximally, in economic progress.

Following World War II, continuing high rates of economic

growth and the virtual elimination of unemployment became the goals of economists, the election promises of politicians, and the taken-for-granted certainties of the American public. These certainties created others—e.g., strong consumer confidence in business leadership; the sustainability of the business cycle's upward curve; positive assumptions about the abundancy of natural resources, particularly land and energy; a belief in the positive consequences of technology, the genius of science, and the scientific discipline to solve social and economic disruptions; and a high birthrate.

In large measure, these postwar economic certainties demonstrated a remarkable degree of continuity between 1947 and 1973, or until an inflated and artificial prosperity gave way to simultaneous double-digit inflation and recession. Thereafter, a shattered public mind became aware that a new set of economic realities was emerging: namely, high unemployment and underemployment; low and even no real growth in GNP; the visible, ever-disturbing fact of inflation and increasing costs for eating, living, and enjoying; high-cost, potentially rationed, possibly dangerous energy sources; resource shortages; a declining birthrate; domestic economic dislocations precipitated by international politics and a linking of American prosperity to the evident weaknesses of the British and Italian economies or the strengths of Germany and Japan; sagging consumer confidence in the value of the dollar, the wisdom and ethics of business leadership, and in the promises of politicians, government bureaucrats, and labor leaders; a vastly altered set of assumptions concerning ecological abundance; and, finally, serious reservations about the miraculous achievements of science and technology.

But while it lasted, the quarter-century following World War II was, to use economic historian John Brook's phrasing, the "Go-Go Years." And its underlying certainties greatly affected banking thought and practice.

Chart 6.2 focuses on one aspect of the postwar prosperity by tracing the increase in Real Disposable Personal Income. Reflected is increased consumer earning and purchasing power. The latter, moreover, was strengthened by the use of instalment debt. In its

Chart 6.2

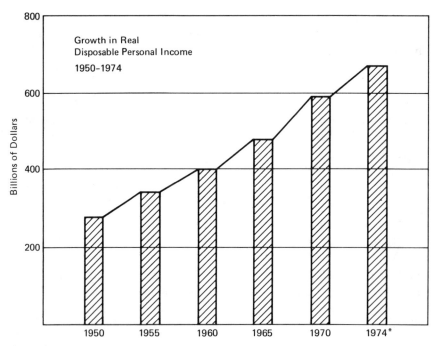

Growth in Real
Disposable Personal Income
1950–1974

Billions of Dollars

800

600

400

200

1950   1955   1960   1965   1970   1974*

SOURCE: Department of Commerce Deflected by Consumer Price Index   *Preliminary

combination with such factors as a pent-up demand for consumer durables, consumer purchasing power helped to further stimulate production (homes, appliances, cars, TV sets) that served to maintain, and even accelerate, prosperity.

Historically, disposable income was not large enough to permit most consumers to engage in an aggressive investment program with their savings; they typically were guided by the thrift motive, and by the desire to build a "nest egg" for retirement. In the postwar years, however, the extremely sharp increase in real disposable income permitted consumers to satisfy thrift *and* investment needs. As shown in Table 6.1, total financial assets held by consumers more than quadrupled between 1950 and 1973. Especially noteworthy is the larger slice of the pie acquired by

Table 6.1. Composition of Financial Assets. Households, Personal Trusts, and Non-Profit Organizations.

	1950	1955	1960	1965	1970	1973
Total Financial Assets Outstanding (Billions)	$447.5	$707.8	$967.9	$1464.4	$1918.9	$2302.3
			Percent of Total			
Demand Deposits	12.6	9.2	7.3	6.4	7.0	7.4
Savings Accounts						
Commercial Banks	7.2	6.2	6.4	7.9	9.8	12.5
Savings Institutions	7.8	8.8	10.7	11.7	12.2	15.1
U.S. Gov't. Securities Short-Term						
Marketable	N/A	N/A	.9	.8	1.2	.8
Other Direct	N/A	N/A	1.7	1.0	.5	.2
Agencies	*	*	.3	.3	.8	.9
Savings Bonds	11.1	7.1	4.7	3.4	2.7	2.6
Tax-Exempts	2.2	2.7	3.2	2.5	2.4	2.2
Corporate Bonds	1.1	.9	1.0	.9	2.1	2.5
Corporate Equities Investment Company						
Shares	.7	1.1	1.8	2.4	2.5	2.0
Other Shares	29.1	39.4	39.2	41.1	35.7	30.3
Life Insurance Reserves	12.3	9.8	8.8	7.2	6.8	6.5
Pension Reserves	5.4	7.1	9.4	10.5	12.4	13.4
Other**	10.5	7.7	4.6	3.9	3.9	3.6
Net Acquisition of Financial Assets as a Percentage of Disposable Income	7.7%	9.3%	7.3%	11.5%	10.6%	14.3%

*Insignificant
**Consists of: Commercial Paper, Mortgages, Security Credit, and Miscellaneous
Source: Federal Reserve flow of Funds Accounts

commercial banks after 1960; a general shift away from low yielding assets such as demand deposits and savings bonds into time and savings accounts at financial intermediaries; the steady decline in the proportion of funds in life insurance reserves, which suggests that consumers became more inclined to rely on this asset for death benefits than as a broad savings vehicle; and the rising proportion of funds flowing into corporate equities and bonds, which suggests that consumers did become somewhat more sophisticated in their investment habits.

Consumer buying and savings patterns, of course, combined with other forces to foster growth and the certainties prosperity engendered. This cycle in no small measure was a consequence of America's investment in Europe's postwar recovery. It also was strengthened by full employment legislation that made employment a national policy of the highest priority. Legislation ranged from the 1946 Act through the deliberations culminating in the Humphrey-Hawkins proposal of 1976 and other incomes maintenance measures. The prosperity cycle was stabilized by welfare programs and government spending imperatives in the fields of health, welfare, and education that effectively placed a floor on poverty. It was stabilized equally by subsidies and incentives to business and agriculture. Perhaps most important of all, prosperity was enhanced by the economic commitments to wars in Korea and Vietnam and to Cold War defense.

But these very stimulants and stabilizers, whether viewed in terms of savings account balances, welfare, two cars in every suburban garage, or thermonuclear overkill, also created the problems undermining the premises of prosperity and the certainties they created. In time, for example, a rebuilt Germany and Japan came to compete too successfully with American industry. A dual commitment to "guns and butter"—to wars against Communist incursions overseas and to equally difficult wars against poverty, illiteracy, racial bias, and urban decay on the home front—proved too heavy a burden in sustaining growth without inflation. In time, these and many other complex forces burst the bubble of prosperity; a new set of economic realities were forthcoming.

IMPLICATIONS FOR BANKING

Many of the implications of this prosperity as they relate to banks
and other financial institutions have been discussed in this chapter.
Others are implicit:

- the rebuilding of the European economy led American banks
  overseas on an unprecedented scale, equally to supply credit,
  later to gather funds, and commonly to seek out opportunities to enhance earnings;
- "guns and butter" occasioned massive Federal budgets and
  deficits to be financed by financial institution holdings of
  government obligations;
- government social programs that developed on an ever-
  widening front impacted credit allocation policies, while
  also bringing about more and more layers of control over
  financial institution management;
- consumers borrowed, saved and spent more than ever before
  causing transaction volume to mushroom, which, in turn,
  encouraged increasing reliance on technology, particularly
  expensive computer-based, transaction-handling systems;
- banking became a relatively "riskier" business as loan-to-
  deposit ratios soared in response to customer demands and
  earnings requirements;
- at the same time loan and deposit growth outran capital
  formation, and this despite the industry's use of the holding
  company structure to tap nontraditional sources of debt and
  equity;
- home construction and home ownership financing became a
  national priority that required heavy and stable inflows of
  low cost funds, especially into thrifts, and led to regulatory
  procedures designed to keep money costs as low as possible;
  in this respect, the virulent inflation of 1973–1975 forced
  the disintermediation of funds from thrifts and virtually
  closed down housing; and
- the higher levels of inflation that, in the main, stemmed from
  the burden of a "guns and butter" economy, squeezed banks

and other financial institutions at the margin, and led to the placing of more credits on a flexible rate basis and similar adjustments on the liability side of the ledger.

These few generalizations (they are just part of a long list) nonetheless indicate that the retail banking revolution was influenced immeasurably by the combining and interplay of external changes in banking's operating environment during the postwar era. These alterations have been categorized as *Competition*, *Lifestyle Changes*, *Education*, and the new economic certainties brought about by the *Postwar Boom*. We also have seen that the anchoring premise of prosperity was brought into question with the inflation and recession of 1973–1975.

Finally, we have assessed some of the methods employed by commercial banks in dealing with these external changes in the marketplace—branching, the certificate of deposit, consumer credit, the credit card, and the computer among them. Another method of accommodation was the holding company movement.

The Holding Company Era: "At the Edge of Change"

The modern bank holding company movement flourished chiefly as a means of circumventing legal and regulatory constraints limiting geographic expansion and product extension. Some observers subscribe to the notion that its ultimate goal is to become redundant; that it is an expedient rather than an end in and of itself.[6]

By design, the holding company would enlarge the nature of the banking business through the acquisition of "closely related" activities such as factoring. It also would overcome limitations of geographic expansion by erecting statewide systems of banking affiliates, a process that concurrently would weaken and eventually overcome long-standing taboos against branching and supposedly undue concentrations of economic power. These bank and bank-related units in time would be consolidated and integrated into "department stores" of finance that incorporated the fullest possible range of financial service and expertise under one roof. Eventually, the singular geographic constraint would be an organization's *natural trading area*, whether or not it involved the crossing of state boundary lines.

Viewed from today's perspective—the troubled years following 1973 notwithstanding—this potentiality still appears promising. To be sure, the holding company movement has been buffeted badly by its excesses and, to some degree, its successes. It did come "too far, too fast, and on precious little capital."[7] Nonetheless, the underlying premise of integrating financial service and enlarging the industry's product and geographic base remains viable.

But if the bank holding company movement emerged in the 1960s as a means of challenging constraints and the perceived inequities its proponents maintained they fostered and perpetuated, then the movement's singular achievements created other competitive disparities that resulted in a series of actions designed to offset them.

THE UNWELCOME CONGENERIC

It is not surprising, therefore, that many smaller, community-oriented, independent banks initially fought the holding company movement, then later elected to become affiliates or even leaders in forming comparable organizations. By the mid-1970s, the movement in fact had become three-tiered: the money-center banks, primarily with their one-bank organizations; the regionals with their multi-bank, statewide systems and an array of bank-related units (often active well beyond regional trading areas); and a third tier of what can best be typified as smaller, common-interest groupings in which the "time sharing" of people, skills, and technological capacities was much in evidence. There also was a noticeable tendency among smaller independents to accept a general liberalization of state branching statutes.[8]

The thrift industry, on balance, responded in similar fashion. The savings and loan service corporation virtually duplicated the holding company concept in purpose. Further, savings banks and savings and loans responded to holding company expansion by intensifying their push for legislation facilitating their ability to become "full service family financial centers," an objective comparable to banking's determination to evolve into "department stores" of finance.[9]

To be kept in mind, however, is that not all thrifts, nor all commercial banks, for that matter, shared or are likely to share these objectives.   Schisms run deep among financial industry competitors. There is no accepted banking objective, and not all thrifts think alike concerning the future. This point is exemplified by noting that over the past decade both thrifts and smaller independent commercial banks often worked side by side (in effect, if not in fact) to stem the tide of holding company expansion. Chiefly through legislation, their common objective was to place constraints on its growth in order to maintain competitive parity; no less, and particularly in the case of thrift institutions, they sought to earn a time span in which their own goals could materialize and be absorbed operationally.

RHYME AND REASON

Holding company leadership in the mid-1960s and thereafter did not publicly contend its interest in circumventing the status quo. This interest was assumed, believed in deeply, and argued over bitterly during Congressional hearings leading to enactment of the 1970 Holding Company Act Amendments, and still later as the Hunt Commission reforms evolved as legislative proposals.[10] But other reasons were cited to advance the need for and credibility of the holding company movement; generally, these reasons recognized the external social and economic forces changing the banking landscape.

For one thing, the holding company held out the pro-competitive prospect of breaking up the money center monopoly. It would create a system of strong regional organizations that would be less dependent on Wall Street, State Street, and LaSalle Street; thereby, less business would go to New York, Boston, and Chicago. Business would remain at home to be more efficiently served by larger, better capitalized (this meant a larger lending base) and better managed financial congenerics. The regional holding company similarly would assist smaller corporations and municipal authorities in obtaining continuous flows of adequate financing; it would free these "captives" from the vagaries of money center favoritism, particularly during periods of "tight money."

It also was claimed that the holding company would realize certain scale economies in bank operations, equally in terms of financial and human resources.   In many respects, presumed economies did not materialize; bigger was not necessarily better, nor even cheaper.[11]   However, in one area a much needed "economy" seemingly was achieved.   Many medium-sized and even large-sized regional banks could not afford to employ experts in fields such as marketing, investment portfolio management, computer technology, corporate financing, banking law, and planning.   As the holding company structure combined units, it could afford such experts—people that very quickly became necessity.

Third, the holding company concept encouraged many regional organizations to view the multi-national marketplace as one in which they reasonably might compete successfully.   Their experience between 1965 and 1975 on the whole was mixed.   For some regionals, it proved a profitable method of diversification providing contracyclical earnings strength with a minimum of risk, while at the same time affording an opportunity to service the multi-national business of regional customers.   But for others, international banking led to excesses in zeal, risk, and stupidity.

Finally, holding company proponents maintained that diversification into closely related fields such as factoring and mortgage banking, not to mention consumer financing, equipment leasing, management consulting, and Real Estate Investment Trusts, would enable these organizations to tailor products and services to the needs of customers in a more efficient manner.

THE LIABILITIES

It has been charged by regulators, legislators, bank competitors, businessmen, and even many bankers that the holding company movement led *banks out of banking*. It led them into new fields that they did not really comprehend well, thus spawning unnecessary shareholder and depositor risk. It prompted and spread a "go-go" spirit alien to industry traditions of prudence, risk minimization, and depositor safety. It was especially in the nonbanking field that loans frequently carried a higher degree of risk and a marked need for specialized treatment and knowledge to make them payout profitably. Belief that this know-how commonly accompanied holding company acquisitions proved an illusion in numerous cases. Many acquired firms, especially after the first flowering of the holding company into bank-related fields, were actually available more because of weakness than strength. Detroit Bank of the Commonwealth president Arthur Snyder addressed this point in the editorial pages of the *Wall Street Journal:*

> Banking used to be an industry unto itself. Increasingly, it is becoming only a part of some other vaguely defined industry. Bankers are becoming like everyone else in business, and that is where the danger lies . . . The essence of being a banker is to stand apart from the excitement and to serve business and the community without joining in business activity.[12]

Critics of the holding company also charged that it fostered inappropriate *concentrations of economic power.* The facts and figures, while supporting this concentration (See Table 5.2), fail to prove that this ingathering of financial resources into fewer and more powerful hands was inimical to the national welfare, nor even anticompetitive. Moreover, either prospective danger was counterbalanced by strong doses of regulatory medicines.

Finally, many critics (and any number of proponents!) bewailed the fact that the holding company excited far too much interest in earnings performance, in *the bottom-line.* Historically, bankers measured growth and success with the yardstick of total footings. Each year (it was hoped) assets or deposits grew at least 10 percent. For years, this performance measure was held out to the public, to the media, and to investors (although in the preholding company era investors were few, mostly loyal, mostly interested in dividends, and generally uncritical of industry or individual bank policies). The holding company changed much of this by turning to the money and capital markets and to institutional or professional investors for growth, expansion, and operating capital. In this environment, earnings and p/e multiples marked performance, and thus an ability to attract additional capital.

One consequence is that earnings became *now-oriented:* now, this quarter; now, this year or the next at the very least. In turn, this orientation encouraged greater levels of risk exposure to support better spreads. No less, it emphasized the expediency of the moment while lessening tendencies to invest in the future. A "now-orientation" appeared only a minor problem during the formative years of the holding company movement. Many organizations began expansionary drives with an excess capital position. Then, too, the economy was working in their favor. Finally, the holding company was new, a fresh breeze that stirred and excited professional investors. Banking, that dreary industry, had come alive, become modern, become part of a "go-go" world, and it basked in this new sun. In time, notably as inflation and recession altered economic certainties, this heady breeze deadened and hung heavy; the fickle professional investor who pushed and leveraged bank stocks and p/e multiples to unprecedented highs led what *Business Week* editors termed "The Great Banking Retreat." This publication charged that "a decade of supergrowth led to superproblems. The result: slower growth, tighter loan policies, more conservatism." It said, quite simply, that the banking industry now was responding to a new set of economic realities. The postwar era had come to a fork in the road.[13]

CONCLUSION

Throughout the postwar period, two pervasive elements appeared to define banking thought and practice. They stood out as distinctive threads separating past and present, while simultaneously pulling together the many-hued varieties of banking experience. One of these threads was *liberality*, whether seen as turning to consumers for more business, seeking relationships overseas, or

Often the past and the future can be separated by posing a series of questions. Here are some that appeared uppermost in the thoughts of banking leaders as the Bicentennial year drew to a close. Such concerns and especially the answers they generate signal the essence and immediacy of strategic planning.

- Could inflation be brought under control? Were we entering a period of permanent inflation and slower real growth? Would economic cycles be sharper and shorter in duration?
- Could we absorb the cost of consumerism? Could we turn around what seemed to be a rising antibank and antibusiness sentiment?
- Would the projected heavy costs of electronic banking prove too great a burden? Would it keep us from doing other things, from expanding in other directions?
- Would consumers—even our employees—readily accept the electronic mode? Could we close the gap between projected systems capabilities and their needs and wants?
- Which was the future? The credit card, the debit card ... plastic or banking by phone? Which was the future? ATM, POS terminal? And what about bricks-and-mortar offices?
- Who was the future? A variety of state and Federal regulatory authorities, or a single Federal Banking Commission?
- Would there be enough capital to go around? Would there be a shortfall? If so, how big? How does one manage to get an acceptable share, and then some?
- Was the threat of unionization just a shadow with no substance or a probability as certain as taxes and death?
- And above all else, there were the many questions and doubts concerning the legitimacy of profit-seeking enterprise. Had capitalism had its day? Was the market economy just extra baggage?

simply breaking away from established, though often obsolete operational patterns. Liberality put aside traditions inherited from Depression experiences or shaped by life in a less mobile America of small towns and farms—an isolated America suspicious of internationalism, urbanization, and concentrations of economic power.

Liberality, moreover, was the growing belief that banks have products and services to sell; it was revealed in the practice of reaching out to customers and in using marketing techniques to determine their needs and wants. Liberality also was the belief that bottom-line performance counted as much as size.

The other thread was *technology*. It was first the credit card and became the point-of-sale transaction terminal or automated teller machine. It was, more broadly, more significantly, a computer-based operations network that made possible high-volume activity in the sorting and posting of customer transactions.

This veritable revolution in a bank's backroom supported and then prompted an ever-widening range of customer services that all too quickly gave birth to others. Technology chiefly has meant the computer and the plastic card. The former provides efficient, inexpensive methods of handling uncountable billions of financial information units each year; the latter, either as credit card or debit card, is the access instrument to the machines and interfacing systems of an electronic age.

By the 1970s, if not somewhat earlier, it had become clear among financial industry leadership and Federal and state regulatory authorities that the industry had reached the dawning of an electronic era. Technology had become a principal determinant in shaping the future. The same was true of liberality, that underlying conviction that commercial banks along with other financial institutions are moving unalterably toward a more competitive environment characterized by a freer interplay of marketplace dynamics and a minimization of institutional specialization with its consequential protectionist codes.

Both of these threads are woven through the other chapters comprising Unit Two.

The Age of the People

In our estimation, a third thread will become profoundly influential in planning future responses or strategies in an era of electronic banking and heightened competition.

The future is also *The Age of the People*. It is consumerism. It is expanding application of public interest imperatives to banking practices. It is people who will seek out and insist on the best rates, the finest deal, the greatest convenience, the most efficiency, and the highest standards of quality. It is government in its desire to most effectively manage socio-economic conditions in a world society. It is the imperatives of high employment, economic stability, the optimal utilization of natural resources, and social equality.

Leonard L. Berry and James N. Donnelly, Jr. in *Marketing for Bankers* make this point clearly:

> . . . banking, like other industries, should not expect to escape from The Age of the People's general mandate to business: *the public will be served, not used.*[14]

The closing chapters of Unit Two and the several chapters comprising Units Three and Four in large measure focus on this contention.

FOOTNOTES

1. Thomas W. Thompson, *The Origins of Mutual Savings Banking in America: 1816–1820* (Washington, D.C.: The George Washington University, Unpublished Dissertation, 1977).
2. Especially see Paul B. Trescott, *Financing American Enterprise* (New York: Harper & Row, 1963); Ross M. Roberston, *The Comptroller and Bank Supervision: A Historical Appraisal* (Washington, D.C.: The Office of the Comptroller of the Currency, Department of the Treasury, 1968); and Thomas W. Thompson, *Checks and Balances: A Study of the Dual Banking System in America* (Washington, D.C.: National Association of Supervisors of State Banks, 1962).
3. *U.S. v. Philadelphia National Bank*, 374 US 321 (1963). Also see Charles F. Haywood, *The Potential Competition Doctrine* (Washington, D.C.: Association of Registered Bank Holding Companies, 1972).

4. Theodore Levitt, "Marketing Myopia," from *The Harvard Business Review*, July–August, 1960. The application of this doctrine to banking practice is explained clearly in Wat Tyler, "Organizing the Critical Tasks in Bank Marketing," an address before the 1972 American Bankers Association Marketing Conference. See *Proceedings* for the years 1970–1973 for related discussions on the evolution and application of the marketing discipline in banking (Washington, D.C.: The American Bankers Association). Also helpful is Leonard L. Berry and L. A. Capaldini, ed., *Marketing for the Bank Executive* (New York: American Bankers Association, 1974).

5. Among the countless studies assessing this point and its implications for planning, the work of Daniel Bell stands out. Especially see *The Cultural Contradictions of Capitalism* (New York: Basic Books, 1976) and *The Coming of Post-Industrial Society: A Venture in Social Forecasting* (New York: 1973).

6. Carter H. Golembe Associates, Inc., *The Bank Holding Company Act Amendments of 1970: A Legislative History* (Washington, D.C.: Financial Publications of Washington, 1971). Particularly see its excellent bibliography of materials dealing with the origins and purposes of the holding company movement, p. 849.

7. ——, *4(c)8: Some Thoughts on the Future of Bank-Related Activities* (Chicago: The Bank Marketing Association, August, 1975). For a particularly critical assessment of the holding company movement, see Martin Mayer, *The Bankers* (New York: Random House, 1974), notably its concluding chapter, "Living on the Edge of An Abyss," pp. 521–545.

8. See *Bank Branching: An Analysis of State Laws* (Washington, DC: The American Bankers Association, 1976); *Eliminating Constraints on Banking, Proceedings of a National Conference to Consider the Ability of Banks to Serve the Public* (Washington, DC: Carter H. Golembe Associates, Inc., 1975); and Subcommittee on Financial Institutions, Committee on Banking, Housing and Urban Affairs, United States Senate, *Compendium of Issues Relating to Branching by Financial Institutions* (Washington, DC: U.S. Government Printing Office, 1976).

9. Particularly see speeches and published materials issued over the past decade by The National Association of Mutual Savings Banks and the United States League of Savings Associations. See also similar materials issued by Credit Union National Association. These materials and testimony before House and Senate Committees as well as State legislative committees outline thrift industry objectives in becoming "full service family financial centers."

10. *The Report of the President's Commission on Financial Structure and Regulation* [Hunt Report] (Washington, DC: United States Government Printing Office, 1971). See also various hearings in the House and Senate, particularly those concerning *The Financial Institutions Act, 1973*, *The Financial Institutions Act, 1975*, and related measures.

11. Samuel H. Talley, *The Effect of Holding Company Acquisition on Bank Performance* (Washington, DC: Board of Governors of the Federal Reserve System, Staff Economic Study (69), 1972) and Thomas R. Piper, *The Economics of Bank Acquisitions by Registered Bank Holding Companies*, (Boston: Federal Reserve Bank of Boston, Research Report No. 48, 1971). An excellent bibliography dealing with holding company operations is contained in *Business Conditions* (Chicago: Federal Reserve Bank of Chicago, December, 1976), pp. 8–9.
12. May 22, 1974.
13. April 21, 1975.
14. Leonard L. Berry and James H. Donnelly, Jr., *Marketing for Bankers* (Chicago: American Institute of Banking, 1975) p. 27.

7 BUILDING TOWARD A WORLD WITHOUT Q

INTRODUCTION

What will tomorrow be like? We have said more than once that we really don't know for sure. We can only offer a related series of reasonable forecasts based on the following considerations:

1. an evaluation of where we are today and how we reached this point
2. an understanding of fundamental socio-economic continuities which throughout the American experience have influenced financial industry practice and thought—e.g., the diversity of America's financial structure and a deep-rooted suspicion of bigness and concentration of economic power.
3. a recognition of presently discernible trends that singularly and in their combination point to major alterations in the nature and scope of banking operations and competitive relationships

In the earlier chapters of Unit Two, we have seen that by and large current trends have been forged and then moved along in an evolutionary manner by technological advances, changing customer habits and beliefs, the emergence of new economic realities, the expanding role of Federal and state governments in creating responses to perceived societal needs, and the real achievements and stated objectives of banking's competitors. We also have measured and evaluated facts and figures attesting to the impressive performance of financial institutions during the decades following World War II. What these data strikingly reveal is an unprecedented degree of change and the potentiality for even greater change in the years ahead. It is this *potential* that necessitates the management of customer, employee, and investor markets through the exercise of strategic planning procedures. However, besides these considerations, there are the anomalies and inconsistencies that challenge the planning discipline.

THE ANOMALIES OF CHANGE

Dr. Carter H. Golembe, chairman of the Washington-based bank research and consulting firm bearing his name, offers this perspective:

> ... the most productive approach to anticipating banking developments is to focus on the *anomalies* which exist in the industry today. The assumption, of course, is that in such situations are to be found the significant clues to future changes.[1]

Dr. Golembe, who sometimes is called banking's "philosopher in residence," discussed two of these "odd, peculiar, or strange conditions" in a *Memorandum: The Anomalies of Banking in an Electronic Era*, that was issued in September of 1976. It merits quoting at some length:

> Our first choice must be the snarl that has resulted from the application of the McFadden Act to the evolution of electronic funds transfers ... (a) particular anomaly that comes as close to deserving the application 'monstrosity' as any that might be found. ...

> When the present system dealing with geographic expansion was finally put into place between 1927 and 1933, at least all of the basic communication devices had been invented and were in use. But no one foresaw the transitor and its spawn: computers, ATMs, CBCTs, and the like. The vision of otherwise sensible

men wrestling with the problem of stuffing this genie back into the bottle is enthralling. . . .

Enormous inputs of time, energy, and ingenuity have gone into overcoming the balkanization of banking that interpretations of existing laws would impose. We have no doubt that much more inputs will be forthcoming—that the revolution in communications cannot be put down. . . .

Not long after Congress passed the McFadden Act it gave us the prohibition of interest on demand deposits, another anomaly that must, in any logical scheme of things, continue to give way in the years to come. . . .

We have, of course, lived for over 40 years with this anomalous interest rule. But times change, as do interest rates, and in this case time has helped to make this 'peculiarity' a 'monstrosity' . . . As we look ahead, it is hard to see how a system of 'thou shalt nots' can be designed with such thorough coverage as to effectively prevent paying interest on transaction balances. The methods that can be used to undercut the prohibition are practically unlimited—more than sufficient to outpace the most brilliant efforts of rule-writers to keep the lid on.[2]

In closing his *Memorandum*, Dr. Golembe made the following observations:

The identification of anomalies is, however, more than a game. The implications of their resolution are of immense importance. We can think of no better expenditure of time on the part of concerned bankers than to fix the close attention of their planning personnel on the possible consequences for the bank when these situations are resolved—and the opportunities that will be available for those who position themselves well.[3]

This perspective is made more convincing by the work of New Hampshire Senator Thomas J. McIntyre, chairman of the Senate Subcommittee on Financial Institutions. In September of 1975, the senator announced that his unit "would undertake a comprehensive study of national policy governing all forms of geographic expansion by banking institutions." One year later, his Subcommittee published an extensive *Compendium of Issues Relating to Branching by Financial Institutions.*[4] The New Hampshire Senator, a Democrat, explained that the *Compendium* would provide the basis for extensive hearings when Congress convened after the 1976 presidential elections. Most important, Senator McIntyre detailed his own views on this complex, controversial, and critical issue:

> For all too long a period of time now, Congress has skirted the issue of national branching policy, a policy which has existed virtually without change for more than 40 years. Yet—as everyone is aware—the nation's economy is vastly more sophisticated and complicated today . . . [What has evolved] is a mishmash pattern of branching laws nationwide. . . .
>
> If there ever was an effective stimulus to reassess Federal branching policy, such stimulus comes from current development of electronic funds transfer systems (EFTS).
>
> Electronic banking, a subject not even dreamed about 40-odd years ago, is inextricably linked to traditional branching policy established then and in effect yet today. National branching policy is therefore even more deserving of prompt attention now.[5]

And finally, there is this brief, but pointed exercise in pragmatism authored by Joseph D. Hutnyan, long-time Washington correspondent for *The American Banker.* In his October 29, 1976 Column, "Washington Bank Notes," Hutnyan assessed the situation in the following terms:

> A lot of bankers will not like it, but is is beginning to look as though payment of interest on demand deposits is a certainty for the near future. . . .
>
> When it finally happens, it is not going to come as a sudden, startling change in the way of doing business. It is going to

creep into the system.   In fact, the 43-year-old law which prohibits banks from paying interest on checking accounts likely
will remain in place. *It will just become meaningless.*[6]

While admitting that there are numerous and quite sound objec-
tions to interest-bearing checking accounts, Hutnyan maintained
that "The overriding consideration is that the competitors are offering this to their customers, and the banks have to respond."[7]

These perspectives identify certain of the anomalies confronting
financial institution managers and planners in their consideration
of the future.   There are others of course.   But these few are illus-
trative of the conditions, their implications, and the reasons why
they *probably* will give way as time passes.   Chiefly, their passing
appears linked to the reasonableness of new approaches; for example, branching prohibitions and related limitations on geographic
expansion in an electronic age are portrayed as illogical and redundant.   Finally, these perspectives, the trends and specific developments which nourish them, and the predictive implications they
raise serve to define the parameters of change.   It is within these
boundaries, we believe, that new competitive relationships and operational procedures will take shape and be refined.

THE LIKELIHOOD OF CHANGE

Change will happen.   The difficult challenge is pinpointing when.
Past experience suggests that the actualization of contemporary
trends will vary markedly over common time periods.   At the time
of this writing, for example, the payment of interest on demand
deposits by commercial banks and, concurrently, the elimination
of banking's historic monopoly in this area, seems eighty percent
probable by 1980.   A new national policy on branching appears
less likely.   The phasing out of Regulation Q savings ceilings within
this time frame seems even less a possibility, even though many
prerequisite developments should continue to fall in place and ag-
gravate the further evolving of free market mechanisms.

Then, too, the sudden reappearance of double-digit inflation
accompanied by a major disintermediation of core deposits from

financial intermediaries could trigger a quick shift from regulated rate ceilings to a market rate. It nearly happened during the 1973–1975 recession and its aftermath search for remedies.

Also influencing probability forecasts about these and other trends are innovation, the consequences of changing national and international economic situations, and certainly, most pervasively, technological advances and the extent to which they induce more widespread customer acceptance and use of tradition-shattering practices. Accordingly, a massive public campaign to stimulate direct deposit of government transfer funds into financial institutions could accelerate the overall transition to an EFT environment and, interrelated, the reconsideration of branching policies limiting this development or existing distinctions between interest-free and interest-bearing deposits.

Dealing with the *unless* or *perhaps* elements therefore emerges as an integral part of the planning process. Its focus is the prospective possible combination of events that alter the odds of probability, that make things happen sooner or later than expected, or that cause revisions in response patterns.

THE TOTALITY OF CHANGE

A final point to be raised before crossing the frontier and exploring "A World Without Q" is the authors' contention that the creation of effective responses to what seems probable or what might occur should the unexpected take place requires dealing with the *totality* of their implications. Both the individual trees *and* the forest must be perceived and comprehended. The ability, welcome or otherwise, to offer interest on checking accounts understandably affects an individual bank's marketing practices, cost of funds, credit allocation procedures, systems management, and profitability (budget) estimates. It also possesses vital implications for the following areas:

- the nature and degree of competitive reactions from other banks and nonbank competitors
- regulatory policies, including reserve requirements; the prospects for interest-earning member bank reserves; and possibly

the extension of compulsory requirements to all commercial banks *and* thrift institutions engaged in providing third-party transfers

- consumer deposit patterns, particularly decisions about where to place traditional "rainy day" savings
- the viability of smaller financial institutions and, interrelated, their willingness to form or affiliate with holding company organizations
- correspondent banking relationships and, especially, methods for paying for services rendered

Not only are there many more implications related to the payment of interest on demand deposits, the phase-out or elimination of Regulation Q ceilings, and the introduction of a new national policy on bank expansion, but each of these possible changes also spawns its own series of actions and reactions. In other words, each creates additional implications and a widening range of consequences.

These implications will be treated in greater detail in the remaining chapter of this unit and throughout the next two units. The particular objective of this chapter is to set the stage for these discussions by targeting on the prospective elimination of controlled, fixed-rate interest structures exemplified by Regulation Q. Our position is not one of advocacy. It only recognizes the existence of forces that presently appear to be pushing toward this fundamental alteration in banking practice.

THE BUILDING BLOCKS OF CHANGE

Over a three-day period in the Autumn of 1975—at a time when interest rates were declining from double-digit extremes to more normal levels—the Senate Banking, Housing, and Urban Affairs Committee chaired by Wisconsin's William Proxmire voice-voted what *The American Banker* termed "the most sweeping restructuring of the financial industry since the Depression years." Major reforms approved by the committee included:

- phasing out Regulation Q ceilings on time and savings deposits of less than $100,000 over a 5½-year period

- eliminating the prohibition against the payment of interest on demand deposits by commercial banks
- authorizing thrift institutions to offer checking accounts
- extending NOW (Negotiable Order of Withdrawal) Accounts nationwide
- granting national charters to mutual savings banks; tacitly, authorizing a nationwide system, with allowance for the conversion of Federally chartered savings and loans
- generally expanding the consumer lending powers of thrift institutions
- authorizing thrifts to provide limited, consumer-oriented trust services
- permitting credit unions to make residential mortgage loans and to offer interest-bearing transfer (checking) accounts

In December, the full Senate passed *The Financial Institutions Act,* "a somewhat distant descendant of the Hunt Commission Report of 1971."[8]   Meanwhile, the House Banking and Currency Committee was readying its FINE study—*Financial Institutions and the Nation's Economy*—for public hearings. Generally speaking, the published FINE study "Principles" went somewhat beyond the Senate recommendations by touching on such issues as foreign bank activities in the United States and the holding company movement.[9] At about the same time, another Senate committee was reviewing Glass-Steagall Act prohibitions on commercial bank investment practices; Senator McIntyre's Senate Subcommittee on Financial Institutions was contemplating arguments favoring a new national policy on branching; the President's Electronic Funds Tranfer System Commission was finally getting underway with its extensive study to determine rules for an orderly transition to an electronic banking environment; and both House and Senate banking units were considering legislative proposals calling for the consolidation of the three Federal bank regulatory agencies (possibly even the Home Loan Bank Board which regulates savings and loans) into a single banking commission.

None of these measures became law during the final session of the 94th Congress. Nor was it expected that they would, especially given their individual or collective degree of controversy in an election year. That they were considered, nonetheless, was significant. That the Senate actually passed the Financial Institutions Act of 1975 was remarkable, even stunning. There was no consensus among various segments of the industry calling for broad-based reform; if anything, the opposite was the case. There was only token interest in financial industry reform on the part of the Ford Administration.

What explains the Senate action? A common view held that the Senate did not expect that the House would concur, and thus sought only to crystalize interest in recognizably long-overdue changes in competitive relationships. In effect, the Senate acted to make reform along these lines inevitable, a matter of *when* and no longer *if*. The agreement in principle evidenced by the House of Representatives tended to support this contention. Now that the air was cleared, Congress, the regulators, and the regulated could begin the serious job of effecting workable reform programs.

Most important for our purposes, the prospect that Regulation Q might be phased out, that interest on demand deposits might be permitted, and that credit unions might soon offer checking accounts or make residential mortgage loans *became* reasonable probabilities. The latter eventually has since materialized.

These proposed reforms, either individually or taken as a whole, possess a long history of advocacy. Most were embodied in the Hunt Commission study and its 1971 report to the President. Many could be traced back to the 1961 Report of the Commission on Money and Credit or to the 1963 Report of the Committee on Financial Institutions to the President of the United States. The point is that there was very little in the Senate-passed Financial Institutions Act or the House FINE study that was radical, much less new; there was nothing revolutionary, but only, as we will see, evolutionary.

The Underlying Purposes

Approved by the Senate and endorsed by the House, the FINE study "Principles" in effect were a long-term plan of action apparently designed to achieve these fundamental purposes:

First, an elimination of deposit distinctions and, explicitly, distinctions among different types of depository institutions.

Second, a more competitive environment for consumer savings—one in which the customer would receive a more economic rate of return on savings and investment-type accounts.

Third, a more competitive environment for depository institutions accepting consumer funds.

Fourth, the virtual elimination of commercial banking's monopoly as primary agent for payments transfers.

Fifth, a minimization of traditional distinctions on the asset side of the ledger in order to optimize competitive equality.

Other projected Congressional studies and legislative proposals considered by the 94th Congress (and which reappeared in the 95th Congress) on balance amplified this basic reordering of the *status quo*.

To contemplate the advent of "A World Without Q" is, therefore, to envision the evolution of a *free market* for consumer savings and investment funds, although one in which the customer will be protected by the imposition, as necessary, of fair-treatment and fair-pricing laws. It is, moreover, to ponder a future in which *full-service* as an operational characteristic applies to both commercial banks *and* to their major retail-oriented competitors.

Pressing Toward the Vital Center

This perceived Congressional plan of action, we believe, represents the coming together of several tangential forces that insist on accommodation. Among them, as we have seen, are the onrush of technology, consumerism, the inflationary bias seemingly present in the economy, and a continuing liberalization of banking codes at the Federal and state level.

Verle Johnston, writing in the December, 1976 *Business and Financial Letter*, published by the Federal Reserve Bank of San Francisco, provided this clarification:

Both of these forces for change—state legislative actions and the new EFT developments—have strong consumer overtones, and herein may lie the means for unraveling the Gordian knot that has tied up the restructuring of the nation's depository institutions.[10]

Taking this point further, Frank E. Morris, president of the Federal Reserve Bank of Boston, in an address before the 61st Annual Convention of the Bank Marketing Association in October, 1976 identified "four forces for intensified competition in retail banking."

The first of these forces, Morris explained, "is a fundamental change in the thinking of Congress on banking law . . . [and] without abandoning [its] objective of avoiding excessive concentration in banking, it seems clear that the Congress is drifting toward the easing of geographic barriers to competition." Consumerism was identified as a second force for change, and Morris argued, "A consumer issue for the future which could have a major impact on competition in banking is the treatment of the small saver under Regulation Q." He then charged that the effect of deposit rate ceilings "has been to subsidize the home buyer at the expense of the small saver . . . [who] had never had an effective champion in matters appearing before the Congress, but perhaps his day is coming."[11]

The third force recognized by the Boston Federal Reserve Bank president "is the entry of the thrift institutions into the payments mechanism." He explained that "In New England, where this trend is much further advanced, competition between commercial banks and thrift institutions is at a much higher level than before," and added the following:

Not unnaturally, the thrift institutions want also to keep the special privileges which were given to them when they were special purpose institutions. As things stand in New England, the thrift(s) . . . have been given new tools with which to compete with commercial banks but are still sheltered from the price competition on commercial banks by Regulation Q. But this competitive shelter may not be long-lived.[12]

Finally, Morris pointed to electronic banking developments as doing "more to change the face of banking in the years ahead than any of the other forces."[13]

This summarization of the pressures developing on several different fronts and combining to compel an intensification of competition in the retail area or, more broadly, mandating a reordering of marketplace relationships, was given added clarity in an *American Banker* editorial:

> There was a time when people saved 'for a rainy day' and to build up nest eggs that could help them in their retirement years. Both of these motives have been downgraded markedly in the changed American economy. . . .

> In sum, the day when banks could look at checking accounts as one service and savings accounts as another is vanishing. The thrifts recognize this and aggressive commercial banks recognize it. Once all bankers recognize this fact, we are likely to see a better understanding on the part of commercial bankers of what their thrift competitors must have to survive.[14]

This is today's battleground. The public mood—what customers want and need—is changing markedly. This largely is due to the emergence and intensification of new socio-economic conditions. Congress and the state legislatures are sensitive to this mood and as one response are drifting toward the easing of barriers to competition. Progressive elements within the banking industry (although perhaps not even a majority) are seeking to respond affirmatively and with strength. As a result, their actions are irritating still further long-standing industry schisms while concurrently obviating them by their achievements. Thrift institutions recognize that the issue is simply survival; their response in turn attacks the structure of competitive equality that had been built up over the postwar decades, thereby necessitating the formation of new structures. Finally, the regulatory authorities interpret the times as beckoning fairer, more just, more rational, and more efficient operational and structural guidelines. Equally significant is their predilection to lead, to be architects in the shaping of change, to play an activist role.

ADDITIONAL FORCES FOR CHANGE

In addition to these very general and broad trends, there are a number of specific developments conditioning enactment of reform programs. Such programs are anchored in the phasing out of Regulation Q, the payment of interest on demand deposits, the liberalization of branching practices, and the elimination of related constraints on the ability of financial institutions to serve customers with a maximum degree of convenience and efficiency. Many of these developments actually occurred in the 1970s, although commonly their seeds were planted earlier and merely matured as part of an evolutionary process. Moreover, the number and significance of these specific developments tended to grow and expand in geometric progression with the passing of each year. It is in their individual and cumulative impact that they are signposts clearly signaling the advent of discontinuity: the axial, generative perception that tomorrow somehow will be vastly different from today.

Alterations in Liabilities, Assets, and Financial Institutions

It is not possible, of course, to list all of these changes in the organizational structure or assets and liabilities of the major financial institutions. Nevertheless, there are certain significant developments that cannot be overlooked.

Liabilities

1. the success of the NOW Account experiment launched in New Hampshire and Massachusetts in 1972 by thrift institutions, their acceptance by commercial banks, and the subsequent spread of NOW Accounts to other New England states, not to mention agitation that they be permitted on a nationwide basis
2. the recommendation advanced by the bank commissioners of several New England states in June of 1976 calling for the elimination of Regulation Q ceilings on an experimental basis in their jurisdictions[15]

3. the several proposals advanced between 1974 and 1976 by then Federal Deposit Insurance Corporation chairman, R. Frank Wille, calling for the indexing of consumer savings rate ceilings to an acceptable Federal barometer such as the Treasury Bill rate

4. the introduction and spread of credit union share drafts— essentially, interest-bearing checking accounts—and the concurrent agreement by many commercial banks to service these instruments

5. consumerist pressure for and the growing institutional acceptance of interest on escrow accounts

6. permission granted by the Federal Reserve Board and the FDIC to commercial banks that authorized their acceptance of corporate savings accounts under $150,000

7. permission granted in 1976 by these regulatory agencies to commercial banks that authorized both "telephonic transfers" between accounts *and* subsequently automatic transfers from savings accounts into demand balances, thereby creating a *de facto* NOW Account

8. the introduction and spreading practice of marketing bank holding company debt issues at market rates in consumer-oriented denominations and maturities

9. the so-called 'wild card' experiment authorized by the Federal Reserve Board in 1973 that, temporarily to be sure, allowed commercial banks to exceed Regulation Q ceilings, commonly by offering an "inflation bonus" on longer term deposits
   (A reaction to the "economics" of double-digit inflation, this action nonetheless served as an important precedent; most significant, it worked as demonstrated by the extent of disintermediation impacting thrift institutions and even smaller commercial banks.)

10. the Treasury Department's several issues of securities in consumer denominations at rates considerably in excess of Regulation Q ceilings, and those long lines of consumers waiting to purchase them at Federal Reserve Banks

11. the introduction of Individual Retirement Accounts (IRAs)

in 1975 and, most notably, the lack of an imposed rate differential distinguishing those offered by commercial banks from thrift institution instruments

12. more generally, the halving of the interest rate differential between banks and thrifts on time and savings deposits from half of a percentage point to a quarter in 1974

13. the evolution and regulatory acceptance of investment instruments, such as Automatic Investment Services and "money desks," that permitted commercial banks to offer directly to consumer customers a portfolio of corporate, government, and municipal securities along with traditional deposit instruments

Many more items could be added to this listing. Taken as a whole, they would add to the fact that these various developments eroded long-standing practices and beliefs concerning the acquisition of bank and thrift institution liabilities. In particular, these developments assaulted the conviction that regulated interest rate ceilings were "engraved in stone," or that checking account interest barriers were insurmountable. They heralded the evolution of new philosophies and operational procedures. Each was an important change; each also was a building block in the process of creating more radical changes.

Assets

The dynamics of banking require that substantive alterations on the liability side of the ledger (how we get funds and what we pay for them) be accompanied by revisions on the asset side (how we allocate funds and what we earn on them). Revisions in recent years include the following:

1. the continued liberalization of consumer lending powers for thrift institutions, including issuing and servicing credit cards

2. the introduction and subsequent growth of public and governmental acceptance of variable and flexible rate residential mortage loans, including payment and maturity structures keyed to such variables as age and earning power

3. among commercial banks, a general trend away from rate-

insensitive commercial loans and a coinciding emphasis on fee-supported corporate customer services

4. activity by savings banks and savings and loans, following practices introduced earlier by retail merchants, to offer accounts receivable financing for commercial accounts
5. increasing emphasis on managing investment portfolios for income-producing purposes as contrasted with liquidity needs

Organization and Structure

These alterations in assets and liabilities performance were, understandably enough, accompanied by advances in the organization and structure of financial institutions. Some of these advances included the following:

1. the continuing elaboration of bank holding company diversification, which enabled these organizations to obtain experience and develop reputations as *lenders* in national markets irrespective of state boundary lines
2. the growth and expansion of international banking, notably among regional holding company organizations, both as overseas lenders and deposit gatherers
3. especially after 1970, the development of savings and loan and mutual savings bank service companies that simultaneously enlarged the nature of their business, enhanced portfolio flexibility and earnings capacity, and provided certain other benefits accruing to holding company structures
4. among commercial banks, even among larger organizations, a disenchantment with the cost of Federal Reserve System membership that led to numerous withdrawals from the System, followed by the System's responsive recommendation that interest be paid on member bank reserves[16]
5. a gradual, but continual breaking down of geographic constraints on interstate and intrastate banking[17]

And finally, there were the many breakthroughs in delivery system methods and structures occasioned by technological advances in the transition to an electronic age.

The Impact of Electronic Technology

The most important among the literally countless developments that have occurred in the electronic banking field will be discussed in Unit Three. The critical point here is that EFT essentially can be viewed as a series of related developments utilizing computer-based technologies for delivering financial products and services to customers through compatible manned and machine systems. The principal force initiating various EFT processes "has been the need to reduce the paper processing load of the present payments system [though recently] . . . we have seen that the quickening pace of EFT activities presents many opportunities for developing new bank services as well as protecting and increasing market share."[18]

Another interpretation is evident in this partial listing of specific EFT advances during recent years: the automated clearing house movement; direct deposit of government payroll and Social Security checks; the proliferation of remote banking terminals providing a widening array of routine consumer banking functions; the advent of the debit card and check guarantee and credit authorization cards; the continued, side by side growth of the bank credit or asset card; the Bank Wire; and experiments with financial transactions through telephonic communications. This interpretation underscores the drive to seek out and fulfill *opportunities;* moreover, it targets the opportunities as efficient, least expensive customer service in a highly competitive environment.

CHARACTERISTICS OF AN ELECTRONIC AGE

The age of electronic banking is dawning. It is taking clearer if not precise shape. It is unfolding in a rational manner. It has become a central element in the planner's conception of what tomorrow most probably will be like. In this sense, EFT is the hub of a wheel. One might consider it in this manner: The totality of the technological revolution, of which EFT is the symbolic reference point, is the most pervasive force currently impacting banking's future. No other force has more influence over the degree and nature of change in the world of tomorrow. Moreover, no other force for change appears as decisive in determining the speed by which change takes place.

What has occurred so far and what appears at the horizon (while admittedly just the initial exploratory steps) nonetheless provides a framework for constructing operational patterns in an electronic mode. Key characteristics at this point in time seemingly include the following:

- recognition that the notion of a checklist society is a myth; the driving impulse is to reduce the volume of paper processed manually
- the objective is to get *your* plastic into *your* customers' hands and then provide them with easy access to their accounts—indeed, to their total banking relationship
- the objective also is to widen *your* customer base by establishing transaction terminals where people live (apartment buildings), work (factories and office complexes); and congregate to shop (grocery and drug stores) or to travel (train, bus, and airline terminals); it is also to enlarge this base by offering different types of access instruments: credit authorization and check guarantee cards and debit cards keyed to depository accounts
- the vital, elemental procedure of familiarizing employees as well as customers with the perceived benefits of electronic technology; this procedure involves concurrent education to stimulate interest and to reduce their instinctive fears, especially the threat of impersonalization and the invasion of privacy
- the development and utilization of facilities to gather and store customer financial data—i.e., Customer Information Systems (CIS) or Files (CIF)—as a marketing tool for selling and cross-selling financial services
- recognition that technology should be utilized to broaden the geographic area served by a financial institution; that indeed, geographic limitations are redundant
- the reasonable assumption that in time EFT standards need to be rationalized, with the goal of affecting a move away from

the existing diversity of access instruments (i.e., debit and credit cards; the plurality of card systems such as Master Charge, American Express and BankAmericard, now VISA) to a single, mutli-purpose, even multi-national instrument that optimizes efficiency and security considerations for customers and for financial institutions

- the mandate that developmental expenses be kept within realistic bounds; the cost of EFT, in sum, should not impact adversely other procedures for acquiring and allocating funds, for supporting asset structures with adequate capital, and for maintaining acceptable levels of profitability

The formation of a National Electronic Funds Transfer Commission, which began its preliminary work in 1976, recognized the necessity of resolving at least three other procedural issues. One was *privacy*. In the EFT Commission's Interim Report to Congress, which was submitted in March of 1977, it observed that consumer apprehensions about electronic payments "are justified" and "genuine," particularly as they apply to safeguarding the private nature of financial records and assuring protection from theft and computer error. The Commission also noted that unless these public interest considerations are assuaged by industry practices and governmental controls, "consumers will reject (EFT) systems."[19]

A second issue identified by the Commission was the need for *competitive equality*. On one hand, the Commission urged the inclusion of thrift institutions and other providers of retail financial services within the emerging electronic network. For example, in its Interim Report the Commission recommended that any financial institution competitively injured by exclusionary practices should be given expedited access to EFT activity by the Federal judiciary. On another level, the goal of competitive equality was addressed by Commission recommendations calling for the deployment of transaction terminals on a nationwide basis for debiting purposes; as well, it urged that electronic deposit-gathering activity be authorized throughout an institution's natural trading area under reciprocal state agreements. If effected, these latter recommendations would tend to place different types of financial institutions, including retail merchants, on an equal footing with respect to locational characteristics.[20]

Third, in all of its preliminary discussions, the Commission evidenced great concern for the *role of government.* This concern took several forms. For example, should an electronic banking system be administered by the private or public sector? If, ultimately, it is the government, then what would be the ramifications for a free market system? More narrowly, what would be the ramifications for bank decision making with respect to credit allocation practices? Looked at somewhat differently, there also was awareness that "by changing consumer saving and spending patterns, electronic banking may pose problems . . . for the managers of government monetary policy."[21]

CONCLUSION

It is the cumulative impact and intermingling of the broad trends and specific developments discussed in this chapter, including those associated with the advent of an electronic era, that compelled the Senate and House reform measures of recent years. For the same reasons, the path toward enactment and implementation appears clearly marked.

This is not to suggest that enactment will come soon, nor be achieved easily. Ahead, most probably, will be years of negotiation, acrimonious debate, and certainly compromise. The building of a "World Without Q" and a competitive environment characterized by a minimum of institutional and operational differences still remains in the future. The same is true of a competitive environment characterized by a continuing relaxation of constraints on the ability of financial institutions to serve customers more effectively and efficiently. But while these characteristics belong to an evolving future, the critical fact is that it is evolving. It is coming. Between now and then the wise must build knowingly.

Our concern as planners is to forecast the time and form of change, predicting the consequences for our organizations. Attention is focused on the specific steps, *if any*, that might be taken now, next month, or next year to cope with the challenges and opportunities reasonably identified with the reshaping of competitive relationships, the easing of constraints on serving customers, and the transition to an electronic era. Our concern is with a vision of tomorrow and the process of successful adaptation.

FOOTNOTES

1. Carter H. Golembe, *Memerandum Re: The Anomalies of Banking in an Electronic Era* (Washington, DC: September 28, 1976), p. 1.
2. Ibid., p. 2.
3. Ibid., p. 8.
4. United States Senate, Committee on Banking, Housing and Urban Affairs, Subcommittee on Financial Institutions, *Corpendium of Issues Relating to Branching by Financial Institutions* (Washington, DC: 94th Congress, Second Session, 1976).
5. Ibid, pp. v–ix.
6. *The American Banker*, October 29, 1976, p. 4.
7. Ibid.
8. See Chapter Six Note 10. See also "The Commission on Financial Structure and Regulation: A Look Inside," an address by Reed O. Hunt, chairman, President's Commission on Financial Structure and Regulation, at The American Bankers Association National Marketing Conference, San Francisco, March 22, 1972; and *Your Future is Here, An Updated Report on Multi-Bank Holding Companies, Hunt Commission Proposals, Savings and Loan Service Corporations, and the Plans of Independent Banks and Thrifts* (Westport, CT: Bankers Research Publications, January, 1974). The latter study provides a detailed analysis of the Hunt Commission Report, its link to earlier studies dealing with financial reform, and relates this "atmosphere of reform" (p. 45f) to the introduction of the Administration-sponsored *Financial Institutions Act of 1973*, predecessor of the 1975 bill.
9. *The American Banker*, November 5, 1975.
10. Federal Reserve Bank of San Francisco, *Business and Financial Letter*, December 3, 1976.
11. Frank E. Morris, "Four Forces for Intensified Competition in Retail Banking," an address before the 61st Annual Convention of the Bank Marketing Association, Miami Beach, FL, October 27, 1976.
12. Ibid.
13. Ibid.
14. *The American Banker*, August 16, 1976.

15. *The American Banker*, June 2, 1976. Also see *The American Banker*, September 21, 1976, "Required *Reading*," p. 4; Reprinted are the remarks of Pennsylvania Secretary of Banking William E. Whitesell before the Union League of Philadelphia relating to this proposal.
16. *The American Banker*, February 4, 1977. Reported is a statement by Federal Reserve Board Chairman Arthur F. Burns to the House Banking, Finance and Urban Affairs Committee in which Chairman Burns said that the Board is prepared to recommend that Congress enact legislation authorizing NOW Accounts on a nationwide basis and authorizing the payment of interest on Member Bank reserves.
17. See Note 4. Also see Chapter 6, Note 8. Especially helpful in tracing changes in branching practice during the postwar years is *A Profile of State-Chartered Banking* (Washington, DC: Conference of State Bank Supervisors, 1975 Edition).
18. ——, *A Digest of Electronic Funds Transfer Systems Thinking Today* (Washington, DC: The American Bankers Association, 1974), p. v. This compendium prepared by the ABA Payments System Planning Division offers excellent summaries (and appropriate bibliographical references) of the principal issues raised by the transition to an electronic banking environment.
19. See reports in *The American Banker*, February 11, 1977; February 17, 1977; March 2, 1977.*
20. Ibid.
21. See note 20.

*A digest of the Commission's Interim Report is printed as "Required Reading" in the March 3, 1977 edition of *The American Banker*.

8 THE EMERGING COMPETITIVE ENVIRONMENT

INTRODUCTION

There are as many views about the emerging competitive environment as there are different types of financial institutions. This is easily understood given the fact that the nation's historically diverse financial system embraces a wide range of full-service and specialized lenders, each of which is determined to retain a viable and distinctive competitive position as the future unfolds.

Their determination to realize this objective—and it is a clear-cut, bottom-line objective—makes it exceedingly difficult to place the advent of significant alterations in financial practices within a reasonable time frame. For example, there are those who believe that in the world of tomorrow commercial banks and other financial institutions will operate either as "department stores of finance" or "family financial centers." Less clear, however, are the following: First, what these goals specifically embrace or should encompass (they mean different things to different competitors and also to the regulatory authorities); and, second, when substantive changes implementing them (a phasing out of Regulation Q or the authorization of interstate branching or trade-area banking) will occur. Nonetheless, the salient fact is that visions of a different tomorrow are *emerging*.

What this means above all else is that for some time to come competitive relationships may be viewed as continually changing. In other words, the American financial industry is slowly, but clearly breaking with a relatively rigid past. Moreover, it will not become sharply defined and structured for a number of years.

To be sure, institutional and even industry segment goals, objectives, and strategies are definable; however, they also are in conflict, some diametrically opposed. And although we cannot pinpoint precisely how and when they will be resolved, we nonetheless are able to draw a series of reasonable conclusions, many of which are indicated by highly visible current trends. We know what seems most likely; certainly we comprehend what appears most rational.

We can calculate how one step leads to another. We can predict and then create appropriate organizational responses. We even can track the current pace of change by charting specific key developments and assessing their impact in raising or lowering the odds that some other and possibly more substantive development will occur, and whether it will happen sooner or later than expected. In this sense, it is important to note that Congressional and regulatory authorization for banks to pay interest on demand deposits (directly or through NOW Accounts) affects the odds of the following financial developments:

- thrift institutions would be granted funds transfer powers
- thrift institutions would be granted a wider range of more flexible retail lending powers
- the prospect that ceilings on time and savings deposits would be phased out or eliminated
- the application of variable or flexible rate structures to residential mortgage lending would become more widespread and also reflect greater degrees of innovativeness
- the prospect that branching laws and related locational constraints would be further liberalized, even eliminated[1]

PREDICTIONS, PROSPECTS, PROBLEMS:
A VISION OF BANKING TOMORROW

What follows is predictive. It is one portrayal of an emerging competitive environment that is based on where we are today and how we reached this point.   We believe it is a cautious vision that recognizes such critical imperatives as the capacities inherent in computer-based technologies; the wants and needs of customers; and the limitations imposed by precedent, public policy objectives, and the realities of existing competitive relationships.   But most important for the purposes of this book, the following portrayal of the future is one that mandates structured, disciplined responses: in a word, *planning.*

"We'll All Be Bankers"

Predicted is the advent of a *three-tier banking* system.   First, some banks and holding companies will operate at a national and multi-national level, although chiefly in principal markets viewed as centers of population or industrial and trade activity.   Second, a large number of banking organizations will operate regionally or within natural trading areas that are not constrained by state boundary lines.   For example, the "natural market" of a billion dollar bank headquartered in the nation's Capitol might range southward from the Delaware Memorial Bridge to the North Carolina border and westward to the Appalachian chain.   Third, a still larger number of banking organizations will compete as aggressive, highly specialized independent units whose foci chiefly will be either particular geographic markets or distinctive customer bases (e.g., within a broad geographic market, a particular industry such as textiles).   At any of these levels, the common tendency will be to consolidate any bank or bank-related affiliates into single administrative units.

Predicted is that this three-tier banking system will be comprised of both today's commercial banks and other "banks" that may have originated as today's savings and loans, mutual savings banks, credit unions, or even finance companies.   Further, this system will be multi-national in scope and character of management; accordingly, financial institutions chartered in other "free world" nations will offer, directly or indirectly, a full-range of financial services to American customers.   So will American-based financial institutions—banks—operating in overseas markets.

A related prediction is that existing restrictions on intrastate, regional, and multi-national operations will break down. Indeed, most geographic restrictions applicable to either the lending or deposit-gathering functions will be rendered obsolete by electronic technology.

Finally, this three-tier banking system will be comprised of *fewer* independently owned and managed financial institutions (perhaps half as many by the mid-1980s as existed a decade earlier),[2] but there will be far more facilities for transacting individual and corporate financial affairs.

Convenience Banking

Predicted is that core consumer financial services (payments transfers, cash dispensing, savings deposits, small loans, purchases now effected through credit cards, utility payments, and other recurring payments for consumer services) will be processed *primarily* through electronic facilities. These *point of transaction terminals* will be located conveniently where people live, work, shop, and travel. Many of these consumer-serving installations will efficiently operate twenty-four hours a day, seven days a week, year-in, year-out, with little more notice than people today give to writing a check or using a credit card.

These terminals, moreover, will be operated by a plastic device (much time and effort already has been employed to condition both banks and customers to accept plastic as contrasted with metallic instruments) that optimizes security considerations in identifying individuals and their account status.

Predicted, if not actually certain, is that the plastic access device *alternatively* will draw against a positive account balance (a deposit account, though not particularly a checking account as contrasted with a savings account) *or* create negative, interest-charged balances (a loan or overdraft).

Foreseen is the exceedingly high probability that these transaction terminals, except where they actually are manned by a bank's employees, will be administered as a *public utility*, not unlike the telephone system. Likely to be standardized (and thoroughly regulated by the Federal government) are the *func-*

tions performed by electronic transaction terminals. In this respect, governmental concern should focus primarily on such features as transaction charges, if any; security; systems interface compatibility; assurance of privacy; accounting standards; and the guarantee that the machinery of electronic banking is available to *all* members of society—i.e., that it is blind to color, sex, and ethnic origin; that it is open to rich and poor alike.

A Tendency to Simplify

Predicted is that electronic banking will not put banks and other financial institutions out of business, except where they are marginally profitable providers of core consumer services. At most, electronic banking will standardize and mechanize routine consumer services (or to be more precise, the methods by which they are transacted) and, to some extent, price structures. Competition for customer accounts will be no less intense. Indeed, the entrance of new competitors from outside the financial industry with more to offer consumers (and business customers) should make competition for accounts *more* intense than presently is the case. Moreover, the impersonalization inherent in electronic banking should cause financial institutions to increase efforts to *personalize* other services and the means by which they are marketed. This contention will have profound impacts on the employment, compensation, training, and education of a banking organization's people resources.

Predicted is that the coming of electronic banking (when related to other trends such as the lifting of the ban on interest payments on demand deposits and the overall blurring of operational distinctions between currently different types of depository intermediaries) will result in some *simplification* of retail banking activity.

Accordingly, as electronic impulses instantaneously debit savings accounts or create a loan balance, they should encourage banks and thrifts simply to pay or charge interest on the remainder. This *one-account* concept means that a consumer or small business person would at once be depositor-borrower. He or she would be viewed as being either in the red or the black—to what extent (savings or debt levels) and for how long (maturities) probably would determine rates charged or paid. Thus, a larger surplus maintained for a longer period of time would earn the highest rates.

At some appropriate level, as determined by the customer with the guidance of his or her personal banker-financial counselor, any additions to surplus would be channeled into investment-type instruments or retirement programs. Essentially, cash management techniques now applicable to corporate customers would be utilized in serving proven and/or desired retail customers.

Particularly influencing this trend will be systems capacity; that is, the computer-based technologies applied effectively to reduce the cost of processing retail volume. Simplification also appears entirely consistent with consumerist objectives, notably as it emphasizes fairness, efficiency, convenience, and personalized treatment.

The Character of Retail Competition

Predicted as a result of some simplification in retail banking practices is that the character of institutional competition will evolve along these lines:

- an enlargement of consumer product lines, with increased emphasis on *distinctive* packaging, pricing, sales, and marketing techniques; indeed, the promotion of institutional and product line distinctiveness will emerge as a primary retailing strategy
- a greater focus on services (for example, budget planning and credit counseling) to attract account relationships, rather than interest rates and related pricing mechanisms—i.e., quality of service will be the critical determinant, not the cost
- a declining emphasis on overall share of market—that is, total volume—and increasing stress on that portion deemed most profitable and, as a measure of profitability, most loyal
- the utilization of major credit commitments, notably the residential mortgage, as a means of anchoring durable customer

relationships and providing on-going opportunities to market (cross-sell) other retail products and services
- a strengthening of personal, one-on-one relationships with retail customers by increasing direct visitations from better trained, more skilled, and better motivated employees—that is, by *reaching-out*

These and a series of related strategies will be discussed in greater detail in Chapter Ten.

The Thrift Industry Response

Predicted—indeed, it already is one of today's realities—is that mutual savings banks, savings and loan associations, credit unions, and finance companies will become more banklike in their retail operations. They will in time become little different from banks, if not actually retail banks in the fullest sense of the word. In this emerging period, they will probably acquire the authority to conduct bank-related activities such as:

- provide for payments transfers
- engage extensively in consumer lending and related activities necessary to their development as "family financial centers"
- offer retail trust packages, and probably individual and corporate plans for small businesses and partnerships
- join with commercial banks in expanding beyond the customary savings account relationship into the investment of consumer income
- place portions of their assets into business loans, particularly credits associated with construction lending and with small business development

The entry of new competitors into the retail banking field—most notably the grocery, drug, and department stores—already is occurring. *Predicted* is that it will intensify. The ability of these organizations to effect funds transfers and provide credit is discernible, as is their unparalleled ability to attract consumer customers. People *need* to go to department and convenience stores.

To the extent that these stores can facilitate core financial transactions, then it follows that people need to go to banks less often.

Somewhat less discernible at the time of this writing is their
prospective capability to provide consumers with a wider range of
services: budget planning, accident and life insurance, travel
planning and financing, car loans, income tax preparation, home
modernization financing, and both capital and equipment financing for businessmen. Most are in existence, being planned, or at
least talked about—and most make sense for them to offer.

Structural Unification

Predicted is that the current trend toward structural concentration
will not abate and will intensify in the near future, chiefly in the
bank-related areas. This will especially be so as the weaknesses and
shortcomings of the holding company movement are corrected.

At one level, thrift institutions will seek consolidations through
mergers and holding company affiliation in order to achieve scale
economies and maximize operational capabilities and market
position. Concurrently, they will utilize diversification to expand
in areas of existing service expertise (e.g., the mortgage lending
field) while also seeking to acquire expertise and customer affilia-
tions in new operational areas (e.g., consumer lending and trust
management).

In turn, smaller and medium-sized specialized institutions such
as mortgage and title companies, even independents active in the
commercial financing area, will be integrated further within larger
multi-purpose financial institutions.

Finally, the now separate bank-related commercial, consumer,
and real estate financing subsidiaries of holding companies will be
integrated into the congeneric's banking activity. Factoring, for
example, will become part of a banking organization's commercial
services area—a specialty, but only in terms of service, not structure. This pattern likewise will develop as holding companies are
authorized to further diversify: What they acquire and gain in
management experience eventually will be integrated. No doubt,
there will be exceptions to this general practice; however, they prob-

ably will be occasioned by strategic rather than structural purposes. In any case, the vehicle to be utilized probably will remain the multi-unit holding company, although, as previously discussed, the holding company format will use its growth and expansion capabilities to acquire and then consolidate its achievements.

Even at the time of this writing, there are a number of trends that suggest that growth capital will be at a premium in the years ahead. Outright acquisition purchases, therefore, could become more difficult to effect. Other current trends prompt the view that public sector antipathy toward undue concentration of economic power will not weaken but intensify.

Predicted are projected responses that lead to consortium approaches to holding company relationships among banking organizations as well as between commercial banks and other types of financial institutions. The design of a consortium would be to develop structured relationships seen necessary to the achievement of common objects without raising the spectre of bigness and agglomeration. It also is reasonable to anticipate evolution of the following:

- organized, nonequity alignments of banking networks (within and even outside natural markets) in order to offer or participate in the providing of commercial services in a national and multi-national environment
- the general expansion of correspondent activity to embrace nonbank financial institutions in a highly competitive, broad-based manner
- the development of quasi-correspondent or nonequity partnership interrelations, especially those stressing a "sharing" of the burdens associated with the introduction and expansion of electronic technologies

Recognition of the "capital crunch" facing bank and nonbank holding company organizations is critical to any understanding of the emerging competitive environment. More institutions, current status notwithstanding, over time will be competing aggressively for a growing, although probably inadequate, supply of debt and equity funds. The pool will expand, but not nearly as fast as the thirst. Obtaining a fair share of these scarce capital funds is viewed as a major problem facing financial institutions as the future unfolds.[3]

Bricks-and-Mortar

It has been common in recent years to argue that the present number of 14,000 commercial banks; 6,000 savings banks and savings and loan associations; and many thousands of credit unions, finance companies, mortgage banks, mutual fund brokers, etc. will diminish greatly as time passes. They would become victims of concentration and consolidation and of the prospective achievements of electronic banking. Likewise, it frequently is assumed that many of today's 40,000 bricks-and-mortar commercial bank branch offices in time will be rendered obsolete by convenient and comparatively inexpensive electronic terminals.

Predicted as the most probable changes are the following:

- substantial elimination of banks and other financial institutions—especially in areas in which performance is marginal, present or anticipated competition is most intense, or (as always has been the case) the changing population patterns and economic conditions question their viability
- many marginally profitable bricks-and-mortar branch units that currently provide consumer core services *only* in an overly competitive market or, conversely, in a stagnant one, would be discontinued or replaced by mini-offices or electronic facilities minimizing personal contact
- profitable branch locations in vital consumer and commercial markets would be continued, although many core services would be automated; on the other hand, customer service contact as applied to noncore services probably would be substantially expanded. (In effect, these offices would become "full-service banks." Their market penetration by design would be enhanced through on-line utilization of computer-based information systems, closed circuit television interface with support systems, and the intensified

application of employee time and skills for direct customer sales efforts.)
- the sharing of branch and even main office buildings with the communities they serve in a manner that furthers community identification and optimizes institutional distinctiveness; accordingly, *The* First National Bank's auditorium is where consumer education programs are held on Tuesday night and on Thursday evening 'golden oldie' movies are shown

It is also projected that there will be an absolute decline in the number of high risk, high rate lenders of consumer credit. Loan sharks and the like probably never will pass from the scene. However, it must be presumed that the advent of electronic banking and the proliferation of transaction terminals, when combined with public interest imperatives, will serve to bring greater numbers of people into the financial mainstream; these individuals will then be assured of the fairest rate structures and treatment. Viewed somewhat differently, the financial community will do a better job of serving the poor and the disadvantaged; this will result because such activity will eventuate social tradeoffs for expanded financial industry powers. It also can be pointed out that the expansion of government direct deposit programs to include welfare payments should facilitate this trend.

Regulation and Supervision

Throughout this chapter it has been implied or stated explicitly that the role of government—*the public interest imperative*—would become more pervasive during the transition to an electronic era and a more competitive environment. This is hardly a prediction. The expanded role of government is a certainty.

The present thrust of regulation and supervision appears to be moving along two parallel paths. The first is the enlargement of the government's *police powers*. This trend would mitigate conflicts of interest. It would assure fuller disclosure practices. It would reduce discrimination in credit and employment. It would curtail abusive credit collection practices. And it would assure that credit allocation procedures are designed to best serve public policy objectives, at least as they are determined by regulators and legislative policy-makers.

The second and congruent trend is *rationalization.* It is best explained with a series of questions: Given a blurring of distinctions between types of financial institutions, is there any reasonable need for three Federal bank regulatory agencies as well as Federal agencies to administer savings and loan associations and credit unions? Given a trend toward interstate and multi-national banking systems is there any reasonable need for state supervisory activity? Given the anticipated proliferation of banking activities (particularly in the electronic mode or through holding company diversification) and the policing of these activities by other Federal regulatory authorities (i.e., the Securities Exchange Commission, the Federal Trade Commission, etc.), is it not reasonable to unify these often overlapping, even at times, conflicting jurisdictions within a single powerful body such as a Federal Banking Commission? Finally, given projected alterations in the structure and mix of deposits, is it not reasonable to tighten control over the management of the nation's money supply? Can the Federal Reserve System continue to administer monetary policy efficiently lacking reserve requirements applicable to all commercial banks and even to thrifts engaging in *de facto* payments transfers?[4]

Many more questions can be raised. What they point to, as do the foregoing, is rationalization.

Chart 8.1 depicts the existing system of financial industry regulation by Federal and state authorities.[5] The shared role of Federal and state authorities, and the clear divisions at the Federal level, explain the character and workings of America's dual banking system.[6] It is intricate. It is complex.

On one hand, it is "a banking system of almost unbelievable complexity. . . . without rhyme or reason. . . . [that] has given rise, not only to great confusion, but, more important, to competitive inequalities among different classes of banks."[7]

Conversely, as explained by former Comptroller of the Currency James E. Smith, "The greatest single advantage offered by

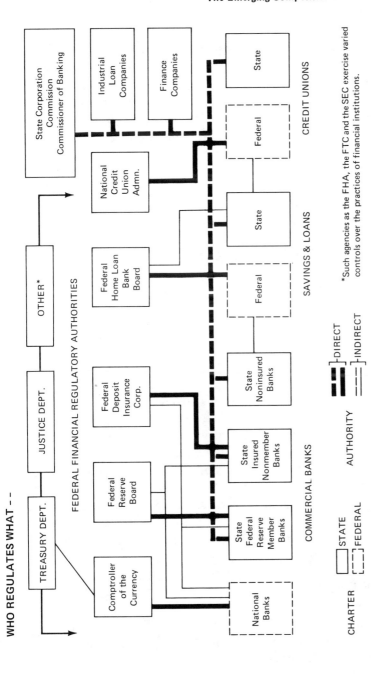

State-chartered financial institutions are directly supervised by the State Corporation Commission. The Federal Reserve Board, while it does not charter banks as does the Comptroller of the Currency or the Corporation Commission, exercises direct control over State Member Bank operations and less directly over National and Insured NonMember banks. The Federal Deposit Insurance Corporation occupies a similar supervisory position. In certain areas, moreover, the authority of nonbank Federal Agencies and the Justice Department is influential. This same duality of Federal and State controls applies to savings and loan and credit union operations. In one key respect, State government exercises authority over Federally-chartered institutions: Office expansion is limited to state boundary lines, and then, by state law within each state respectively.

the duality of our system is its capacity to foster fruitful experimentation." He added that in effect, "we have 51 (the 50 states and the Federal government) banking laboratories. Results of changes in regulatory stance soon become apparent to all authorities. False starts can quickly be amended without widespread impact; salutory changes can spread rapidly into other jurisdictions."[8]

These views are indicative of the arguments raised in support of or in opposition to a rationalization of the dual banking system. This controversy, moreover, has been the subject of extensive hearings in nearly each session of Congress over the past two decades. Often it is initiated by the introduction of legislation calling for the establishment of a Federal Banking Commission. Into this agency would be consolidated the regulatory and supervisory functions of the Federal Reserve Board, the Comptroller of the Currency, and the Federal Deposit Insurance Corporation. Variations on this proposal have called for combining the activities of two of these agencies into the third, either into the Federal Reserve Board or the FDIC. To date, extensive hearings have been held, but no proposal has come to a vote in the House or Senate.[9]

The Corporate Citizen

Any discussion of future regulatory trends also necessitates at least brief mention of *corporate citizenship.*

Predicted is that social responsibility, whether viewed as opposition to environmental decay, the improvement of inner-city life, or race and sex equality, increasingly will be pressed upon capitalistic institutions.

Performance as "good corporate citizens" will become vital in determining banking's ability, on one hand, *to resist* greater degrees of governmental intervention in the marketplace and, at another level, *to identify favorably* with a better educated and more discerning customer base.

To be faced directly will be the question of whether capitalism (and its primary institutions!) is a more viable, more humane, and more productive alternative than a managed economy. Words spoken or written in defense of the existing system will not be enough. There must be achievement. The system, and not its critics nor its regulators, must by its own actions ensure its credibility as the future unfolds. Most important, we believe, conduct and achievement must be real, readily perceived, and generally understood by the public and its legal and moral representatives.

Norborne Berkeley, Jr., president of Chemical New York Corporation and Chemical Bank, added this perspective in a 1974 address at a banking industry public affairs conference:

> We must demonstrate by our actions that our goal is not profit for profit's sake, but profit for the good of many. Only then will the confidence [in the business system] that has been so badly shattered be restored.
>
> The very nature of our business [banking] makes it an economic force of major importance. What I think we must now recognize is that we cannot afford to restrict our activities to the world of business and finance. We must think in terms of banking as a significant social force in this country—and the world—for indeed we are. And this capability carries with it a responsibility to use our resources and talents to find solutions to more than purely financial affairs. . .
>
> Let me conclude by emphasizing my belief that our effective involvement in public affairs is essential to the future of our industry. The past has proved what neglect can do; the present has demonstrated what results can be achieved, and it now remains for us to intensify and expand our effort to insure the future.[10]

The Parameters of Change

The numerous predictions outlined in this chapter—not to mention the earlier evaluation of the trends or specific developments that prompted them—constitute merely one view of the emerging competitive environment. Moreover, it is only a partial picture at that. We believe, however, that these predictions define the parameters of change. It is within these rough boundaries that existing competitive relationships *continually* are to be reassessed and new relationships forged.

Our view may be too bold or, more likely, not bold enough. Our assumptions regarding "when" may be wide of the mark; things may happen sooner or later than anticipated, or events may prove more sharply felt in their impacts on existing relationships. This especially could be the case with electronic banking developments. And probably a recurrence of "stagflation" would invite a range of unexpected actions and a speeding up of timetables affecting such concerns as the rationalization of regulatory practices or the extension of additional banklike powers to institutions that now tend to borrow short and lend long.

Boldness and accuracy notwithstanding, the salient fact remains that our discussion of *Predictions, Prospects, and Problems* identifies change. It signals a transition from now to then and demonstrates that "need for the wise to build knowingly."

THE PASSING OF REGULATION Q

Throughout Unit Two, we have maintained that the phasing out or outright elimination of Regulation Q ceilings on time and savings deposits should be considered a likely and evolutionary occurrence within the bank planner's working time frame. It is an eventuality that can be discerned and possibly prepared for.

It also has been suggested that a transition from regulated consumer deposit structures to an "era of purchased funds" is a distinct possibility. If this occurs, it will be an era in which deposit structures will be determined, as they already are for commercial liabilities, chiefly by interaction within the marketplace.

Subsequently, a number of specific developments were identified that collectively appear to mandate the eventual elimination of Regulation Q, either as an actual constraint on the deposit-gathering function or as a symbol of prevailing regulatory philosophy. In this largely psychological sense, the passing of Regulation Q can be interpreted as a major discontinuity affecting competitive relationships.

As a realistic guideline for banking practice and philosophy, it already has become outdated by technological advances, competitive pressures, altered consumer habits and expectations, and the emergence of new economic realities. Like branching restrictions or prohibitions against the payment of interest on demand deposits, Regulation Q is an "anamoly." The fact that the Senate in 1976 characterized the "phase out" of Regulation Q as a critical element of financial industry reform attests to this view. To be sure, the passing of Regulation Q as a specific event seems no more or less important than the liberalization of branching codes or the breaking down of Glass-Steagall Act restrictions on commercial bank activities in investment banking. Yet it is more important —as an emotional issue; it excites schism; and it is clear recognition that a competitive environment and new relationships visibly have arrived. It is a "watershed" because of its inherent cause-effect implications for other banking procedures and, in turn, the responses they generate.

Finally, we have offered the view that the passing of Regulation Q probably will not come about quickly unless, for example, a sharp and adverse alteration in economic conditions occurred. But its eventual passing appears a possibility; it is likely that we will move into an era of purchased funds. Therein lies its importance: *when Q goes, what then?*

The following speculations are designed to raise a series of questions. The ways in which they might be answered form much of the substance of the several chapters comprising Unit Four. Our procedure for handling these speculations will center on banking's *customer markets*; the *people resources* employed to serve them; the acquisition of a capital base from *investor markets* and its allocation among competing uses; and the methodology, or the *delivery systems*, utilized to bring the product to customers in a manner that satisfies their wants and needs at a profit.

Competing in a World Without Q

The most dramatic and profound impact of the removal of Regulation Q will be on retail banking. The areas most affected will be: the manner in which funds are procured; the cost of funds; the return on consumer credit; the number and diversity of competitors;

and, in all probability, the profitability of retail banking. Clearly, the most important area of concern is profitability.

Traditionally, retail profits have been garnered from the substantial spread between the interest cost of consumer deposits and the much higher interest income generated by the add-on charge of instalment lending. More recently, this spread has been threatened by sharp fluctuations in the business cycle, disintermediation, inflation, and the skyrocketing costs of paper processing and branch installations. Thus, retail banking has not been as profitable as it once was. Looking ahead, how will the removal of Regulation Q affect the attractiveness of retail banking? At this stage, the answer is not yet clear. But a careful examination of the components of profitability provides some valuable insights.

The long-standing argument in favor of promulgating and retaining interest rate ceilings on deposits has been that without them financial institutions would excessively raise rates paid to acquire funds. These costs then would have to be covered by investing in high-yield, high-risk assets. Carried far enough, this process would lead to massive loan losses and eventual failure. Considerable research has shown this scenario to be inaccurate; moreover, it is a call for irrational behavior.[11] Only in rare exceptions have banks actually engaged in such practices and even then there was no follow-the-leader effect. Furthermore, the incentive to survive and to be profitable mitigates against such behavior.

Thus, there is little reason to expect an all-out competitive war pushing up interest rates on deposits following the elimination of Q. Some overzealous and aggressive institutions may engage in irrational practices over the short run, but they would not survive to be a factor over the long run.

What can more reasonably be expected is that broad market forces will establish rates paid on deposits at levels commensurate with rates available on alternative instruments. Important determinants of broad market forces are factors such as:

- relative degrees of risk (insured deposits versus Treasury bills versus commercial paper versus subordinated notes)
- convenience and miscellaneous costs
- entrance barriers (e.g., $10,000 minimum on Treasury bills)

- broad economic conditions (tight money versus easy money, or the rate of inflation)
- local economic and financial conditions

Given the influence of all of these factors, if there had been no Q between 1973 and 1977, the interest cost of deposits to banks would have been much higher than existing ceilings during 1973, 1974, and early 1975. Alternatively, costs actually might have been lower during much of 1975, all of 1976, and early 1977.

If economic conditions in the years following the removal of Q are predominantly periods of a minimum inflation rate of 5%–6% and firm to tight financial markets, then there will be marked upward pressure on the average interest cost of consumer funds over the business cycle compared to the regulated costs experienced during the cycles of the 1960s and 1970s. The generally higher rates available in the open market, combined with a substantial need for funds to accomodate hefty loan demand, would necessitate paying competitive (higher) rates to acquire needed funds.

Since the lifting of Q ceilings on savings and time deposits either would be preceded or accompanied by removing the companion zero rate ceiling on demand deposits, their interest costs definitely would rise unless the public could be persuaded that the value of participating in the payments system was sufficient reward for holding demand deposits. Such could well be the case in periods of easy money and low interest rates.

On balance, it appears that the elimination of Regulation Q will tend to increase interest costs if generally accepted forecasts of high inflation and sharp fluctuations in economic activity eventuate. Interest costs, however, are only a part of total costs, with the other major component being operations costs.

Consumer deposits have been and will continue to be expensive to obtain and process, requiring extensive branching networks accompanied by electronic devices and huge back-room operations. In particular, the shift into an electronic world will be extremely costly initially and will not pay meaningful dividends for some time. If Regulation Q is lifted during this period of electronic development, the entire process could be speeded up as financial institutions seek alternative means to gain a competitive edge. Thus additional upward pressures on costs would emerge.

Since deposit interest costs began moving up in the mid-1960s as a result of higher interest rates in general, the shift in the demand/time deposit mix, and the expanded use of the higher cost consumer certificate, banks have responded by raising rates charged for loans. Both consumers and businesses have felt the pinch of higher loan rates in varying degrees. Inevitably, banks will attempt to cover future cost increases in the same way. On the retail side, however, this approach may be thwarted by the forces of consumerism and competition.

Consumerism, either informally or via legislation, probably will put pressure on banks to keep consumer rates as low as possible. Nevertheless, recent experience has shown that consumers can understand and tolerate higher loan rates during periods of generally higher interest rates. Thus, in a world without Q, but perhaps with higher inflation that causes higher interest costs, the bulk of those costs probably can be recaptured through cyclically higher consumer loan rates (at least to the extent permitted by prevailing usury laws).

Then, too, there is every indication that national policy will continue to require that residential mortgage credit be priced as inexpensively as possible. Concurrently, credit allocation formulas may be imposed that assure ample and stable flows of credit into housing; particularly, banking's contribution would be increased. The same reasoning appears valid with respect to the financing of Federal, state, and municipal debt.

As explained in earlier discussions, banks will face more competitors in the retail market in the future. Thrift institutions and retail chains, for example, are expected to become much more aggressive purveyors of consumer credit. Outside of small, local markets, however, competitive conditions in the retail credit market have been stiff since banks "discovered people" in the 1950s. Moreover, competitive pressures to lower loan rates are likely to be strongest during periods of easy money and weak loan demand—times when the cost of funds is lowest.

What will be the net impact of the removal of Regulation Q on profitability? Separate analyses of costs and income indicate the following:

- the interest costs of deposits will rise markedly *only* if interest rates in general rise
- operations costs will be high over the near-term future as electronic technology is used more widely to acquire consumer deposits
- income will rise to offset higher costs, but could be partially restrained by consumerism and competition

Thus, it is possible that profitability could be affected adversely, essentially the retail spread. Unless circumstances change dramatically in the latter 1970s, however, most medium to large banks will not be in a position to sacrifice earnings. They will not bid up the cost of funds beyond open market levels, and they will maintain revenues by passing on costs and increasing the proportion of higher yielding assets—most likely business loans. Some smaller financial institutions with substantial local market power, however, when subjected to the more competitive world of electronic banking and no deposit rate ceilings, may suffer earnings erosion. The artificial barriers to entry into their markets will be set aside and they will have to compete more actively.

CONCLUSION

In sum, a central issue raised by the prospective elimination of Regulation Q is a narrowing of the spread. This critical challenge to bank management requires either the consideration of new responses or, at the very least, the intensification of what banking now does best as an industry or as an individual bank. It requires, for example, reviewing such strategies as those calling for the minimization of retail banking activities—that is, to perhaps focus on a smaller but most profitable market share—while concurrently increasing commercial banking activity with its potentially greater earnings margins and higher degree of risk. By the mid-1970s, in fact, a number of regional holding companies were indicating their adherence to this general strategy.

The very same point can be made about any of the predictions or prospects mentioned in this chapter; similar logic also can be applied to those forecasts not dealt with in this text. Coping with the opportunities and challenges that will be presented in the emerging competitive environment will require the systematic, creative, and disciplined allocation of human and financial resources through compatible manned and machine systems that satisfies customer needs and wants. Performing this task well will become the hallmark of institutional as well as social profitability.

FOOTNOTES

1. Particularly see Robert E. Barnett, chairman, Federal Deposit Insurance Corporation," H. R. 1901: Regulation Q, NOW Accounts, and the Payment of Interest on Demand Deposits," an address at the 49th Mid-Winter Meeting of the New York State Bankers Association, New York, January 24, 1977. In this policy statement, the FDIC chairman recognized "the natural expansion of NOW Accounts on a nationwide basis." He also noted that "the expansion of thrift institutions into the payments business, and the payment of interest on checking accounts are two important aspects of the NOW Account."

   In his address, chairman Barnett also provided an excellent analysis of Regulation Q and the implications its removal or modification would have for different types of financial institutions. A similar analysis was made with respect to the payment of interest on demand deposits.
2. Remarks by Carter H. Golembe at the 61st Annual Convention of the Bank Marketing Association, Miami Beach, FL, October 27, 1976. See also remarks by K. A. Randall, then president, United Virginia Bankshares, Inc., Richmond, VA, currently President of the Conference Board, and former chairman, Federal Deposit Insurance Corporation, at Eliminating Constraints on Banking: A National Conference to Consider the Ability of Banks to Serve the Public, December 7–9, Chicago, IL.
3. Frederick Deane, Jr., chairman and chief executive officer, Bank of Virginia Company, Richmond, "Capital Needs in Banking," an address at the 26th Assembly for Bank Directors, Pinehurst, NC, November 7, 1976.
4. An excellent analysis of this issue is found in Ross M. Robertson and Almarin Phillips, *Optional Affiliation With the Federal Reserve System*

for Reserve Purposes is Consistent With Effective Monetary Policies (Washington, DC: Conference of State Bank Supervisors, 1974).

5. A more detailed portrayal of current regulatory and supervisory practices is found in *A Profile of State-Chartered Banking* (Washington, DC: Conference of State Bank Supervisors, 1975 Edition).

6. Particularly see Carter H. Golembe, "Our Remarkable Banking System," *Virginia Law Review*, May, 1967. Also see Note 2, Chapter Six.

7. Howard H. Hackley, "Our Baffling Banking System—Part Two," *Virginia Law Review*, June 1966, pp. 824–830.

8. Remarks by James E. Smith, Comptroller of the Currency, at The American Bankers Association Convention, Honolulu, HI, October 18, 1973.

9. The idea of a Federal Banking Commission was first proposed in an address by Federal Reserve Board Governor J. L. Robertson in May of 1962. In testimony before the House Banking and Currency Committee in May of 1963, he restated his thesis as modified. The concept in its essentials has remained virtually unchanged since that time.

    In both his 1962 speech and in subsequent congressional testimony, Governor Robertson charged that bank supervision as then (and currently practiced) was

    > A hodgepodge affair . . . that has grown up like Topsy; it has been divided among several agencies with resulting overlapping, inefficiencies, inconsistencies, and conflicting policies.

    A succinct analysis of Governor Robertson's proposal, with major modifications, is contained in *Proposals for Modernizing the Bank Supervisory Structure* (Washington, DC: National Association of Supervisors of State Banks, March, 1964).

    The American Banker on January 13, 1977 reported that W. Michael Blumenthal, then President Carter's nominee as Secretary of the Treasury, told a Senate Committee that we would give "serious attention to whether the bank regulatory agencies would be consolidated."

10. Norborne Berkeley, Jr., "How a Banker Views Public Affairs," an address at the Bank Marketing Association/The American Bankers Association Public Affairs Conference, Atlanta, GA, February 11, 1974.

11. See Albert H. Cox, Jr., *Regulation of Interest Rates on Bank Deposits*, Michigan Business Studies, Vol. XVII, No. 4 (Ann Arbor: University of Michigan, 1966); Charles F. Haywood and Charles M. Linke, *The Regulation of Deposit Interest Rates* (Chicago: Association of Reserve City Bankers, 1968); George J. Benston, "Bank Investment Behavior," *Journal of Political Economy*, Vol. LXXII, No. 5 (October 1964).

UNIT THREE: THE MARKETS APPROACH TO PLANNING

9 MARKETING AND A FRAMEWORK FOR PLANNING

INTRODUCTION

Although an environmental analysis of the future and the other steps in the planning process (such as setting objectives and strategies) are valuable managerial tools, their benefits are not maximized if they are undertaken in an inconsistent or *ad hoc* fashion. A single study of the likely effects of EFTS or the removal of Regulation Q is useful, but it is not likely to bring about a coordinated, company-wide response unless some common structure exists for integrating future circumstances into current decision making. Similarly, randomly developed objectives are not likely to be achieved without a common theme that is relevant to all areas of a financial institution's activities; this is the case even if specific strategies appear to be sound. What is needed is a reference point, a framework that is applicable equally in the lending division, in the operations area, and among various staff divisions.

A recurring theme in Unit Two's analysis of the future operating environments for banks and thrifts is the greater intensity of competition for *customers, employees,* and *capital resources.* Ongoing legislative efforts to reform and rationalize the structure of the financial industry, coupled with the expanding use of electronic technology, eventually will make existing financial institutions more comparable and equal; as a result, the industry will be introduced to new sellers of financial services. Simultaneously, more knowledgeable and demanding customers, employees, and investors, along with more diligent and scrutinizing regulatory authorities, will expect higher quality performance from financial institutions.

The impact of these external changes will fall on the markets where financial institutions meet the competition. These markets represent the combined interaction of their participants—the buyers and sellers of goods and services. How buyers and sellers interact reflects the structure of the market as shaped by custom, practice, legislation, and regulation. Interactions between buyers and sellers also reflect their needs and abilities as shaped by their attitudes and preferences, the availability of resources, economic conditions, and the state and application of technology. Changes in those external or environmental factors that shape the structure, needs, and abilities of market participants will alter the nature and characteristics of the market.

MARKETS AS REFERENCE POINT AND FRAMEWORK

We believe that the markets in which a bank or thrift must perform against the competition provide a valid reference point for evaluating the likely impact of more competitors, greater competition, and other forms of environmental influence. Moreover, performance in competitive markets is common to all facets of the banking business, thereby providing a framework for establishing the purpose, objectives, and alternative action strategies. In fact, performance in markets captures the essence of the purpose of the business institution as defined by Peter Drucker: Business is to satisfy customer needs through efficient use of scarce, wealth-producing resources.[1]

In general, a financial institution's performance in its markets may be described by the concept and mission of marketing: the profitable, efficient, and responsible satisfaction of the needs that comprise a market. The concept of marketing may be explained in terms of its tasks. The first task is to know the market, to identify customer needs. The second is to satisfy those needs by developing appropriate products and services and creating an effective demand for them. Often this process is characterized as having the right product; at the right price, time, and place; with the right promotion and packaging.

IMPORTANCE OF THE MARKETING MISSION

Many banks and thrifts still adhere to the misconception that the marketing mission is separate and distinct from the overall management mission stated so clearly by Drucker. Many bank executives view marketing as a set of specialized activities (such as research, public relations, or advertising) that are planned and developed by a specific group of personnel who comprise the marketing department. Actually, these activities are the basic tools used to implement marketing strategies. These strategies evolve from the broader definition of marketing as "a philosophy of doing business . . . that must permeate the entire organization."[2]

Each bank employee is a marketing person. Marketing is what a teller does in communicating with a depositor. Marketing is what a telephone operator does in responding to a customer inquiry. Similarly, the clerk responding to a customer inquiry about an overdraft or late credit card payment is marketing. Thus, marketing is an attitude, a perspective, a business philosophy. The marketing department provides tools for developing and implementing this attitude: training, promotional materials, staff morale incentives, and so on. The marketing department's clientele, as can be seen, is twofold: first, external customers being served by the bank; and, second, the bank people providing this service. This assignment affects what is being provided and the methods for delivering it.

By any measure, the profitable, efficient, and responsible satisfaction of market needs is a top management responsibility. To view this responsibility as wholly owned by the marketing department, in effect, is to turn over the institution's destiny to this department. After all, what is the future of the organization if it keeps losing customers to competitors whose top management does a superior job of implementing the mission of marketing? Customers supply the revenue that provides the potential for profit, and the potential for profit is the incentive for investment in the business, which leads to the actual investment needed to sustain the business. These realities summarize to the overall reality that "the customer is the business."[3] That is, without customers, there is nothing. And surely, if "the customer is the business" then the customer is the ultimate responsibility of top management. Clearly, the marketing mission is not distinct from the overall management mission; it is an integral part.

The Marketing Task

The marketing mission of profitably, efficiently, and responsibly satisfying market needs inherently presents a central marketing *task* if it is to be accomplished on a continuing basis. The task: *initiating internal, controllable change to adapt to external, uncontrollable, market-impacting change.* Why this task? Because, as we have seen, external change directly affects the behavior of market participants. Service offerings, distribution strategies, pricing approaches, and promotional tactics that satisfy market needs today will not necessarily satisfy market needs tomorrow.

Whereas a given institution typically cannot prevent the shape and nature of its markets from changing because of external forces (such as high inflation, women's liberation, or the modification of Regulation Q), the institution does not lack for actions that can be taken. The relevant question becomes *what should we do that we can do* to respond to the changing needs of our present customers and of our noncustomers that we would like to have as customers? How can we prepare today for a tomorrow that will include diminished purchasing power, a new kind of female consumer, and the reality of having to bid for deposits in the open market against new as well as old competitors? Such questions are *marketing questions* that *management must answer*, preferably through the management tool of strategic planning.

The Market as Object of Change

Consider the relationship between a bank, its competition, the market, and selected environmental forces that affect the market.

Impinging upon this market are changing socio-economic, legislative-regulatory, and technological forces that are serving continuously to change its shape and nature. As these forces change the market, so must the financial institutions serving the market change. If the market changes in a material way and Bank A adapts to this change and Bank B does not, then Bank B should expect to lose some of its previously held influence in the market in terms of persuading market members to patronize it.

In other words, the influence of any given financial institution in terms of persuading members of the market to participate in the desired transaction relates directly to how well that institution meets the changing needs of the market relative to the competition.

If the legislative-regulatory environment acts to permit interest-bearing negotiable order of withdrawal (NOW) accounts in a given geographic area, the market for consumer deposits is going to be affected. Some financial institutions are going to exercise the option of paying interest on demand deposits and more than a few consumers will be willing to change financial institutions to avail themselves of this new service (as already demonstrated by the NOW account experience in New England during the early and mid-1970s).[4]

In brief, developments in an institution's external environment (such as consumerism, the women's movement, or EFTS serve to alter the shape and nature of markets and, because institutions competing in these markets do not always respond the same way to these new circumstances, some business will change hands.

The vexing challenge to management is to develop alternative potential strategies to the changing needs of customers *before the main thrust of the change occurs*, before it is too late.

Improving the probabilities of accomplishing timely internal change in response to evolving or sudden external change requires studying and monitoring environmental forces, predicting how and when these forces will influence the market. In short, in today's and tomorrow's world of banking, it is not enough to study the customer as he or she presently is. Well-managed institutions also need to study carefully the changing society in which the customer lives to better estimate what he or she will become and when. To do otherwise is to increase the probability of initiating needed internal change *before* or *after* the market has changed, instead of *as* it is changing. To do otherwise is to react after the competition has won away profitable customers, instead of *before* they have done so.

THE PRINCIPAL MARKETS

If the markets in which a financial institution performs are to constitute its reference point for analyzing the impact of environmental change and also its framework for strategic planning, those specific markets need to be identified. We submit that customers, people resources, and investors are the principal markets; in other words, it is these markets that provide the common reference points and overall framework for a strategic planning effort.

A market can be defined as *people with the capability and the inclination to use this capability to make a certain type of transaction.* People in a market may act independently (for example, consumers), on behalf of an organization (for example, corporate executives), even on behalf of society (government).

Therefore, a market is people—a certain kind of people. Both the wherewithal and the motivation to make a certain type of transaction must be present. A market can be comprised of consumers, able and willing to exchange economic resources for certain types of goods or services. A market can be comprised of people resources, able and willing to exchange time and energy for compensation of one type or another. A market can be comprised of investors, able and willing to exchange economic resources for the prospect of eventually receiving in return even greater economic resources.

Customers are proposed as a principal market because these are the consumers, businesses, and governments from whom banks and thrifts receive funds (traditionally in the form of deposits) and to whom they provide loans and other financial services. Customers of financial institutions, whether retail or commercial, are purchasing a collection of financial services to satisfy real and perceived needs. Banks and thrifts must be prepared to satisfy them on a profitable basis. Chapter 10 focuses on retail customers and Chapter 11 focuses on commercial customers.

People resources are proposed as a principal market because they make possible the availability and delivery of financial services for which banks and thrifts are compensated in the form of revenue. Financial institutions do not now have, nor can they reasonably expect to have in the future, ready and easy access to an unlimited supply of people having the background, skills, and motivation required for optimum organizational performance. Accordingly, the best people for given jobs must be competed for with other prospective employers in much the same way as companies compete with each other for larger shares of customer markets. It is erroneous to think only in terms of executives, line managers, staff officers, and technicians when considering people resources. This is certainly tomorrow's leadership element; they are vital decision-makers. However, the skill, awareness, and motivation of banking's back-room, customer-contact, and support staff also are critical elements in achieving satisfactory organizational performance. They make decisions that distinctively satisfy customer insistence for friendliness, efficiency, privacy—i.e., the countless reasons a customer selects *your* bank, not *your competitor's.* Chapter 12 deals with markets for people resources.

Investors are proposed as a principal market because these are the people—individuals and professional fund managers—who provide the capital, both equity and long-term debt, that so many financial institutions depend on to support growth in deposit and lending activity. Just as banks and thrifts cannot assume the easy and ready availability of customers, or of capable employees, neither can they assume the easy and ready availability of capital. Among other factors, the "go-go" bank holding company years of the late 1960s and early 1970s, when banking found the capital markets eager to purchase their securities on attractive terms, gave way to the credit crunch and recession of 1973–75. During this time, huge real estate loan losses, substantial bank earnings declines, and even outright bank failures provided not easily forgotten proof to many burned investors that banks, just because they are banks, are not risk-free investments.

Ultimately, all investment funds come from individuals, but they do not always purchase securities directly. In fact, the trend for some time has been for larger and larger sums of investment funds to be channeled through institutions (pension and profit sharing plans, bank trust companies, mutual funds, insurance companies, etc.) as the direct purchasers of securities. Thus, participants in investors' markets include, in addition to individuals, institutional fund managers, brokers, and analysts.

It is necessary to draw an important distinction here. Investors supply banks and other shareholder-owned financial intermediaries with funds—i.e., the operating and capital funds that comprise a bank's *financial resources.*

Although depositors also supply financial resources, we do not include them in the investors market, but rather in the customers market. To discuss the market for retail customers is, therefore, to focus on the consumer in his dual role as saver and borrower. It is to develop strategies that deal successfully with each of these roles and their component parts (i.e., the consumer differentiated as car-buyer, home-buyer, or credit-card user).

Normally, the customer is not a risk-taker in his or her dealings with a bank. The bank is where funds are safeguarded, where deposits are insured, and where credits are collateralized or protected by bad debt reserves or a capital structure.

The *investor,* however, is willing to accept some risk. He or she is chancing that a bank will grow and produce profits. The investor in an enterprise society is the ultimate provider of institutional as well as societal growth. Chapter Thirteen focuses on the investors market.

Delivering Products and Services

Connecting a financial institution to its markets is a *delivery system*, through which varied offerings are made available to customers, employees, and investors. Chiefly, these offerings are financial services and products. In the case of the market for people resources, however, a delivery system would focus on employment, compensation, training, education, and motivation procedures.

Our concern at this point is with the more traditional concept of offering a financial service such as credit counseling or a financial product such as a consumer loan or savings account through manned and automated, computer-based networks. These networks include bricks-and-mortar buildings, electronic terminals, loan production offices, the "plastic branch" or credit card, and other limited-service facilities.

In recent years, an inordinate degree of attention has been targeted on the emergence of an electronic banking system—the new, modernistic mode of delivery. Beginning with the 1970s, even sooner in a great many respects, the magic term was EFTS. This concept embodied not only a transition from a paper-based funds transfer system to paperless entries, but also a spiraling, ever-proliferating array of hardware and software concepts: POS terminals, automated teller machines, debit cards, direct deposit programs, bank-by-phone experiments, Federal Reserve and bank wire systems, and even computer-based elaborations of traditional banking practices such as NOW accounts and credit verification systems.

By mid-1977, it was estimated, for example, that the nation's financial institutions were operating some 6,000 ATMs that dispensed cash; accepted deposits (with some even permitting overdraft loans); and reported checking and savings account balances. In addition, approximately 11,000 POS terminals were operating in retail stores, chiefly verifying checks. A National Commission on EFTS was preparing a report to the President and Congress that dealt with long-range developmental policies. Automated clearing houses and switching centers were functioning in major cities to handle a large volume of checkless funds transfer transactions.

For all of this, however, the electronic banking revolution appeared to be slowing to a halt. In its April 18, 1977 issue, the editors of *Business Week* magazine made the following observations:

Suddenly it appears that the great electronic banking revolution that has been "just around the corner" for a decade may never arrive at all. It has been halted by consumer resistance, soaring costs, legal and legislative snarls—and by a growing belief among bankers that they really do not need and cannot afford a nationwide electronic funds transfer system. This is a dramatic turnabout. Until recently, most experts considered EFT both inevitable and highly desirable. In the widely envisioned "cashless society," dominated by magnetically encoded plastic debit cards, funds would be rocketed across the nation in seconds, eliminating checks and saving both the time and money it takes to process them. With electronic terminals in every retail outlet—and maybe in homes and offices as well—there would be no need for people ever to go near a bank to carry out routine transactions. They would simply use the card for purchases, deposits, withdrawals, payment of bills, and even borrowing money.[5]

There is considerable truth in the *Business Week* assessment. The transition to an electronic banking mode had cooled, and largely because of "customer resistance" and "soaring costs," particularly for hardware applications. Nonetheless, this movement had not ground to a halt nor was it in the process of disappearing. Too much time, energy, and dollars already had been invested; moreover, the need for a simpler, less expensive, less labor-intensive method for processing customer financial transactions remained. What was moving to a back burner—if not actually off the stove and into deepfreeze—were the more visionary notions associated with electronic banking, especially those connected with the sooner-than-later advent of a checkless and cashless society where people required neither money nor bankers.

In sum, it had become clear by 1977 (much earlier for those who closely followed the literature of electronic banking) that the electronic mode was a pervasive, critical element in the industry's delivery system. Furthermore, it would become more so as the future unfolded. However, just as clear was the realization that it would not rapidly become—if indeed, ever—the *only* element or even the *primary* one. Finally, it was recognized that the most immediate impact of EFTS and related technologies would be to facilitate—not take the place of, but complement—the handling of routine consumer transactions in a convenient manner. Accordingly, the electronic terminal would accommodate a customer's convenience requirement by operating twenty-four hours a day, seven days a week as a deposit-taking, bill-paying, account-transferring, cash-dispensing "teller" and "bookkeeper." More-over, a computer-based, on-line customer information system would help identify prospective customers and pinpoint wants and needs.

Electronic banking would be a helpmate. Indeed, it is notable that any number of banking organizations introducing ATMs in the mid-1970s told their employees that Tillie, Ginny, or Suzie (the personalization of machine technology) would be their *friends:* They would work during hours when the bank was closed; make the employee's job easier by handling customer overflow; and so on. EFT was not to be a competitive procedure for deliver-ing products and services to customers but a helper that permitted staff members to have more time to perform their jobs better, thus creating more meaningful career opportunities.

People, Places, and Machines

In the tomorrow of banking that is just ahead of us, or within the planning dimension, it is certain that the industry's products will be delivered to customers by people utilizing a wide range of manned and machine-based systems; it is also evident that their reliance on machines will increase. What appears revolutionary (but really is evolutionary) is not the advent of electronic technol-ogies but a general expansion along *many* fronts in ways and means for more effectively delivering financial services. No less exciting is the evolving of a marked change in management atti-tudes, particularly in the notion that financial organizations must reach out to customers rather than wait for customers to come into a banking office.

This multi-front enlargement of the delivery systems utilized in financial institutions can be discerned from a retail market model developed as part of one bank holding company's strategic plan. By 1980, this organization believed that at the very least it would be operating on a statewide basis in terms of serving its market for retail customers and throughout a "natural trading area" embracing several states in serving its commercial customers.

Retail Market Model

Manned Offices

- Central headquarters
- Regional headquarters offices providing full-service activity for customers *and* back-room and related support capacities for customer contact personnel (including training, credit administration, marketing, and operations support)
- Full-service, "bricks-and-mortar" branches located in key markets—i.e., those characterized by *profitable* actual or potential customer usage criteria
- Limited-service branches oriented toward viable customer-population segments:
  - . . . inner-city, store-front offices
  - . . . self-standing, remote drive-in facilities
  - . . . mini-bank facilities in high traffic areas, airline terminals, shopping centers, office complexes
  - . . . community center offices located in key communities, such as retirement centers, staffed by counselors providing regular depository services and specializing in trust and estate planning and investment advisory assistance; additionally, these offices would be designed for after-hour use as community activity facilities
  - . . . preferred customer personal banker teams
  - . . . community newcomer visitor teams; part-time employees utilized for calling (phone and personal solicitations) purposes and working out of their own residences
- In-plant manned and/or machine mini-banks at major industrial firms
- Local offices of the holding company's consumer finance affiliate

- Regional, single-service offices, chiefly utilizing rented space to provide the following:
  . . . trust services
  . . . residential mortgage lending services
  . . . investment and brokerage services (if legally authorized)

Electronic Offices

- Envisioned is the installation of free-standing *or* manned office-associated electronic banking terminals in high traffic areas—e.g., travel terminals, working centers (factories and office buildings), recreation centers, shopping centers, housing centers (apartment complexes and housing developments)
- Where necessitated and practicable, a telephone and/or closed-circuit television linkage to regional headquarters offices would be established to optimize customer service transactions

This holding company developed a comparable model delivery system for its commercial customer market and, significantly, also focused on the market for investor funds. In the latter case, attention was given to programs and projects rather than offices; thus, the content and circulation of the holding company's annual report, quarterly statement of condition, and other corporate communications forms were viewed as part of a delivery system along with programmed presentations to financial analysts in major money markets and to investment brokers and community leadership groups located within that organization's primary retail and commercial marketplaces.

Its delivery system for commercial customers understandably stressed the excellence of people resources; the integration of traditional commercial lending activities and the more specialized approaches utilized by the holding company's bank-related units, particularly leasing, factoring, and accounts receivable; commercial term and capital financing; and the integration of trust and international banking skills.

This organization's retail market model—or in planning terms, its action strategy—testifies adequately to our contention that a marked expansion is occurring in delivery system techniques as well as in attitudes. This expansion appears to be influenced by several factors. The first, of course, is technology and the development of an electronic banking mode. A second factor is cost. Not just the cost of technology, but also the soaring costs of people and places—i.e., what it costs to hire, train, and retain competent employees; what it costs to build or rent bricks-and-mortar offices.

A third important factor is the holding company movement. On one hand, the holding company movement has changed and continues to change state laws governing office expansion. More to the point, it has facilitated a breaking down of restraints confining banking organizations to one or a few locations. At the same time, the holding company movement has enabled banking organizations to acquire nonbank subsidiaries in a variety of fields, thus enlarging the scope and nature of their operations.

Finally, the emerging delivery system is being influenced by the conviction that banking organizations must reach out to customers in selling products and services, an attitudinal change that will be explored in greater depth in the following chapters.

The Back Room

So far, we have seen that a financial organization's approach to delivering products and services tends to focus chiefly on people, places, and machines. This approach is action-oriented: Here is the front line where it happens, where business is conducted, where people buy (loans and other services) and sell (deposits and investment funds).

Customer centricity can hardly be challenged. Indeed, it is a primary theme of this book. Nonetheless, efficient delivery systems that satisfy customer wants and needs at a profit will be anchored in the excellence of their back-room support. Customers will measure delivery system (and bank!) performance by the accuracy of monthly financial statements; the treatment accorded by collection department representatives; the up-time of ATMs; the hours a branch is open; the candor of a bank's advertising; the efficiency of a telephone operator in channeling customer calls to the "right people"; and even the clarity of a bank's credit, new account forms, and procedures.

In sum, tomorrow's delivery system has two essential components: first, the *mechanisms* by which and through which services and products are offered to customers; and second, the operational *mechanics* that make them viable, distinctive and appealing.

Why the Markets Approach to Planning

It is the basic nature of financial institutions that suggests the markets approach to strategic planning. Banks and thrifts, in essence, employ people and capital resources to establish relationships with customers that involve the acquisition of funds from them and the offering of financial services to them. In short, they require customers, people resources, and capital resources to function. The problem is that prospective customers, employees, and investors often have alternatives from which to choose and do not have to select a particular institution with which to make a transaction.

To develop solid capability in the attraction of desired customers, personnel, and investors necessitates that a given institution effectively serve the needs of these people relative to competitors also seeking their patronage. But these people keep changing in their ability and inclination to make certain types of transactions; they keep changing because they are constantly buffeted by social, economic, legislative-regulatory, and technological change. And as they change in what they require from a transaction partner, so must the transaction partner (in this case, the institution) change accordingly; otherwise, valued members of the market can be expected to be lost to competitors providing a more attractive offering.

How does a bank or thrift improve its capability for serving the changing customer, people resource, and investor markets in which it operates? The answer is that it invests in strategic planning oriented towards the initiation of change within its control to respond to market change beyond its control.

CONCLUSION

Markets for customers, for people resources, and for investors (as linked by the delivery system) provide a satisfactory reference point and framework for the strategic planning process. The market is the object of change and thus a reference point for evaluating the effects of changing environmental conditions. As a framework for establishing the corporate purpose and objectives and formulating alternative response strategies, the markets approach permits external change to be systematically integrated into all phases of institutional activities in a consistent and coordinated manner.

Customers, people resources, and investors were selected as the markets of interest because of the nature of financial institutions. In effect, they employ capital and people to acquire funds from customers and to channel funds and other financial services to customers. Customers, people resources, investors—and the delivery systems linking a bank or thrift to these markets—are all necessary to function; therefore, they provide useful reference points for evaluating the effects of changing environmental conditions and developing strategic responses.

FOOTNOTES

1. Peter F. Drucker, *Management: Practices, Responsibilities, and Tasks* (New York: Harper and Row, 1974) p. 29.
2. C. Jordon Jelliffe, "Special Report: Marketing," *Banking*, August, 1973, p. 19f.
3. Peter F. Drucker, *Managing for Results* (New York, Harper & Row, 1964) Chapter 6.
4. Jelliffe, p. 21.
5. "Electronic Banking," *Business Week*, April 18, 1977, p. 80.

UNIT FOUR: STRATEGIES – MAKING PLANNING PAY

10 ACTION STRATEGIES: RETAIL CUSTOMER MARKET

INTRODUCTION

Chapter Nine proposed a framework for bank planning that focuses on a bank's principal markets: the customer market, the people-resources market, the investor market. It was suggested that banks require customers, people resources, and capital resources to function; moreover, it was posited that a given bank's capability for attracting quality customers, personnel, and investors in good supply cannot be assumed.

Customers, employees, and investors have bank and nonbank alternatives from which to choose in terms of financial services, employment, and investment; as such, it becomes important for a bank to provide offerings that effectively serve these markets relative to the competition. As earlier chapters have pointed out, however, markets are dynamic rather than static. In the case of banks and thrift institutions, a period of awesome, industry-shaking change is already well underway. How individual depository financial institutions respond in the next several years to the changing shape and nature of their principal markets will go a long way toward determining their strength of presence, or even survival, within these markets during the 1980s.

The next four chapters concern some of the actions that banks might well consider today in preparation for the very different tomorrow that awaits them. This chapter and the next one address customer markets. Chapter 12 concerns the people-resources market, and Chapter 13 concerns the investor market. Delivery systems, which provide the linkage among capital resources, people resources and customers have already been discussed in Chapter Nine.

PREPARING TODAY FOR TOMORROW

The process of change already has begun affecting retail markets. Changes tomorrow promise to be even more dramatic.

Electronic funds transfer, so complicated, so novel, so enmeshed in conflict among vested-interest groups, is invading the world of banking. Bankers everywhere are unsure of what EFT train or trains to get on, when to do it, how to do it, and how to pay for it.

Regulation Q, vulnerable to such naked realities as its fundamental unfairness to small savers and its massive contribution to disintermediation, appears on its last shaky legs as this book is being prepared. What this means is that funds acquisition for depository financial institutions is going to become far more price competitive.

Also on its last shaky legs is the other major component of Regulation Q, the prohibition against the payment of interest on demand deposits. It is crumbling piece by piece in the face of such developments as interest-bearing NOW accounts, telephone transfers from savings accounts to checking accounts, and EFT terminals at the point-of-sale. In short, banks not only will pay competitively for savings and time deposits, they also will pay directly for demand deposits for the first time since 1933.

Confronted with this era of unprecedented change (a confusing, uncertain, and unsettling time), how is a bank or thrift to respond? What plans should be devised that result in actions today that lessen the likelihood of being left behind tomorrow? We do not pretend to know the answers to these questions. For one thing, we cannot be certain that all of the forecasts we have made in this book will materialize. This book is about probabilities not certainties. For another thing, a given institution's response should be shaped by such specific environmental criteria as the competitive realities and the cultural climate existing in the geographic areas in which it functions; the existing share of the various segments of the retail and commercial markets of interest to it; and its strengths and weaknesses with regard to people, capital, and delivery-system resources.

For these and other reasons, the material that follows in this and forthcoming chapters is not meant as a "laundry list" of what every institution should do. Rather, the intention is to indicate a series of responses that would very likely result from a strategic planning process. The emphasis is on the responses—the action strategies. The other steps in planning such as external and internal analyses and the formulation of purpose, objectives, and goals will not be discussed. Most financial institutions will articulate where they want to go in similar terms such as "best," "dominant," "profitable," "increased market share," etc. Differentiating one institution from another is *how* they achieve their objectives. What specific strategies do they devise? How do they implement these strategies? Thus, given the more competitive world of tomorrow and the resulting need to address banking in terms of its principal markets, what action strategies are more likely to result in high performance?[1] This is the subject of the remainder of this chapter as well as the ensuing three chapters.

PERFORMING IN CUSTOMER MARKETS

Our analyses in Chapters Seven and Eight of the forces changing the shape and nature of customer markets suggest that in order to achieve their objectives, America's best managed banks will implement over the next decade or so action strategies characterized by some or all of the following:

- an emphasis on "relationship banking," i.e., developing complete or total financial relationships with retail and commercial customers
- considerable attention to the production of fee income
- intensified efforts to provide higher quality, more personalized service in circumstances where EFT is resisted, nonapplicable, or requiring of human intervention

- genuine acceptance of the philosophy of tailoring marketing strategies to segments of markets rather than to markets
- recognition of the need to apply substantial marketing resources and sophisticated marketing tools towards commercial banking and not just retail banking
- recognition of the mortgage loan's potential as a prime instrument in solidifying long-term, multiple-service *relationships* with retail customers
- minimization of marketing and service delivery expenses not justified in terms of contribution to bank objectives, more reliance on "one-time" approvals for retail credit access, and more "hard-nosed" pricing of both retail and commercial services
- greater focus on consumerism and public affairs programs as potent means for doing good and winning business at the same time

Devising a set of action strategies reflecting these characteristics in the context of the retail market is the purpose of the remainder of this chapter. The following chapter then focuses on the commercial market.

THE RETAIL MARKET AND RELATIONSHIP BANKING

Over the next decade, the retail sector in banking will represent a combination of necessity, challenge, and opportunity that will test even the most astute bank management. The basic necessity of performing well in the retail sector is that consumers supply about four dollars of loanable funds for every dollar they borrow. For all but the largest banks that have developed worldwide sources of funds, consumer dollars provide the bulk of financial resources.

In looking toward the future, many commercial banks, and notably larger regional organizations, possibly will decide to intensify business lending activity at the expense of retail banking. This is not to imply that they will curtail consumer lending, but rather that the proportionate increases in new credit extensions will be more heavily oriented toward business lending, presuming, of course, that requisite economic conditions are satisfactory.

This approach, moreover, will not obviate the importance of acquiring and maintaining acceptable levels of consumer deposits, whether in the form of transaction, savings, or investment accounts. The various strategies examined in the chapters comprising Unit Four recognize this duality, this need to be aware at all times of where funds come from and what they cost, as well as how they are employed. In this sense, asset management and liability management techniques are interdependent functions.

The challenge of retail banking is that it will be characterized by intensified competition from nonbanks, by a possible narrowing of the spread between the cost of funds and earnings on those funds, by unrelenting inflation that impacts retail banking disproportionately (e.g., facilities, labor), by the complexity and high stakes of EFT, and by consumerism. But the retail sector is not without opportunities. On balance it is immensely large and for the most part underserved.[2]

How should a banking institution interested in the retail market approach it? Suggested here is that a vital strategy for the future is relationship banking, which in turn makes crucial a number of other marketing concepts related to the acquiring and retaining of desired bank-customer relationships.

Good marketing people long have recognized that what customers really buy when they venture into the marketplace is the satisfaction of certain felt needs. That is, a "checking account" is not what the bank customer is buying; rather, what the bank customer is buying is a safe, convenient, and recordable means of transferring funds.

The reality that people venture into the marketplace to satisfy some type of felt need (for example, the need for recreation or the need for nutrition) is central to the potential for relationship banking. If people enter the marketplace to satisfy a certain need, why not attempt to profitably satisfy all of it rather than just part of it? Why not design a coordinated package to satisfy the totality of the customer's needs? Instead of offering services in bits and pieces, create a relationship with the customer. In other words, the need to safely and conveniently and recordably transfer funds is but part of a much more comprehensive constellation of needs that falls under the rubric "personal financial management."

In banking, and in other businesses as well, there are substantial and measurable cost justifications for concentrating on increasing the amount of business done per customer, for concentrating on satisfying most or all of the customer's need rather than just a little bit of it. The fixed costs of enticing the customer into the bank (buildings, people, product/service development and promotion) are not only large but also the same whether the customer signs up just for a checking account or a full array of financial services. Moreover, a total relationship establishes greater loyalty, which is the key to a stable customer base. The tradition of retail banking, however, is one of satisfying the overall financial management need of consumers in bits and pieces i.e., selling checking services if the consumer asks for checking, a savings account if that is requested, perhaps a safe deposit box, or an installment loan. We submit that the drawbacks of the "bits and pieces" approach will become increasingly glaring in the future and that the better route, at least for a great many banks, will be through strategies designed to facilitate long-term, multi-service relationships with individual households. Three vehicles for doing this—and some banks will use all three simultaneously—are *predetermined service packages*, *the personal banker*, and *the home mortgage*.

The Predetermined Package

One strategy for satisfying the totality of the consumer's financial management need is the predetermined package of financial and financially related services directed to specific segments of the market. A number of existing and/or new services are grouped and sold together. The package might be available for a flat monthly fee or in return for the establishment of a specific relationship, for example, the opening of a savings account.

At this writing, the concept is both familiar and misunderstood. It is familiar because in February 1973 Wells Fargo Bank in California introduced just such a customer service package, the "Gold Account." The bank achieved significant success with it; as a result, the concept was widely imitated by banks throughout the United States.

In its original form, the Gold Account customer received unlimited check writing; personalized checks; a credit card; safe deposit box; overdraft protection; unlimited travelers checks, cashiers checks, and money orders; reduced interest rates on personal loans; and an identification card for check-cashing purposes. The monthly service charge was $3. The Gold Account was positioned in the market as a service package for "very important people," hence the name (Gold Account) and the steep, prestige-seeking price.

By the end of 1973, Wells Fargo had received 90,000 applications for the package and, during the first six months of the year, increased its market share of new checking accounts from thirteen percent in the previous year to twenty-eight percent in the six-month period.[3]

When well conceived, service packages are attractive to many consumers because they more conveniently provide fuller satisfaction of financial (and, in some cases, nonfinancial) needs. Such packages are attractive to banking institutions because they facilitate consumer access to, and usage of, a broader range of services and because they offer an approach for building identification and relationships with specific market segments.

Yet, more than a few banks attempting packaged banking in the last few years have not fared well. Perhaps the most common reason was that the concept was not well understood by those using it. Instead of researching the needs of a market segment, and then designing a package of services to meet these needs, far too many banks merely grouped together a number of existing services and sold the package in "shotgun" fashion—i.e., to their total market rather than to a segment of it. In short, the concept of marketing a *need-meeting* package of services to a *specific segment* of the market was violated.

The success of the "Young Nashvillian Club" (First American National Bank, Nashville, TN) and "Dimension 60" (Citizens Bank and Trust, Park Ridge, IL.) illustrates the potency of properly executed service packaging.

As the name implies, the "Young Nashvillian Club" was targeted toward young adult households, specifically the 18–34 age group. For a monthly service charge of $3, Club members received a group of services including: unlimited checking, personalized checks, travelers checks and cashiers checks, a $10,000 accidental death insurance policy, merchant discounts (announced each month in the Club magazine, ranging in value from ten to twenty percent), Club travel (ski weekends, theater tour to London, Kentucky Derby), and special event programming (tax seminars, fashion shows, children's events). Between the Fall of 1974, when the Club was first promoted on an intensive basis, and the Fall of 1976, Club membership grew from 10,600 accounts to 23,000 accounts.[4]

"Dimension 60," launched early in 1974, was targeted toward consumers 60 years of age or older. In return for opening a savings account, customers received a package of services including: unlimited checking, personalized checks, a photo-identification card usable for guaranteed check cashing and merchant discounts, trust and will review, financial seminars (the initial seminar on social security and medicare was attended by over 750 people), and travel packages designed exclusively for elderly people. Ninety days after the program was first marketed, over 1,000 "Dimension 60" accounts had been opened with an average savings balance of approximately $8,000. This is an impressive figure when viewed in the context of the bank's structure and size at the time—unit bank, with $263 million in deposits.[5]

In sum, packaged banking works best when it is designed to fulfill the needs of a specific segment of the market. In the future, inventive financial institutions will achieve profitable market share gains through well-researched packages for young adults, for senior citizens, for women, for professional people such as physicians and, as we shall see later in this chapter, for home buyers.

The Personal Banker

A second strategy for developing long-term, multi-service relationships with consumers—and one that can be employed along with service packaging—is personal banking.

Assuming proper implementation of the concept, personal bankers develop one-on-one, full-service, continuing, "client" relationships with those retail customers assigned to them. The personal banker opens new accounts and sells bank services, makes loans and provides financial consultation, cuts "red tape" when client problems arise, and, in general, is available when clients need service of a nonroutine nature.

Personal bankers, in short, function in much the same way as public accountants or attorneys might function—i.e., on a client basis. Although the personal banker will have many more clients than the accountant or attorney, and will often have a less involved and less complex relationship with these clients, nevertheless the similarities are more striking than the differences. In each case, the individual consumer has a "someone" with a name, a face, and a telephone number to contact when the need arises. Instead of a faceless bureaucracy, the consumer has a somewhere to go, a someone to talk to; in other words, the consumer has his or her own "personal banker."

Personal Banking Is Going to Spread

Success with personal banking is neither easy nor inexpensive. Nevertheless, many more banks will have implemented such programs by the early 1980s than is now the case. Why? There are a number of reasons, including the following:

1. Service delivery in retail banking means not only the delivery of services *where* and *when* consumers want them delivered but, also, *how* consumers want them delivered. We believe that in an increasingly impersonal and computerized society, full of poor service, red tape, and bureaucratic nonsense, more and more bank executives will recognize that for many consumers the right way to deliver bank services is to do it in a personalized way, in a way that helps customers feel good rather than not good, adequate rather than inadequate, confident rather than not confident. The personal banker approach is a means for distinctively positioning a bank, relative to the competition, as a "personalized bank."
2. The marriage of electronic technology and plastic cards

means increasing similarity among competing banks and other financial institutions on (a) convenience of routine service delivery (as there are more and more shared EFT installations at nonbank sites) and (b) quality of routine service delivery (since quality of human service delivery varies much more than quality of machine service delivery). More simply put, banks will find it difficult to differentiate themselves from competitors solely on the basis of long standing criteria such as more and better locations and longer hours.

3. As this likely scenario unfolds, it will become increasingly important for a bank to achieve competitive superiority in the delivery of *nonroutine* bank services. When the consumer does need to come to the full-service branch, when a machine in a supermarket won't suffice, the personal banker is a prime vehicle for outcompeting the competition on the nonroutine.

4. The onrush of interest on demand deposits and of modified or eliminated Regulation Q ceilings on savings and time deposits is likely to mean a narrowing of the spread between the cost of retail funds and the price of retail loans. Usury laws, public policy objectives, consumerism, and intensified thrift industry competition for consumer loans could discourage banks from passing on all of this new cost in the form of higher retail loan rates. Two ways of combating these worrisome realities of retail banking are to increase business (the theory of the discount store: lower margins but increased volume) and to make more money without money (in other words, fee income). The personal banker provides the means to do both. Because of the quality of his or her training and experience, the personal banker is in a better position than the typical new accounts representative to customize a package of financial services tailored to the specific needs of a consumer originally coming to the bank only to open a savings account. Whether total or only partial customizing of the service package (i.e., modification of a flexible, predetermined package by adding or deleting service) is the strategy, the concepts of *market segmentation* and *relationship banking* are operative.

The personal banker, in brief, makes the phrase "full-service bank" more than just a phrase that consumers hear but don't understand. The personal banker represents a means for the bank both to make money on money (for example, personal bankers making loans over the telephone or preauthorizing personal credit lines) and to make money on expertise (for example, personal bankers providing, on a fee basis, trust services, nondeposit investment services, financial counseling services).

Making the Concept Work

Not all banks that attempted personal banking in the 1970s have made the concept work. Personal banking is neither easy nor inexpensive. Some brief implementation guidelines can be formulated.

First, candidates for becoming personal bankers should be selected from among the most people-oriented and career-oriented personnel available. Whereas banking and financial management fundamentals can be learned, a personal commitment of serving people should be present from the beginning. Also, turnover among personal bankers needs to be minimized; hence, it is important to attempt to identify people most likely to stay with the bank.

Second, management must be genuinely committed to investing in intensive preparatory and ongoing training for personal bankers. Expertise cannot be faked and personal bankers need expertise.

Third, personal banking must genuinely mean just that—personal banking. If personal banking is seen merely as an opportunity to sell some services to new customers and then forget about them, it will not be productive. For personal banking to realize its potential, the personal banker must be readily available to clients, and, in general, must view the personal banking role as one of periodic client contact.

Fourth, personal bankers should be assigned to specific clients. If they function merely as customer service representatives, available to any customer who enters the bank, then little has changed from when the bank didn't have "personal banking."

Fifth, personal bankers need the assistance of technology to effectively handle a large client base. In particular, personal bankers need to make extensive use of the telephone and, ideally, need a means for instantaneously displaying an individual client's financial profile for reference prior to or during client contact.

In summary, personal banking is attractive because it addresses the need that many consumers have for personalized, complete financial management. Moreover, it meets the rising need of banks and thrifts to outperform the competition on the nonroutine and to develop multiple-service, fee-producing relationships with retail customers. Furthermore, personal banking is a means for commercial banks to rescue the home mortgage from the periphery of the business and to make it pay. We now turn to an examination of this point.

The Home Mortgage

As an industry, commercial banking traditionally has been only modestly interested in making home mortgage loans.[6]   At year-end 1975, savings and loan institutions and savings banks held a combined total of fifty-six percent of all home or residential mortgages while commercial banks held only sixteen percent. There is no particular mystery why banks have not been enamored by the idea of making mortgages: These instruments have been less profitable than other modern era credit extension opportunities. Making long-term, fixed-rate loans in an environment of fluctuating funds costs has not been as attractive as making short-term loans wherein adequate spreads between the return on funds employed and their cost could better be assured.

Why then do we emphasize the importance of taking a fresh look at residential mortgages? Our reasoning revolves around forecasts that banking's future will include these realities: many consumers conducting their routine financial business electronically; thrift institutions having full funds transfer (DDA) powers and, in general, enjoying the same retail service opportunities as commercial banks; and the prospect that the Federal government will force commercial banks to assume their "fair share" of residential mortgages if sufficient response is not forthcoming voluntarily. Finally, it had become readily apparent by the mid-1970s that there was a pronounced and increasingly acceptable trend away from fixed-rate loan structures to flexible-rate formulas, thereby "sensitizing" this asset to economic fluctuations and their impact on the cost of funds.

As we prepare this book, there are still institutional distinctions between banks and thrift institutions which, in effect, require many consumers to patronize both types of institutions. Generally speaking, if the consumers want checking accounts, credit cards, or personal loans, they still need a bank. The question arises, however, as to what happens when banks no longer offer these services on an exclusive basis? *Why, then, will the consumer still need a bank?* Most people buying homes require mortgages and if mortgages are chiefly available only through a thrift institution, then a relationship with this type of institution becomes necessary. And if the thrift institution also offers the same services as banks do— at the same rates, and with the same convenience and quality— then why will the consumer still need a bank?

We see the residential mortgage loan and the totality of financial services related to buying and maintaining a home as strategic opportunities for banks to *reach* customers. By virtue of the relatively long-term nature of the mortgage, it becomes a means to *anchor* a continuing, multi-service relationship with them. Homebuyers tend to represent an attractive market segment. (Consider their relative affluence, savings orientation, and their variety of home-related and family-rearing needs.) Creative challenges such as the following must be met if this opportunity is to be optimized:

1. enhancement of the *direct profitability* of the residential mortgage through nontraditional pricing
2. enhancement of the *indirect profitability* of these loans by using them as stepping stones to a multi-service customer relationship.

This second point requires additional emphasis. The suggestion here is that the mortgage loan itself should be seen as a part of a more comprehensive bank-customer relationship. Banks making mortgages need to enhance their profitability directly, and of critical importance, the profitability of the entire relationship. The mortgage, in short, should be viewed as a way both to bring the customer into the "store" and to keep him or her there.

The challenge of making the residential mortgage more profitable, and hence more attractive to banks, requires fresh thinking about loan components, rate structures, and the provision of related and complementary home-life services. Also required for certain of the proposals that follow are changes in existing banking law and regulation. These changes can be defended in terms of the public policies that have been proposed to help consumers purchase homes and to encourage banks to make the necessary low-rate loans for such purchases.

Loan Components

The mortgage instrument long has been viewed as a fixed-rate loan amortized over fifteen to thirty-five years, requiring an up-front downpayment between five and twenty percent. In addition, settlement and related service charges are generally paid up-front on a one-time basis. What all of this means is that the total *entry cost* for a $50,000 home may well be as much as $9,000 to $10,000 and perhaps more—$5,000 for downpayment, $2,000 for settlement charges, $2,000 for relocation costs (moving possessions, personal transportation, setting up the house, etc.). The combination of a twenty percent entry cost and the dramatically escalated price of homes in recent years has, in effect, forced many prospective home-buyers out of the market completely and others to the fringes of the market.

In terms of public policy objectives, it has "frozen out" younger families and lower income groups. By the mid-1970s, the commonly held view was that there was a critical shortage of new homes costing between $25,000 and $40,000 geared to individuals or families earning less than $16,000 annually.

In response to these realities, banks can expand and make more flexible the components of the mortgage loan. For example, the following programs could be proposed:

1. offer the basic amortized mortgage
2. offer an option whereby the purchaser can buy the home but lease the land (The lease might be only for a short-term period, possibly five years, after which time the home owner

would either exercise an option to purchase the land at its appraised value or see it sold to a permanent investor.)

3. amortize the downpayment, settlement charges, and selected relocation costs either over the life of the mortgage or for a shorter period of time, for example, five to ten years, thus reducing entry costs

4. include as part of the loan package a preauthorized line of credit for the express purposes of home improvement and modernization (Rate structures and maturities could be linked to earning levels at the time the line was exercised and the option might take effect only when a predetermined level of homeowner equity was achieved to assure ample collateral.)

5. minimize refinancing provisions, making them simpler, less costly, easier to effect and, in general, less penalizing to the homeowner

6. include as part of the amortized mortgage a fuller range of insurance options directly related to the home-life environment; for example, investment items (jewelry, antiques, and art), automobiles, life insurance, and credit life insurance

Evident from the foregoing discussion are these basic themes: (1) viewing the home mortgage more broadly than has been customary by integrating within the loan certain related activities; (2) providing consumer-oriented options designed to attract customers and cement long-term relationships; (3) making access to home-ownership easier; and (4) providing recurring opportunity for dealing with mortgage customers on a personalized basis. In brief, the mortgage loan is being looked upon in this book not as a one-time interface between bank and customer, but as a continuing interface that is serviced by a competent, multi-skilled banker (ideally a personal banker) and that is generative of a variety of streams of income to the bank and a variety of desired services to the consumer. Thus, the mortgage loan can be a major strategy for accomplishing retail objectives in the more competitive world of tomorrow.

Rate Structures

As already referred to, mortgage instruments have historically been of a fixed-rate nature, resulting in uncertain profitability for lenders since the cost of loanable funds fluctuates over time. Because of this inherent weakness in the fixed-rate, there has been in recent years growing interest among bankers, thrift institution executives, and public officials in the concept of variable-rate mortgages (VRM). With VRMs, rates vary, upward or downward, according to an acceptable, predetermined index, such as the interest rate on U.S. government securities. Financial institution executives are interested in VRMs from a profitability standpoint and public officials from a credit availability standpoint.

The VRM has also fostered considerable suspicion by some consumers, consumerists, and politicians who view it as a means of shifting risk from the lender to the borrower. That the VRM does shift risk to the home-buyer is true; equally true and more significant, however, is the stark reality that the availability of mortgage loans relates to their profitability and sensitivity vis a vis other funds allocation opportunities available to lenders. In recent years, the result of placing the entire risk burden on the lending institution has been that although mortgage rates were relatively low, mortgage money has sometimes been unavailable. If a consumer can't obtain any mortgage money to buy a house, it doesn't do him any good if the interest rate is low, or even zero for that matter.

We would suggest that the fixed-rate mortgage loan no longer meshes with today's and tomorrow's economic realities, that it is archaic, and possibly even discriminatory with respect to low-income groups. The challenge presented is one of finding approaches more acceptable to both lender and borrower. It is in this vein that the following variable or flexible rate alternatives are presented:

1. semi-annualize or annualize the posting of the appropriate plus or minus charge to a single mortgage payment to avoid more frequent variations in monthly charges

2. effect indexed rates by adding to or subtracting from equity, or by altering the maturity schedule (Adjustment in dollar terms would then occur when the home is sold or the mortgage is paid off.)
3. provide the home-buyer the alternative between fixed and variable-rate instruments with the fixed-rate mortgage priced appropriately higher than the VRM (The lower rate for the VRM would explicitly recognize that the VRM does provide some benefit to the lender not provided by the fixed-rate mortgage. An alternative approach might be to assess a one-time charge for the fixed-rate option.)

These are just some approaches. By the mid-1970s, a growing number of other alternatives were being evaluated and placed in use on an experimental basis by banks and thrift institutions. One popular proposal was the "stepped rate" or "graduated" mortgage payment keyed to family earning power. Accordingly, a young family might start making payments of less than the full principal and interest due each month; later, payments would rise in keeping with income increases.

Another idea occasioning growing interest was the "reverse mortgage," which would allow older homeowners, especially those at or nearing retirement age, to generate income by mortgaging portions of their equity to a lender. When a home was sold or the owner died, the lender would subtract total payments made to an owner and accumulated interest from the mortgaged property value. The remainder would be paid to the owner or to his or her estate.

The vital point is that the financial industry was considering the most effective ways of moving from a fixed rate, fixed maturity formula to approaches that equally and equitably satisfied distinctive customer needs *and* the lender's concern for loan stability, sound collateral, and asset sensitivity. The emerging emphasis was on creativity.[7]

Related and Complementary Services

Traditionally the home-buyer and home-seller primarily have interacted with real estate agents and attorneys in effecting property transactions. The banker has been that seldom-seen middleman who either approves or disapproves the loan application and, if the decision is to approve, provides the paperwork and monthly coupon book. Indeed, many banks commonly sell the originated loan to permanent financiers.

It seems reasonable to suggest that if the home mortgage is to become a prime entree to a multiple-service relationship with the consumer, one place to begin is to make available, on an optional basis, a variety of fee and interest-producing services relating to home buying and to home selling. Appraisal services, staff counsel for title searches and other legal requirements, educational seminars on residential real estate transactions, home-buying or home-selling consulting (for example, advising on needed refurbishing to optimize a property's sales potential), and bridge-loans all exemplify means for increasing a bank's *visible* role in the home-buying and home-selling process. They are proposals that can profit both the bank and the consumer.

The rationale for the bank to add related and complementary services is to make the mortgage relationship itself more profitable. The rationale for the consumer is that more of the *total* financial/ shelter need will be satisfied because there will be more guidance and because the services will be available from one source. Moreover, if the bank's management is "relationship-oriented" enough to offer these added services at reasonable prices, the consumer can possibly save money as well. But above all else, the bank and the customer are linked.

CONCLUSION

The purpose of this chapter, the first of four on banking's principal markets, has been to propose a series of action strategies for implementing and achieving objectives in the changing retail customer market—changes that, in one way or another, should merit the attention of bank management.

More specifically, it has been suggested that such environmental challenges as intensified nonbank competition for retail customers, a narrowing spread between the cost of retail funds and the price of retail loans, and the growing pervasiveness of electronic funds transfer systems all point to the desirability of the retail strategies encompassed in "relationship banking." In other words, these challenges clearly elucidate the drawbacks of the customary "bits and pieces" approach to bank customers.

The central idea of relationship banking is to develop with customers total or complete financial relationships. Three strategies for developing long-term, multi-service relationships with consumers —*the predetermined service package, the personal banker*, and *the home mortgage*—were discussed in some detail. Suggested was the notion that some banks will implement all three approaches. That is, in some banks personal bankers will be selling service packages and home mortgages and/or home mortgage service packages.

Also suggested was the notion that good execution of relationship banking depends upon capability for marketing to *market segments*; for providing *high-caliber, personalized, and responsive service*; and for *making money without money* as well as with money.

We now turn, in the next chapter, to a discussion of responses to the changing commercial customer market. The reader should find of interest the similarity of responses called for, despite the relative dissimilarity of the two markets.

FOOTNOTES

1. A close observance of the components of action strategies (customers, products/services, people resources, delivery system) presented in Chapter Four has not been attempted here. Each of the strategies discussed here contains each of these components, but they are not discussed explicitly.
2. John S. Reed, "Consumer/Retail Banking," a speech delivered before the Citibank Correspondent Bank Forum, January 31, 1976, p. 3.
3. Lois Niese, "Customer Service Packages," *Bank Administration*, July 1974, p. 23.
4. Data supplied by First American National Bank, Nashville, TN.
5. "Citizens B & T, Illinois, Finds Package of Services for People Over 60 Good for Image, Business," *American Banker*, May 14, 1974.
6. This section is in part based on the following earlier published works: "Commercial Banks and Home Lending—A Reconsideration—Part I and Part II" in "Commentary" *United States Investor/Eastern Banker*, May 31, 1976, pp. 5–7, and June 14, 1976, pp. 5–6, 9, 11, 18; and Julian W.

Banton, "Rethink the Home Mortgage as the Core of a Broad Relationship," *Banking*, December 1976, pp. 50, 52, 54, 56. The "Commentary" in *United States Investor/Eastern Banker* was written by one of the authors of this book and Mr. Banton, an associate and colleague of the authors, worked with the authors in shaping the residential mortgage concepts presented in this section.

7. William R. McDonough, "Real Estate Finance: Advantages of Innovations in Variable-Rate Mortgages," *Business Review* (Dallas; Federal Reserve Bank of Dallas, December, 1976), pp. 1–7. See also *Bankers Research*, "VRMs and AMIs: Pros and Cons," (Westport, CT: Bulletin 5–7, March 4, 1977).

Chart 10.1

A common view in the mid-1970s was that *today's* bank holding company, with its multiple units would evolve into *tommorow's* "department store of finance." Behind this view has been the understanding that eventually banking structure would be defined in terms of the customer rather than various legal, and regulatory distinctions. The adjoining chart illustrates this rationalizing of today's complex structure into two key customer segments—retail and commercial. Moreover, as discussed extensively in both the preceding and succeeding chapters, the underlying strategy in both segments has got to be relationship banking.

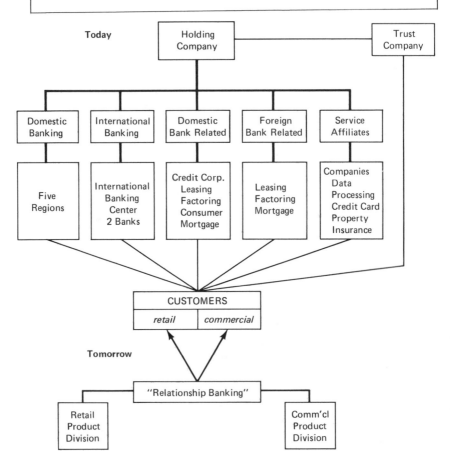

11 ACTION STRATEGIES: COMMERCIAL CUSTOMER MARKET

INTRODUCTION

It is evident from the environmental analyses in Chapters Seven and Eight that effectively serving commercial customer markets most likely is going to become more important, not less so, in the coming years. One reason is that retail banking may well be a less profitable alternative in the more competitive environment now emerging.

On one hand, the expansion of NOW Accounts and the prospect that banks will pay interest on demand deposits (not to mention implementation expenses related to technological innovation in the retail field or the relaxation of Regulation Q ceilings) should combine to foster upward pressures on the cost of acquiring retail funds. The protracted high levels of inflation and sharp fluctuations in economic activity should add to this pressure; similarly, intensified competition from thrift institutions armed with a wider array of lending powers can be expected to increase retail expenses involved in acquiring funds.

Conversely, the prospects for increasing *commensurately* the prices charged for retail banking services appear limited. For one thing, public policy initiatives to control inflation and to support housing by increasing the availability of reasonably priced mortgage credit should serve to constrain price increases. Growing competition with nonbank lenders and the varied but significant impacts of consumerism also should combine to inhibit the price increases possible for retail products and services.

Such influences as thrift industry competition and consumerism should not have immediate effects on commercial lending. Moreover, commerce and industry historically have demonstrated a willingness to pay whatever it takes to obtain credit when credit is needed, which suggests, generally speaking, that it will be easier to protect, possibly even increase, commercial lending profitability in the years ahead.

It should not be implied that banks simply will pass on projected higher costs for consumer funds, including rising acquisition expenses, to commercial customers in the form of steeper price structures. Not at all. But it can be suggested that the commercial customer market may possess the greatest opportunities for optimizing institutional profitability, thus absorbing most easily the impact of rising funds costs. Equally, to enlarge commercial customer service activity does not imply a sharp decline in the retail area. This expectation appears an exaggeration. More likely, the emphasis on *profitable market share* in either customer market will be intensified dramatically.

WHY COMMERCIAL STRATEGIES

In short, one of the most alluring objectives for many banking institutions as the 1970s unfold into the 1980s, especially for those banks that have been disproportionately involved in retail lending, is going to be increasing commercial business. Two studies published in 1976 by the American Bankers Association convincingly suggest why developments in the retail sector will make capability in the commercial sector more rather than less important.

One study assessed the interest-bearing NOW account experience in Massachusetts and New Hampshire during the first several years that this service was offered. Among the researchers' not-very-surprising conclusions: Consumer acceptance of NOW accounts was substantial, the average costs (operating costs plus interest expense) of acquiring these funds was high (8–10 percent depending on size of bank and assumptions made in the analysis).[1]

The second study was based on data derived from the Federal Reserve's *Functional Cost Analysis, 1974 Average Banks* in which 905 participating banks were placed into one of three deposit-sized categories: under $50 million, $50 to $200 million, over $200 million.

Table 11.1 portrays the average experiences of the sample banks with regard to net yields for various types of assets. As indicated, for banks above $50 million in deposits, the best yielding category of assets was commercial loans. In commenting on Table 11.1, Charles Haywood wrote: "Payment of interest on demand deposits would provide incentive for each bank to reallocate funds from lower yielding assets to the higher yielding assets . . . The incentive would be strongest to shift from assets below the average for loans and investments to assets above that average."[2]

To be sure, shifting the asset mix in the direction of better yielding assets will not by itself fully offset the higher funds costs associated with interest on demand deposits and "purchased" savings and time deposits. Nevertheless, it is one option that can help the situation, and, accordingly, many banks can be expected to take it.

PERFORMING IN THE COMMERCIAL CUSTOMERS MARKET

Banks desiring to enlarge and improve their performance in the commercial customer market will be required to develop strategies that address a range of old and new issues: risk management; credit administration; the pricing and costing of commercial products and services; portfolio balance and sensitivity; the integration and cross-selling of financial services that currently are functionally alike but frequently are separated as bank or bank-related activities; the enhancement of people skills that matches, at the very least, the ever-growing complexities associated with commercial customer operations in a high technology, multi-national environment; delivery system methodologies; and marketing practices.

In a probable economic environment of higher than customary levels of inflation and sharper fluctuations in the business cycle, risk policies and continuing credit administration procedures—

Table 11.1* Major Types of Assets and Net Yields

Under $50 Million		$50–200 Million		Over $200 Million	
Investments	3.17%	Commercial loans	3.28%	Commercial loans	3.54%
		Investments	3.10	Investments	2.80
ALL LOANS AND INVESTMENTS	2.70	ALL LOANS AND INVESTMENTS	2.83	ALL LOANS AND INVESTMENTS	2.75
Installment loans	2.63	Installment loans	2.36	Real estate loans	2.22
Commercial loans	2.54				
Real estate loans	2.28	Real estate loans	2.18	Installment loans	1.35
		Credit card loans	-0.05	Credit card loans	0.87
Credit card loans	-2.28	Cash	-4.98	Cash	-5.55
Cash	-4.81				

*Based on the table appearing in Charles F. Haywood, "Possible Effects of Payment of Interest on Demand Deposits," in *Studies on the Payment of Interest on Checking Accounts* (Washington, DC: American Bankers Association, 1976), p. 6.

particularly, effective "early warning" programs—will be more carefully determined along with portfolio balance considerations. Similarly, more attention will be paid to the costs of commercial products and services in order to make sure they are priced competitively and profitably. In this respect, the long-standing debate over balances versus fee income will take on greater meaning.

Looking toward the future, an especially important feature of commercial strategies will involve the application of marketing approaches customarily associated with retail banking activity. In a 1974 speech at the American Bankers Association National Marketing Conference, Allan F. Munro supplied some of the reasons why:

> The competition for large corporate banking business is intense . . . almost fierce. The reasons are clear: Suppliers are saturating the market. Close to a thousand banks are competing for the business of about fifteen hundred large corporations.
>
> The buyer is a pro. Each corporate financial executive spends a large amount of his working hours on banking relationships.
>
> The market is well-informed. A constant stream of bankers quickly provides the financial executives with the latest information on how to use banks and their services.[3]

In a very real sense, the application of retail marketing techniques to the commercial customer market is a revolutionary notion. Indeed, in all but the largest and most sophisticated banks commercial marketing as such has been virtually nonexistent. Perhaps the chief reason was a matter of attitude: Customers *sought* commercial bank relationships; banks did not seek them. Looked at differently, the bank was the only game in town and did not need to market its services to a relatively captive audience. But this view of things is changing.

Officer call programs in which virtually all bank officers are expected to make calls and, more or less, do so, uneasily, ill-prepared, and wishing they were doing something else, will not be sufficient in the future. Commercial marketing strategies largely oriented to maintaining a traditional image rather than forthrightly selling financial expertise, a wide range of properly priced products and services, and an ability to solve a customer's financial problems will not be sufficient.

In sum, it is our belief that most of the marketing strategies presented in the previous chapter dealing with the retail customer market will be applicable, appropriate, and necessary to successful performance in the commercial customer market. The new game in town will involve reaching out to an audience searching for the best deal.

THE MEMBERS OF THE TEAM

Another important feature of future commercial strategies will involve teamwork—in particular, the combining of traditional commercial lending activity and the types of specialized financial services now provided by factoring, commercial finance, or equipment leasing firms.

The bank holding company movement led to the organizational integration of many bank-related financial specialties. In recent years, some progress has been made in consolidating personnel and concepts along functional lines. Cross-selling and referrals are increasingly more common. Factors and commercial banks and trust people, it is frequently claimed, are "talking to each other now and trying to understand each other's business"; they even are discovering they are in the *same business* from the customer's point of view.[4]

This is a trend, however. In very few banking organizations today is it a common practice. At best, bank and bank-related commercial activities appear as complementary services with distinctly different ends in mind; in many instances, moreover, they remain competitive approaches to the same markets.

The long term trend, we believe, involves consolidation along functional lines. It entails the packaging of a full range of financial services and marketing them to fit the specific needs of an individual commercial customer; it entails recognizing the *interdependence* of commercial services and expertise—i.e., the fact that the bank is a "team of talents" serving the needs and wants of commercial customers. This point can be taken a logical step further: The interdependent team also utilizes, as extensively as possible, the disciplines of marketing, trust, and international banking; it employs computer-based technology as a tool, not only as a support mechanism.

We now turn to a discussion of three important strategies for realizing the objective of enlarging and improving performance in the commercial customer market: image building, relationship banking, and unbundled pricing.

IMAGE BUILDING

It has become customary for many organizations to look initially to IBM when in the market for computer products and services. A principal reason why is that IBM has *credibility*.[5] Prospects for data-processing equipment know that IBM will stand behind its products, will service them, and will not be going out of business in the foreseeable future.

In short, one of IBM's most crucial marketing advantages is its "image." Installing a computer system is a "high stakes" proposition for most organizations; it is not the type of transaction in which there is much sentiment for "taking chances" on a company of unknown, uncertain, or erratic capabilities. Unquestionably, a commercial customer's principal banking relationships also fall into the "high stakes" category.

What are the critical elements of a strong image in commercial banking? In a 1975 speech, the chief executive officer of First Chicago Corporation stated that in assessing banking's environment and future, his bank had determined that it wanted to stand for four things:

First, we want to stand for reliability. When we give a line of credit or an accommodation to a customer, we never want to have to tell that customer, 'Please don't use it. It is not comfortable for us if you come and use it.' We must expect that, if we give a line of credit, it is going to be utilized at a time when it is least comfortable for us and most commodious for the customer.

... Second, we decided that credibility is important. To have credibility means that you have to limit the real amount of commitments you make to the maximum levels you can fund in a crunch.

... We also said that we want to stand for capacity. Having capacity has a number of dimensions. There is capacity in the range of services, and capacity in the types of services. ... Capacity also means ... as the business grows, we will be able to accommodate the increased needs.

... Finally, we said we wanted to stand for quality. Primarily, quality means the ability, capability and character of the people in your organization.[6]

These remarks indicate three increasingly important realities about commercial banking. First, bank management must assess the future and, based on this assessment, must determine just what kind of commercial bank (or retail bank, trust bank, etc.) it wants to be. Second, the "high stakes" nature of commercial banking means that many bank-using organizations, whenever possible, are going to select banks perceived as reliable, credible, and capable (capacity and quality). Third, the development of such an image requires performance; rhetoric, illpreparedness, and "fair weather" banking are not the stuff upon which a strong, change-resistant image of reliability, credibility, and capability is built.

How does a bank develop a strong image? Not surprisingly, it does so by solid performance over time and under all types of conditions. It does not do so by suddenly showing up at the corporate doorstep when money market conditions are easy asking: "We were in the neighborhood and wondered if there was anything we could do for you?" It does not do so by making promises that the bank's back-up systems cannot deliver. It does not do so with poorly trained calling officers who "handle" 150 accounts in 60 separate industries. What an organization does do in a strategic as well as a tactical sense is clearly implicit in the following presentation dealing with relationship banking.

Particularly applicable to image building will be the overall excellence and aggressiveness of advertising and promotion targeted at carefully selected and well-researched market segments—especially those in which *primary* commercial customer relationships are most likely to be forged. A good image can be developed through initial call, follow-up, and client relationship administration procedures; community involvement by the banking organization, notably in a leadership capacity; and the relative, publicly understood, *stable* bottom-line performance of the banking organization. Keep in mind, "hot and cold" performers can easily become, from a customer's point of view, "hot and cold" suppliers of credit and financial services—i.e., there when you need them least and seldom around when you need them most.

RELATIONSHIP BANKING

The principle of relationship banking introduced in the preceding chapter actually is rooted in the industry's commercial lending experience. Both bank and customer long have recognized the mutual benefits of establishing and maintaining close relationships.

For the bank it is cost efficient to do as much business with as many *good* customers as possible. The costs of acquiring a new customer are substantial and do not vary to any great degree with the size of the relationship. It is clear that close working ties can enhance a customer's growth and profitability, as well as the firm's creditworthiness. Risk is minimized in most instances by a bank's overall awareness of a customer's financial situation. The concept of relationship banking implies an added dimension, as it involves a continuing, systematic approach to comprehending customer needs.

For the customer, relationship banking means reliability. In particular, it means the availability of banking services (namely, credit) during periods of economic and financial stress.

The rapid postwar expansion of economic activity, along with the accompanying emergence of a multitude of new businesses and banks of considerable size, diverted the establishment of relationship banking for the most part; the only long-standing relationships were between older and larger banks and corporations. Both banks and businesses seeking rapid growth tended to make or take loans and other financial services wherever and whenever they could be found. The inefficiencies and disadvantages of this approach were masked by the virtually ceaseless expansion of the economy and by the high rates of inflation during the late 1960s and early 1970s.

The severe recession of the mid-1970s, however, pointed up the scarcity of financial resources and the importance of credit availability throughout the economic cycle. Looking ahead, environmental analyses suggest a continuation of economic trends that make a relationship banking strategy more important than ever.

As desirable as a relationship strategy may be, it is extremely difficult to implement properly. The following are required:

- knowing and understanding customer needs
- developing the right products and services to satisfy those needs
- equipping and preparing commercial bank people resources to deal in total relationships

Executing these tasks will require the application of sound marketing principles.

Just as in retail marketing, effective commercial marketing means satisfying the *specific* financial management needs of the customer. It necessitates uncovering the real needs of the customer and creatively fulfilling them; it involves selling a coordinated solution to the totality of the customer's financial management problem, of selling a "tailor-made" system of services that goes beyond credit.

Market Research

Satisfying specific customer needs requires that they first be identified. This is no less true with commercial customers than with retail customers. Yet most of the formal marketing research done in banking today concerns the retail market. Why? One reason is that relative to retail banking, commercial banking is characterized by considerable personal interaction between bankers, customers, and prospects. Moreover, it is sometimes assumed that this provides the bank with all the feedback it needs. Another reason is the assumption that because each commercial relationship is unique, there is no reliable and meaningful method of surveying the market. Contemporary research techniques, however, have proven this assumption incorrect.[7]

In truth, many banks do not capitalize on the personal interaction that does take place between calling officers, customers, and prospects. The calling officer receives clues about unmet needs or frustrations with existing bank policies. However, these data very often stay in the calling officer's head. They are not formally categorized, summarized, placed together with data received from other calling officers, and then digested and analyzed as a whole. Furthermore, the research inadequacies that some calling officers inevitably have cannot be overlooked—e.g., the failure to ask the right questions or the inability to detect clues concerning unmet needs that customers cannot easily articulate for themselves.

It is the calling officer and later the account officer—not the customer—who must discover and service a possible need for direct payroll deposit programs, cash management and "lock box" requirements, computer-based inventory control, such alternative methods of financing as factoring and leasing, or a pension trust arrangement.

Moreover, it is not uncommon, for one reason or another, for a bank to fail to contact a number of companies and other organizations that are genuine prospects for its services. These and other realities of commercial banking suggest the implementation of programs such as the following:

1. calling officers should themselves be regularly interviewed about the customers and prospects with which they interact
2. call reports should be designed to best capture information of potential use to marketing personnel involved in new service development work
3. formal marketing surveys (analogous to those done for retail markets) should be made by trained research personnel with both customers (for the purposes of assessing the degree of satisfaction with the relationship and supplementing call of-

ficer feedback) and noncustomers (for the purposes of assessing the degree of satisfaction with current banking relationships and uncovering unmet needs that might exist)

4. up-to-date information concerning different industry categories should be available in a data bank for retrieval as the need arises—e.g., company financial profiles and current banking relationships, categorized by industry; industry-by-industry analyses of predominant types of financial services traditionally required and potentially needed.

In short, marketing research in commercial banking needs to be *formalized*, *broadened*, and made more *sophisticated*.

Market Segmentation

Formalized research into the commercial marketplace provides the information to better know *what to do with whom*. Just as in any business, a valuable strategy for commercial banking is the intelligent selection of market segments—niches in the overall market—and the development of superior, need-meeting services or ranges of services for these segments. The scarcity of capital and people resources mandates their effective and efficient use. Relationship banking in *selected* segments of the market pays much richer rewards than does superficial and fragmented banking in *all* segments of the market. Being effective with relationship banking in selected segments means truly understanding the nature of the "business"—e.g., the problems, the culture, the language. Therefore, if innovative, distinctive, hard-to-imitate, need-filling services are to be designed for these segments, carefully directed research must be done.

An important challenge, of course, is the selection of those segments that are best for the bank; those that make the most sense in terms of the following criteria:

1. *bank criteria*—segments selected should be consistent with long-range bank objectives, resources, and expertise
2. *market criteria*—segments selected should be characterized by present size and by growth potential, unmet financial needs, and sufficient diversity to avoid undue dependence

on the health of a given industry or on a given set of economic conditions

3. *primary vs. secondary relationship criteria*—segments selected should be determined by the bank's willingness to foster viable primary account relationships that, though fewer numerically, may prove more durable and rewarding than larger numbers of subordinate relationships

The above criteria represent an "ideal" and though it may not always be possible to fully satisfy them, they nonetheless merit careful attention since determining the *right* commercial accounts to go after is every bit as important as doing the *right* things with these accounts once they are targeted for action.

Although the practice of many larger banks and holding companies has been to concentrate on developing relationships with the largest corporations, one of the best segmentation opportunities for the future may revolve around small- to medium-sized businesses. It is this sector of industry that traditionally has been most underserved by the banking community, that has a variety of financial needs that banks are in a position to satisfy (ranging from cash management to lease financing to long-term capital financing), and that reflects both diversity of economic activity and some commonality of need by virtue of relatively small operations. Also, there are many more small businesses than larger ones. As one Oregon banker put it in a 1976 speech, "24,000 of the 28,000 businesses in Oregon are small businesses."[8]

One bank that has discovered the potential afforded by small- to medium-sized businesses is Chicago's Exchange National Bank, which in recent years enjoyed noteworthy success with innovative equipment leasing and accounts receivable financing programs, among others. The equipment leasing program was offered to various types of small- and medium-sized equipment manufacturers who were afforded through the bank the opportunity to provide a lease (versus "buy") option to their equipment customers. In effect, Exchange's program was premised on providing a means for equipment manufacturers to increase their sales and profits and, in the process, provide the sales force for selling bank-financed leases.

The accounts receivable program was designed to bring into the bank smaller businesses having, due to the nature of the business, periodic cash flow or short-term capital needs and a continuing fear that the money might not be available when it was needed most. Prospects, including firms that had been borrowing from finance companies, were contacted by telephone and by direct mail. In addition, morning drive-time radio was used. By late 1976, Exchange had developed an accounts receivable financing portfolio of $125 million in approved lines.[9]

The above material implies that total relationship banking can be approached directly through *industry segmentation* and indirectly through *need segmentation.* In its ideal form, industry segmentation directly develops total relationships through the in-depth servicing of multiple financial needs within a given industry and through the utilization of knowledgeable officer call personnel having special expertise in that industry. In contrast, need segmentation provides the first step in developing a total relationship by servicing a specific need shared in common by a variety of industries. The relationship between the bank and the customer firm is much less involved; bank personnel are not expert in the industries involved, and much of their time is expended on selling the service.

In essence, need segmentation provides a "foot in the door" approach. In one instance, it might be used to assist a young, fledgling company that is not quite ready for a complete banking relationship. In another instance, it might be used to establish credibility with a desirable, but difficult to persuade customer.

In the future, an increasing number of banks can be expected to use both segmentation approaches simultaneously. These banks will target certain industries for relationship banking and will, at the same time, sell specific services to a wide variety of industries, for example, freight payment programs usable in many different types of companies.

The industries selected and the specialties offered, of course, will depend on a variety of internal and external factors. As explained, researching them carefully becomes the critical first step in the segmentation process; the objective is to match *realistically* capacities and needs, and where the capacities fall short, improve them.

Eventually, some of the industry customers first approached on a need segmentation basis will become total relationship customers. In an enterprise system, the smaller company can and often does become larger; it is this principle that has distinctly characterized American commercial lending practices. Banks have been in the growth-building business first; becoming handlers of financial transactions has been a secondary process.

Professional, Need-Oriented Relationship Officers

There can be no question that the most crucial element in successful commercial relationship banking is the human factor—the quality and knowledge, the ability and authority—of bank personnel soliciting or administering an account. To this point, the phrase "calling officer" has been used to denote this function. However, although this is standard terminology in the banking industry, there are certain inadequacies inherent to the term. For example, for those accounts where the objective is relationship banking, we prefer the phrase "relationship officer." This better describes the requirements of the task if noteworthy success in obtaining or maintaining commercial business is to be achieved.

The desire for personalized, professional, competent, "do-it-all" banking by corporate customers was quite evident in a Greenwich Research Associates study (covering 705 of the nation's top 1,200 companies) in which corporate executives made rather clear what they want from their banker:

. . . he should know our firm's requirements, have new suggestions or new ideas . . .

. . . we look to the calling officer to win our trust, look to him for the services he offers . . . the more he can offer, the stronger will be the bank relationship . . .

. . . quality bank representatives as illustrated by thoroughness and an interest in our operating problems . . .

. . . able to offer specific banking services on a high professional level.

. . . an attitude by the bank calling officer that he and his bank can work with us . . .

. . . the ability to give innovative ideas and describe the areas in which they believe their bank excels.

. . . brevity, knowing their business, fast followup on requests.

. . . has done his homework, has a specific item to talk about, and has learned about our company . . .

. . . an understanding of our banking needs and a flexibility to meet them. They must speak our language and there must be a mutuality of interests and trust.

. . . the brevity . . . and the ability of the person making the presentation to make a commitment. Today some banks tend to send boys rather than ranking officials . . .

. . . know my business, read their file from the last call, be succinct . . .

. . . offer sound financial and economic knowledge, offer sound opinions on new markets . . .

. . . an ability to discuss banking problems, knowledge in the esoteric problems (beyond fundamentals), and the capability of problem solving as an individual.[10]

In commenting on this study, Allan Munro has said: "The theme runs—know me, know my needs, be a professional, don't waste my time, be innovative, and be someone I can trust."[11]

These responses vividly explain what corporate treasurers expect and why the phrase "relationship officer" is more descriptive than the term "calling officer." What is implied by the phrase "calling officer" (and what in reality is often fact) is to "make a call," to "pay a visit." What is implied by the phrase is a sense of casualness, a sense of superficiality.

If banks are going to better serve (and sell more services to) existing customers, then what is needed are blended-function relationship officers (or teams of relationship officers as the case may warrant) who combine into one position sales, credit, and noncredit service delivery and administration. They know how to develop what initially is a credit-only relationship into a noncredit relationship as well. Or, they also can expand a noncredit relationship into a credit relationship.

A true relationship officer possesses the following:

- an ability to earn, because of his competence and professionalism, genuine acceptance by the corporate customer as a financial consultant
- a complete understanding of the philosophy of marketing: profitably and responsibly serving *the needs of the customer*
- in-depth training in bank operations, credit, bank services, and selling skills
- a thorough knowledge of the companies and industries served
- the ability to design credits that best meet the needs at hand and the authority to make credit decisions
- the image of sophistication and knowledgeability now accorded the investment banker but not the calling officer

In sum, every officer in the bank can and should be a calling officer, but only those with the proper training and skills will be in a position to implement a strategy of permanent, total relationship banking.

One final point should also be made. A "first blush" reaction is that relationship banking appears applicable chiefly to larger banking organizations with sufficient financial and people resources on the line and in support. In a sense this is true. Equally true will be a determination to expand their commercial activity by broadening their customer base, a step which may, as explained, turn their attention to smaller businesses, many of which currently are served by community banks and specialized lenders.

It is no less true, however, that one small bank strategy could be to respond competitively by applying the same techniques utilized to counter large bank and thrift industry challenges in the retail field during recent years. Such techniques have included computer sharing and joint ownership with like-sized banks in a service center providing research, marketing, sales and training programs. Still another strategy may call for a maximization of expertise, personalization, and decision making in serving a narrow but carefully selected customer base. Then, too, organizational purposes and profit objectives may be realized by discovering and nourishing growth accounts and then by steering them to larger banks at the appropriate time. Whatever the strategy, however, the principles of relationship banking apply.

UNBUNDLED PRICING

As a long-standing practice, banks have priced "bundles" of commercial credit and noncredit services on the basis of compensating balances and interest rate structures associated with a nationally determined prime rate. For the following reasons, a rising number of well-managed banks will be less inclined toward "bundled" pricing in the future:

- In recent years, growth in corporate demand deposits has not at all kept pace with growth in corporate lending. Whereas in 1953, corporate demand deposits equaled $28.3 billion, by 1973 the total had grown only to $32.5 billion. In comparison, corporate loans totaled $22.3 billion in 1953 and $141.0 billion in 1973. Over the twenty-year period the annual compound growth rate of corporate demand deposits was about one percent and of corporate loan volume about ten percent.[12]
- The velocity of corporate deposits has been increasing, meaning higher costs to banks. In 1973, for example, the turnover of corporate deposits increased by twenty percent.[13]
- Banks continue to expand the number and the types of services offered to corporations. *Business Week* has noted the following development:

  The pricing problem has been brought to a head by the new services that banks have introduced in recent years, including wire transfers of funds, foreign exchange transactions, and advice on money market investments. But rather than price such items separately, many banks still are reimbursed only by the interest their corporate customers pay on loans, plus what they can earn on the money left as compensating balances.[14]

The sum and substance of balances-oriented pricing is that only recently have banks begun to identify the costs of individual services. In the past, banks only have known what their total costs have been. Thus, pricing, at best, could be done only on a gross basis. With the projected scarcity of capital resources, the pressure on earnings, and the proliferation of credit and noncredit services, especially those linked to technological capacities, there will be a clear incentive to develop cost systems that permit profitable marginal cost pricing. As Lowell Bryan, an early champion of unbundled, fee-oriented pricing, has written:

The trends have been remarkably clear. The activity of corporate demand deposit balances has greatly increased, the level of corporate demand balances has remained stable, and the volume of corporate loans outstanding has grown steadily. Most of the fun and profit has gone out of the traditional methods used to price bank products to corporate customers.[15]

Customer Views on Fee Pricing

Significantly, the presumed unattractiveness of balances-oriented pricing to banks does not necessarily mean that it is attractive to commercial customers. One mid-1970s survey of more than 900 corporate financial executives found sixty-nine percent of them favoring explicit pricing and viewing it as advantageous to both parties.[16] One of the problems of bundled pricing from the customer view is that it does not provide the quality of incentive for service excellence and innovation that explicit pricing would provide.

In a 1976 talk, the chief financial officer of International Harvester made this point by telling the story of when his firm discontinued one of its banks as pension fund manager but continued it as trustee. After discontinuing the bank as pension fund manager, it was learned that there would be no reduction in fee. In other words, when combined with trusteeship, management cost nothing. This incident, according to the financial executive, afforded him a concrete assessment of that bank's management services. In his words, he discovered "a condition which I had suspected through observation of their performance."[17]

The International Harvester executive also stated in the same speech:

> I believe that the traditional pricing structure has also discouraged innovation. The more progressive banks that have developed superior services at considerable expense often have had difficulty marketing these services because corporate treasurers were obtaining the same services, often admittedly inferior, and being allowed to pay for them with double-counted balances.[18]

Similarly, as the chief financial officer of TRW stated in a 1974 panel discussion, "I think I am typical of most corporate financial officers in that I am willing to pay the banks' price for good service, but don't want a poor service—even if it's free."[19]

Given the myriad problems associated with balances-oriented pricing, both from the bank's view and from the customer's, there is every reason to expect more well-managed banks to adopt explicit pricing strategies in the years immediately ahead. Such strategies should contribute markedly to achieving bank objectives of improving and stabilizing earnings performance.

Making Fee Pricing Work

The Bryan and Clark approach offers insight into how this new pricing strategy might work.[20] They contend that the most valuable service banks provide to most corporations is the assurance of available credit when it is needed. Thus, in the period of sluggish loan demand following the severe recession of the mid-1970s many banks began to offer lines of credit on which they charged a specific lending fee based on the amount and type of credit involved and the degree of risk assumed. These fees replaced compensating balances and provided a considerable portion of the profit created by the credit transaction.

Bryan and Clark also suggest that all noncredit services extended should be priced separately and at a level that justifies selling them. Of course, only those banks with adequately detailed cost accounting systems will know how to price services properly. If they preferred to do so, customers could pay for access to credit, credit, and noncredit services with demand deposit balances but only in a manner as fully compensatory to the bank as unbundled pricing. Even here, costs must be known.

A Word About Costs

Commercial banks for many years have been accused of not knowing what it *really* costs to place money and financial services in the hands of either retail or commercial customers. In a sense the costing of commercial services has been a follow-the-leader exercise, with the national money-center banks establishing a "prime" price determined by the availability of credit. This price then is scaled for commercial customers according to such variables as creditworthiness, the size of a demand balance, and the overall nature of a bank's relationship with a particular customer. Costing as a means of determining marginal profitability simply becomes submerged in this equation.

This approach, we believe, will not be adequate in a future characterized by intensified competition in the market for commercial customers. Effective pricing strategies will presuppose a more realistic determination of total costs, including indirect expenditures such as customer education, sales programs, or expenses related to the replacement of outdated product lines. The cost of the total package or any major component parts should provide a better handle in establishing competitive "prime plus" scales.

Total costs can be divided into two basic categories—first, research and development expenditures (what it costs to enter the marketplace) and, second, the maintenance expenses during the projected life of a product (what it costs to make the product successful in terms of understood corporate objectives—e.g., income, image, market share, or market positioning).

A basic formula often can be utilized to assess ongoing costs:

- processing and systems operations
- systems maintenance, including product processing equipment
- cost of funds, including deductions for reserves and recognizing proportions allocated from different and differently priced funds sources (e.g., demand balances, savings accounts, time deposits, etc.)
- promotion and merchandising expenses
- customer contact personnel expenditures, including training and education expenditures
- administrative overhead, including taxes, licenses, insurance, etc.
- support staff charges

To these total ongoing costs, a bank then would add expenditures for research and development amortized over a predetermined period of time. Profit expectations then are built in.

It should be added that research and development costs not only include tangibles such as mailing solicitations and advertising programs, but also intangibles such as *people-time.* For example, how many manpower hours will be required for relationship officers to learn all that is needed about a new product or marketing strategy? Moreover, how much of this expenditure will come at the expense of merchandising existing products or in failing to maintain high levels of customer contact calls? Another intangible cost may be associated with possible legal ramifications. There is also a cost linked to the competitive response from another financial or banking organization; interrelated, there is the cost of not acting, of not being competitive.

All of these considerations impact costs and, therefore, pricing strategies.

CONCLUSION

The purpose of this chapter has been to suggest some valuable action strategies for achieving objectives and for performing in the commercial customer market—a market that will become more important, not less so, in the years ahead.

Increasing a bank's penetration of the commercial market, however, is not an easy, automatic process. Moreover, assuming that it is quality business that is being pursued, it is not likely to be a rapid process. Therefore, the bank that desires to substantially reallocate its asset mix in the direction of commercial credits five years hence must begin now to facilitate this objective.

The key to achieving such an objective requires a thorough understanding of marketing concepts and their application to commercial strategies. Thus, strategies should be emphasized that focus on identifying customer needs, developing those needs into an effective demand, and satisfying those needs in a profitable and responsible manner. Developing a professional and sophisticated image, effecting relationship banking, and unbundling prices are strategies that meet these criteria. Basic to each, moreover, is an improved understanding of costs.

With this two-chapter discussion of the customer market now behind us, we turn in the next chapter to a discussion of another of banking's principal markets—the people resources market.

FOOTNOTES

1. Charles Hoffman and Earlene Herman, "NOW Accounts in New England," in *Studies on the Payment of Interest on Checking Accounts* (Washington, DC: American Bankers Association, 1976), pp. 36-37.
2. Charles F. Haywood, "Possible Effects of Payment of Interest on Demand Deposits," in *Studies on the Payment of Interest on Checking Accounts* (Washington, DC: American Bankers Association, 1976), p. 6.
3. Allan F. Munro, "Why the Competition for Large Corporate Banking Business Is So Intense," in *Competition-Action or Reaction*, Selected Speeches from the 1974 National Marketing Conference, American Bankers Association, March 1974, Bal Harbour, FL, p. 24.
4. See William G. McNinch, Jr., "Commercial Banks in a 'Buyers Market,'" in *Profits, A Business Publication of Bank of Virginia Company*, Spring-Summer, 1977, pp. 6-8.
5. The term "credibility" is used here in a broad context to suggest such factors as reliability, size, strength, and quality. Robert Abboud, quoted in this section, uses the term "credibility" in a more specific context.
6. A. Robert Abboud, "Management/Marketing—A Partnership in Transi-

tion," in *Management/Marketing . . . Meeting Tomorrow's Challenges Today*, Selected Speeches from the 1975 National Marketing Conference, American Bankers Association, March 1975, Chicago, IL, pp. 2–10, 11.

7. For example, in the mid-1970s the Wachovia Bank in North Carolina conducted a major and detailed research survey of its commercial market in three states. It reveals business preferences among various banks in those states as well as what corporate treasurers seek in a banking relationship.

8. Donald McClave, "Marketing Strategies: Small Business Market," remarks made before the Annual Convention of the Bank Marketing Association, October 26, 1976, Miami Beach, FL.

9. Alan B. Eirinberg, "Marketing Strategies: Small Business Market," remarks made before the Annual Convention of the Bank Marketing Association, October 26, 1976, Miami, FL.

10. Munro, pp. 24–3, 4.

11. Ibid., p. 24–4.

12. Lowell L. Bryan, "Put a Price on Credit Lines," *Bankers Magazine*, Summer 1974, p. 45.

13. Lowell L. Bryan, "Pricing Corporate Credit and Financial Services," in *Competition—Action or Reaction*, Selected Speeches from the 1974 National Marketing Conference, American Bankers Association, March 1974, Bal Harbour, FL, pp. 35–2.

14. "The Unbundling of Full-Service Banking," *Business Week*, October 27, 1973, p. 69.

15. Bryan, "Put a Price on Credit Lines," pp. 45–46.

16. "Unbundling," *American Banker*, November 4, 1976, p. 4.

17. Ibid.

18. Ibid.

19. Remarks of Charles R. Allen in "Competition—Corporate Banking Markets," in *Competition—Action or Reaction*, Selected Speeches from the 1974 National Marketing Conference, American Bankers Association, March 1974, Bal Harbour, FL, pp. 13–4.

20. See the works of Lowell Bryan cited earlier or Lowell L. Bryan and Simon G. Clark, *Unbundling Full-Service Banking* (Cambridge, MA: Harcomm Associates, 1973).

12 ACTION STRATEGIES: PEOPLE RESOURCES MARKET

INTRODUCTION

Banks and thrifts are in the service business, which means, among other things, that they are labor intensive. In other words, much of what customers buy from them is labor, human acts, or performances. Although EFT will continue to spread into banking's customer markets, the human element of banking's "product" will remain crucial to the level of satisfaction attained by those who consume it.

Indeed, the emergence of EFT enhances rather than diminishes the importance of having high quality, effective personnel. On the one hand, the human and economic costs of EFT foul ups require quality personnel in the "back room" attending to the upgrading of "fail safe" capability and to the immediate redressing of those problems that do occur.

On the other hand, and of even greater importance, EFT will make financial institutions more alike in the delivery of *routine* services and correspondingly will make effectiveness in the delivery of *nonroutine* services more important. Quality personnel will be a key part of any bank's efforts to outdistance the competition on the nonroutine: *to remain distinctive.*

In short, the neglect given to selecting, training, motivating, communicating with, compensating, and otherwise effectively and efficiently managing personnel represents an error of considerable magnitude that will grow rather than decline in significance. In circumstances where EFT is avoided by customers, inapplicable, or requiring of human intervention, these customers interact directly with bank personnel. These personnel *are the bank* to the customer. When they are impersonal, careless, slow, or uninformed, they are impersonal, careless, slow, or uninformed in the *presence of the customer.* From the customer's perspective, an impersonal new accounts representative or an uninformed relationship officer is, at least on that day, an impersonal or uninformed bank.

THE PEOPLE RESOURCES MARKET: CHALLENGES AHEAD

Attracting high quality personnel and keeping them on the job, both literally and spiritually, is a task laced with challenge in the near-term future. Among the most significant challenges are these:

The New Values and the New Worker

There is a new attitude toward work evolving in America, an attitude that rejects the traditional Puritan tenet that work is innately good and dignified. Rejecting the innate goodness and dignity of work, however, is not the same thing as rejecting work. In-depth research into the attitudes of contemporary workers, for example Terkel's *Working,* [1] suggest *not* a desire for leisure, for play, but a desire for work with meaning, for work that attracts recognition and feedback, for work that is big enough for the human spirit.

As one of the authors wrote in a 1976 *American Banker* column:

> Many people who work in banks today want to live on the job, not just off the job, when they work, not just when they go home. They want to grow as individuals and advance in the organization as they do so, make real contributions to the organization's success and to be recognized for having done so, play on a "team," not just be a "muscle." And they want all of this and more, not because they work in a bank, but because they

are people, real people, living in a society that is beginning to recognize that people are more important than things, that the quality of life is more important than the quantity of life . . .[2]

In an *Age of the People*, personnel policies must emphasize more than ever the individual rather than the job or machine, the human side of work rather than the technological side.[3]

Affirmative Action

No personnel challenge will more test tomorrow's banker than the challenge of redressing years of societal and industry discrimination against women and minorities in terms of employment opportunity. Although a 1976 American Bankers Association study indicated some progress resulting from affirmative action programs directed towards women and minorities, the thrust of the challenge still lies ahead.[4]

One reason the thrust of the challenge lies ahead is that the supply of qualified females and minorities for managerial positions in banking at this writing remains inadequate to meet the demand. Using the criterion of "full utilization" (women and minorities in managerial positions in proportion to their representation in the labor force), a 1974 study of 2,845 banks with 100 or more employees revealed these banks employed about 18,000 female and minority employees that would qualify for promotion to a management level job but needed over 42,000.[5] Attempting to make up this difference by recruiting outside the banking industry is to confront the dual realities that banking is *not* the only industry with affirmative action pressures and that from an all-industry standpoint there is not now a sufficient supply of qualified women and black managers and executives to go around.

An additional reality arising from the affirmative action issue is that markedly increasing the percentage of female and minority managers makes the avoidance of employment discrimination against white males extremely difficult.

Still another facet of the challenge lying ahead is that successful affirmative action requires enlightened management not just at the top, but at the middle levels as well. In commenting on the absence of progressive thinking often found at these middle levels, one bank CEO made the following remarks to the National Association of Bank Women in a 1974 speech:

> Where we have a problem is with middle-aged, middle-management. You can communicate, lecture, and even knock heads, but you won't see dramatic, progressive changes in attitudes unless, for example, "affirmative action accountability" is used to measure *their* job performance. Even then we are fighting "heart and heritage." The battle won't be lost. Neither will it be won overnight, and assuredly, it will test your patience and mine.[6]

In sum, hiring and advancing into management the increased numbers of females and minorities mandated by government edict, by the threat or actuality of litigation, and by what is right (and avoiding at the same time the sacrifice of performance standards and of employees and employment candidates who are neither female nor minority) will be anything before it will be easy.

Growing Personnel Competition Between Banks and Thrifts

Increased competition with industry in general for talented, college-educated females and minorities will not be the only form of heightened personnel competition to confront banks and thrifts. In addition, thrift institutions can be expected to become increasingly interested in luring away from banks certain types of expertise. The reason is that thrifts will need experienced bankers to help implement the banklike powers most likely in store for these institutions. In particular, banking can expect thrift industry interest in bankers experienced in funds-transfer operations, consumer lending, and retail trust services.

In short, thrift institutions confronted with authority to offer financial services for which they have little or no experience can attempt to develop the expertise internally or can attempt to produce it overnight by hiring people who already have it. We believe there is little doubt as to which alternative many will take.

Managing More Specialists

Implementing the types of action strategies presented in the previous two chapters will require a steady increase in specialists—for example, computer technicians, attorneys, communication specialists, planners, marketing researchers, perhaps even social workers to provide household financial counseling services.

A number of these specialists will come to the bank with nonbanking backgrounds and once there will never deal directly with customers; they will never analyze a credit application, never extend a credit line. Indeed, many won't really consider themselves as bankers; they will be professionals in their respective fields.[7]

Melding these specialists into a banking culture, while respecting their professional identities and accurately evaluating the quality of their work and their overall contribution to bank objectives, represents one of the challenges implied by the growing proportion of staff specialist personnel to line personnel in banking.

Accentuating the challenges of fitting these "round pegs" into banking's traditional "square holes" will be those personnel from holding company affiliates, such as leasing and factoring specialists, who are brought into the bank as the result of holding company diversification and subsequent organizational consolidation.

Fostering Salesmanship

Personal selling at the consumer level is a more important marketing tool in some industries than in others. For example, many nationally branded convenience goods (such as packaged food and cosmetics) are presold through advertising and require little selling from store personnel. In circumstances where products are relatively complex or risky and where consumers have relatively limited knowledge, personal selling tends to be quite important to successful marketing. As such, one finds particular emphasis on personal selling in such product/service categories as stereo equipment and insurance.

Because the importance of personal selling relates to what is being sold, it is possible to think of selling in terms of two broad levels: *low-level selling* (making a sale to a customer who already knows what he wants and who often seeks out the seller, in other words, "order-taking" selling) and *high-level selling* (uncovering unmet needs, determining the best alternative for satisfying those needs, informing, and persuading the customer-prospect).[8]

Clearly, much of banking's retail service mix requires high-level selling but in fact most banks provide only low-level selling. The consumer enters the bank in search of a checking account and leaves the bank with a checking account. It is not surprising that at this writing banks sell an average of less than two services to each of their retail customers.

There is no question that well-executed, high-level selling will become even more important in retail banking (and in commercial banking, too, as discussed in the last chapter); accordingly, banking industry deficiencies in this regard could become increasingly costly if not corrected. The reasons, once again, relate to such environmental influences as EFT (and the corresponding need to capitalize fully on those fewer occasions when the customer is face-to-face) and the rising costs of loanable funds (and the corresponding need to develop long-term, multi-service relationships with customers—to sell them more for a longer period of time).

As one holding company executive put it in a 1974 speech:

> . . . electronic banking will foster the creation of new responsibilities, and, furthermore, should encourage more of our people to spend more time calling on actual or prospective customers . . . reaching out to them with service packages and financial know-how more directly . . . Tomorrow's "branch" could be an officer with a briefcase . . . the car used by a housewife working two or three hours a day visiting a community's new families and selling them on 'her bank.' . . . Emphasis will shift from bricks-and-mortar *places* to competent and energetic *people.*[9]

If personal selling in banking, already important, is going to become more important, then two especially significant challenges for the future will be the hiring of more "sales-oriented" personnel and greater emphasis on and effectiveness in sales training. The reasoning is that a salesperson's performance is considerably influenced by personal attributes and selling skills and knowledge.[10]

Concerning personal attributes, research has consistently shown that bankers do not tend to have sales personalities.[11] It is probably true that many entered banking in part to *avoid* selling, and it is undoubtedly true that vast numbers of bankers do not think of their jobs as sales jobs.

Based on seven years of work, one study on traits common to superior salesmen concluded that good salesmen possess two basic qualities:[12]

- empathy—the ability to feel as the customer feels
- ego drive—the desire to complete the sale, and not only for the monetary gain involved

Attracting more people to financial institutions with these and other attributes conducive to selling is a task that should not be taken lightly. Furthermore, investment in sales training should not be taken lightly since, in addition to the right kinds of personal attributes, successful selling requires selling skills and knowledge of the bank's service mix, the needs and behavior of the customer-prospect, and the strengths and weaknesses of the competition.

Growing Size and Complexity of Banking Institutions

Most observers of the banking scene agree that banking's future includes larger, more complex, more geographically spread-out institutions. How to communicate with, "turn on," and create a sense of belonging for personnel in branches or affiliates located throughout states, regions, the country, and the world are formidable challenges; moreover, they will become even more formidable in the future.

The model of the smallish, noncomplex unit or branching system, where "eyeball" contact between senior executives and middle- and lower-level personnel often occurs on a regular basis, will not disappear from the banking scene, but it no longer will characterize or adequately represent the banking scene. Banking is moving away from this traditional model and is moving towards bigness, geographic freedom, and broadened service mixes. In this evolving climate, creating an organization in the truest sense of the term "organization" (people working together towards common goals) will become ever more difficult and challenging.

Unionization

At the end of 1975 there were thirty-two unionized banks in America, mostly smaller banks of under $50 million in deposits.[13] In other words, effective unionizing of banking's more than 900,000 employees had not yet happened. The realities that financial institutions are currently one of the least unionized of major American industries, and that there are a variety of potentially fruitful issues upon which unionization campaigns might be built, suggest that a relevant management question is what to do today to prevent unionization tomorrow.

How bank and thrift executives handle the "low pay" tradition, especially at the lower levels of employment (the teller line, the collection department, the operations backroom); how they handle career advancement for women; how they handle job displacements due to automation in general and EFT in particular are some of the crucial challenges ahead. At the present time, there is not any reason to be smug that these issues will be effectively handled. As one magazine put it in a 1976 editorial:

> ... it should be noted that currently there is more discussion about the types of jobs that will be eliminated by technological advance than the types of new career opportunities that will be opened. This emphasis needs to be changed if organizational activities by the unions are to be blunted.[14]

Cost Control

Along with delivery system expense, compensation expense represents the bulk of noninterest costs in financial institutions. If the stable and superior earnings performance required to attract investors is going to be achieved, costs must be carefully monitored and controlled. Because, as the ensuing discussion will emphasize, paying insufficient salaries is simply not feasible; a more sophisticated approach known as productivity analysis will be required. Finding ways to help people perform more efficiently and productively is the key to cost control.

INTERNAL MARKETING

Just as banks compete with banks and nonbanks for customers, so do they compete with banks and nonbanks for people resources. That is, banks compete in a market comprised of people able and potentially willing to exchange their time and energy for the compensations of employment. The most attractive members of this market—in terms of background, skills, and personal attributes—can be expected to have the most exchange alternatives available to them and to select those alternatives which best meet their needs.

In short, the "best" employees must be fought for in the same sense that the "best" customers must be so pursued. Not unlike other markets, the people-resources market is buffeted by environmental forces that change its shape and nature.

Managing this people-resources market—creatively responding to it and coming away with a healthy share of it—requires good marketing or, more specifically, good internal marketing.

Internal marketing is the discipline of *thinking of employees as internal customers, thinking of jobs as internal products, and, just as with external marketing, endeavoring to design these internal products to meet the needs of these internal customers while satisfying the objectives of the organization.* Internal marketing, in other words, is applying the marketing philosophy of profitably satisfying human needs, of exchanging value for value, to the people resources that serve the external customer in the hopes that the best possible people can be employed and once employed, they will do the best possible job.

Importantly, the crucial matter is not so much that the phrase "internal marketing" be the phrase of choice but, rather, that the implication of the phrase be understood—i.e., by satisfying the needs of its internal customers, a bank or thrift upgrades its capability for satisfying the needs of its external customers. As Sasser and Arbeit put it: ". . . the successful service company must first sell the job to employees before it can sell its service to customers."[15]

The importance of relating marketing—and its research, product design and communication thrusts—to personnel matters is strongly suggested by a University of Chicago study of more than 1,800 company situations in the late 1960s. Concluded was that the roots of employee discontent were primarily the result of three management deficiencies:

- key decisions affecting employees were often made in ignorance about what employees really wanted because no one listens to employees
- dissatisfaction, griping, and complaints were considered normal and disregarded; pressure tactics and exhortation were used to obtain improved efficiency
- employees were often given some information about the company but quite often the information provided was not well-related to the employee's own personal circumstances, e.g., personal goals and achievement[16]

The remainder of this chapter concerns internal marketing. More specifically it concerns action strategies and implementation programs designed to improve and enhance the internal products (jobs) that banks and thrifts sell. Our analysis of the changing shape and nature of the people-resources market suggests that over the next decade or so, the internal marketing efforts of America's best managed banks and thrifts will be more or less characterized by action strategies in the following areas:

- organizational communication
- career development and growth
- compensation

We now turn to a discussion of each of these areas.

ORGANIZATIONAL COMMUNICATION

It is difficult to argue with the general proposition that people working in organizations will be more effective in their jobs if they know what's going on in their company, if they know where they fit in the overall scheme of things, and if they know how they are doing.   In brief, effective organizational communication is important.

Norwood Pope addressed this issue in the following terms:

> ... it is people who make this thing happen. We can talk to investors and analysts until we are blue in the face ... We can sit down and write marketing programs that will just overwhelm you. But unless we begin to tell the message to our own people ... and to intrigue our own people ... and to make them a part of what is happening, we have lost sight of the name of the game.[17]

Research conducted at Syntex Corporation on the differences in behavior between effective and ineffective managers reveals just how difficult it is to overstate the importance of good communications. The following list summarizes what effective managers do. Explicitly and implicitly, the list reveals the dominating role of internal communications:

- taking responsibility for group performance: passing on credit for successes, absorbing blame for failures
- goal setting: involving employees in establishing work-unit goals aligned with overall division or company goals
- honest communication: free and open feedback, information, and discussion
- team building: fostering mutual trust and respect among members of work unit
- problem solving: prompt, resourceful handling of difficulties as they arise
- controlling: keeping unit moving toward objectives; when necessary, taking prompt corrective action
- climate building: establishing high standards of performance and a success pattern for the work unit
- decision making: seeking and considering alternatives, making sound decisions despite time pressures[18]

We submit that good organizational communication starts at the top, that open and honest and continuing communication throughout the organization won't occur unless top management genuinely wants it to occur and consistently works at making it occur.

Good organizational communication is more likely to take place when various communications programs are institutionalized, when openness and honesty and sharing are rewarded rather than punished, when top management is itself personally active in upward and downward communication. Indeed, if senior management wants good communication, then it must demonstrate that this is so by *deeds*.

Top Management Contact and Dialogue Throughout the Organization

One of the most common mistakes that senior executives of larger banking institutions make is that they lose touch with all but the inner circle of executives with whom they regularly interact. Face-to-face contact and dialogue with employees in the field and at lower levels of the organizational hierarchy is deemed impractical. The bank is too large, too spread out. There are too many other demands on one's time.

We believe otherwise. Difficult and time-consuming? Perhaps. Impractical and not worth it? No. Regularly getting into the field allows a bank's top management to demonstrate they care; to acquire information about bank realities they might not otherwise acquire; and to better assure that the bank's values, purpose, objectives, key policies, and strategies are understood.

When he was Board Chairman at Bendix Corporation, Michael Blumenthal, who made it a practice of frequently visiting the 100 or so cities Bendix operates in and of personally delivering memorandums he wrote to people who worked in the same building, said in an interview:

> You can't operate successfully in any organization if you are cut off from your people. You've got to reach out toward them—out beyond the tight little group you work with daily—and let them know they can reach you when they feel they have to.[19]

A banking system CEO who spends considerable time in the field visiting branch and affiliate offices, who regularly invites small groups of employees from all levels to nonagenda dialogue sessions to find out what's on their minds, who periodically eats in the employee cafeteria to be more accessible—this is a bank CEO who is demonstrating by deeds that communications, exchange, dialogue, are serious and important business.

There are some executive officers who just can't play this role. They become uncomfortable doing it and discomfort the people they're trying to communicate with. One alternative is for the organization's number two or number three executive to handle this responsibility. Another is to stress written forms of communication; for example, a management "state of the company" letter prepared quarterly and mailed to the homes of all employees, or a "Dear Al" letter that recognizes an employee's personal achievement or standout job contribution. These communication forms are not as good as the CEO personally visiting with staff members, but they are better than doing nothing.

Commitment to Formal Planning

Emphasized in Unit I of this book, but meriting a repeat mention in the present context, is that the planning *process* itself is valuable to communications and not just because of the planning documents produced as a result of the process. One reason is that the planning process mandates organizational communication—horizontal and vertical.

By its very nature, planning involves people talking out loud to each other, one-on-one and in small groups. It is a process that involves "brainstorming," "idea sharing," and "negotiation." And it is a process that ideally requires "out-in-the-open, on-top-of-the-table" decisions about where the bank is going and how it is going to get there.

Moreover, the planning documents spawned by the planning process are communications devices in that by their very nature they indicate information to be read, understood, and followed until such time as the plan is modified. More simply put, a genuine commitment to formal, long-range planning means an institution-alized encouragement of organizational communication.

Personnel Opinion Surveys

Regularly surveying personnel concerning perceptions of supervision quality, working conditions, compensation and benefits, company policies, and other job-related matters provides several important benefits.

First, management receives formal feedback (to supplement the informal feedback received in other ways) concerning the degree of satisfaction "internal customers" have with the "internal product" for which they are exchanging time and energy. In other words, surveying internal customers is just as appropriate as surveying external customers. Such systematic feedback helps isolate those components of different jobs that need to be improved.

Second, systematic personnel surveying is a quality control activity, a means for identifying policy violations or other organization breakdowns. For example, a question asking employees if they believe bank rules and regulations are enforced fairly and consistently and a follow-up question asking them to explain if they answer "no" to the first question would normally identify those managers violating certain types of policy. Because managers know this type of surveying is regularly conducted, the survey itself discourages policy violation.

The Marriott Corporation affords an example of effective use of employee surveying. At Marriott, specially trained personnel representatives visit each hotel property and conduct a meeting of all employees; at the meeting, the survey is explained and frank, open participation by everyone is urged. Employees do not sign the questionnaires which require "yes" or "no" responses to a series of questions (e.g., "I get paid for all the hours I work," "I have been properly trained to do my job," "Our work load is reasonable"). In addition, employees may add anonymous comments about each statement in subsequent interviews with personnel representatives. The survey responses are compiled and two weeks later a second employee meeting is held to discuss the results and to solicit additional comments. Four weeks after that, still another meeting takes place to announce any actions that will occur in response to the survey. Also, results of surveys made in previous years are often presented for comparison with the latest survey.[20]

Internal Publications

Internal publications, for example, bank-sponsored newspapers, newsletters, or magazines, offer the potential communications advantages of "speaking" with one voice, of disseminating important information on a mass and regular basis, of "publicly" recognizing individual or group accomplishments, and of encouraging the perception that the bank is an organization in spirit and not just in name.

One firm that apparently believes in internal media is United Airlines. United publishes a daily newsletter for all personnel, the *Employee Newsline,* and a biweekly newsletter for first-line supervisors, the *Supervisors' Hotline.* In addition, United publishes a monthly newspaper that also goes to all personnel. Discussing *Employee Newsline* in a *Harvard Business Review* interview, United CEO Edward Carlson said:

> We use the *Employee Newsline* to tell our employees about immediate company and industry news, policies, plans and objectives; it's also used to quash rumors before they spread. Employees are really interested in news that personally involves them . . .

> The *Newsline* is the fastest way to communicate with all employees at once. It enables us to speak with one corporate voice on corporate and division issues. This is really important for a company as big as United.[21]

Important to note is that internal publications are like any other organizational communications program in that the key is execution—i.e., doing it the right way is important. Employing a professional communications specialist to put out the publication(s), developing publications to contribute to specific corporate objectives and action strategies, avoiding talking down to personnel, building credibility through candid treatment of material, mailing the publication to the employee's home rather than in bulk to the bank—these are some of the implementation tactics meriting management consideration.

How many and what kind of internal publications commonly will be determined by the organization's size and complexity. A statewide holding company with a score of affiliates operating in four or five identifiable geographic regions may publish a corporate newsletter on a monthly or a quarterly basis. Each region, in turn, might issue a monthly letter; one that is usually less formal and less typed than the corporate newsletter. Large departments might find morale enhanced and productivity improved by occasionally publishing a highly personalized four to eight page "poop sheet." International departments and bank-related units may sense a similar need to convey their distinctive work, mission, and priorities to staff members.

The singular requirement that must pervade all corporate, affiliate, or departmental communication forms is that corporate management policy be expressed in a consistent manner. Managerial decisions mean just one thing; confusion develops if they are clumsily interpreted and misunderstood.

One-on-One Feedback

Behavioral scientists are virtually unanimous on the importance of feedback. People at work want to know how they are doing, where they stand, whether anyone is taking notice, whether anyone cares. After taking an exam, the student breathlessly waits for the instructor to grade and return it; the student waits anxiously because he or she wants to know the result.

Wanting to know is no less true for people at work. Work tends to be a high-stakes endeavor with the respect and acceptance of co-workers, one's self-image, present and future income, and career prospects involved. It is not surprising, therefore, that many workers thrive on bits and pieces of praise and are forever attentive to nonverbal clues (or rumors) emanating from the immediate supervisor and from others higher in the organization.

In writing about ways to increase employee productivity, John Zenger emphasizes the importance of feedback, stating: ". . . continuous, accurate supplying of performance data (to the employee) could well be the real key."[22]

Writing in the *California Management Review*, an author team of four behavioral scientists claim that job responsibility, job meaningfulness, and *knowledge of results* are the three crucial psychological states for determining a person's motivation and satisfaction on the job.[23]

How does a bank or thrift better assure that its employees receive regular, accurate, constructively given feedback? For one thing, it builds formal feedback sessions into its performance appraisal system. That is, one-on-one feedback is institutionalized so that it is a policy violation if it doesn't occur.

Also, management recognizes that in the Age of the People, people put in charge of people need to be more than just good technicians. They need to be managers as well. Selecting the right people for these managerial positions helps assure that a crucial form of feedback—informal feedback—will flow in addition to institutionalized feedback. Pats on the back, congratulatory notes in response to significant accomplishments or excellence in overall performance, constructive criticism, reprimands, publicly recognizing an individual's contribution to a specific achievement—these are the types of informal communications that tend to come quite naturally to some who supervise. More simply put, feedback is in part a function of who is in charge. Therefore, managerial personnel should be selected with this in mind—i.e., these individuals should be sensitive yet capable of being tough, constructive yet honest, intuitive yet consistent, easy to talk to, yet leaders who stand apart.

DEVELOPING HUMAN POTENTIAL

The traditional perspective of human resource management is getting things done through people. In the Age of the People, we submit for consideration an alternative perspective: developing human potential so that individual goals and organizational goals can be simultaneously fulfilled.

What people demand from their work is changing and there is today compelling evidence in the research literature that one of the most important ingredients in satisfying employment is the opportunity for personal growth, for mentally moving forward.

Anthony D'Ermes writes: ". . . the potential of the average human being for creativity, personal growth, cooperation and productivity is considerably greater than has been recognized in the past,"[24] We agree and further believe that not only is there a gap between what most people are and could be but, also, there is a growing desire on the part of many of these people to close this gap, to, in Maslow's words, "self-actualize." Those organizations recognizing this reality, and then doing something about it, should be better able to attract and to keep the best people. Moreover, in such firms individuals will do their best work.

Education and Training

The banking industry has perhaps done more than any other industry to provide educational opportunity for personnel at the various levels of the organizational hierarchy. The number of banking schools, American Institute of Banking classes, banking conventions and conferences, and "in-house" seminars that convene on each average workday in America is impressive indeed.

Still, there is opportunity to both improve and increase current educational activities. As indicated earlier, there are not enough college-trained women and minorities to fill the number of management positions that government, vested-interest pressure groups, and conscience are mandating be filled by these people. One response is for individual financial institutions to take the initiative in providing educational opportunity to those female and minority employees who have the ability and the willingness, but not the background, to assume the higher-order responsibilities.

Moreover, there are today many "dead-end" jobs in banking leading nowhere—e.g., clerical jobs, teller jobs, operations backroom jobs. With automation implying the elimination of some of these jobs, and with climbing personal aspirations dulling the energies of certain employees holding them but wanting more, banks increasingly will be confronted with the need to provide more career options and possibilities to people at the lowest levels of the organization chart. Education and training necessarily will be a central activity in this endeavor.

Also, financial institutions are undergoing a period of awesome, industry-shaking change (as Unit II of this book attempted to demonstrate). Banking will emerge from this tumultuous era as quite a different industry. The fiercer competition, electronic delivery systems, the new "rules of the road," an expanded service base, the multiple effects of a society beginning to put people ahead of things, a new set of economic realities—these and other developments will require more sophistication and more background at all levels, As a result, people in financial institutions will need more and better education and training. For example, personal bankers will need in-depth knowledge of human behavior, retail banking, and personal finance; the CEO will need to understand a range of matters from women's liberation to applied psychology.

In-house educational programs; bank-sponsored college and AIB tuition-assistance programs; a policy that every officer attend a minimum of five days of management development coursework per year; active support of appropriate local, regional, and national banking schools and meetings; rigorous entry training for specific jobs—all of these actions have at least one thing in common and that is the prospect for developing human potential.

In 1975, the Bank of Virginia Company initiated an educational seminar, "Issues in Banking," to which all Richmond affiliate employees were invited on a voluntary basis. The seminar was held after hours in the evening, once a week for six weeks, and covered such topics as EFT, consumerism in banking, and the economic environment. Although banks commonly sponsor in-house educational programs, there are two noteworthy aspects of this program. First, all bank employees were invited, not just bank officers. Second, attendance from all levels of the bank far surpassed forecasts. Indeed, a postseminar survey revealed that attendees believed such a program was long overdue; moreover, they wanted more like it. Bank of Virginia Company responded with a more extensive Issues in Banking series in 1976.[25]

At about the same time as Bank of Virginia initiated "Issues in Banking," the U.S. National Bank of Oregon was implementing an in-house, affirmative action program entitled "General Banking Educational Program" (GBE). The program was designed to help female employees qualify for advancement to managerial positions.

What is unusual about this program is its *depth* (twelve courses varying in length from five to eight weeks, three hours per course per week); its *focus* (emphasis both on personal attributes such as increasing self-confidence, initiative, achievement motivation, and interpersonal skills and on general management and banking topics); and its *technique* (a broad range of experiential approaches including video taping, case analysis, and a bank management game). Also unusual is the manner in which the program was developed. Predesign interviews conducted with bank personnel revealed one consistent difference between men and women aspiring to managerial positions: the amount of business-related college education in individuals' backgrounds. Three particular benefits of having a college-level business background were identified: provision of a business vocabulary; introduction to models of analysis; and development of self-confidence for mastering new subject areas. The GBE program was designed to remedy deficiencies in these areas.[26]

Aside from formal education/training investments of one form or another, there is an additional consideration meriting mention at this point. In the earlier section on feedback, a number of qualities important to good management were enumerated. One quality was left off the list, reserved for emphasis at this point. Left off the earlier list was the notion of manager as *teacher*. By the type and quality of feedback given, by the time taken with individuals, by the depth of knowledge and the willingness to share it, by the example set, the manager is in the position to foster the personal growth of others. Those organizations that recognize the profound impact that managers can have on subordinates, for better or for worse, and that select and develop managers with this reality in mind, will be taking a very significant step forward in the education/training area.

Career Pathing

In the years ahead, America's best managed financial institutions will sell "careers" to people, not merely "jobs." To cut the costly turnover rates that have long plagued banks and thrifts at the lower levels of the organization, to respond to affirmative action dictates, to deal with the problem of "dead-end" jobs, more and more organizations will become interested in the concept of formalized career progression programs.

Affirmative action, in particular, calls for investment in career pathing. Much more so than with men, women have tended to be slotted—to be made public relations officers or branch managers, for example, then to perform the same job year in and year out. This tendency has been even more marked lower in the organization where relatively little thought has been given to the idea that a teller or someone in the operations backroom could eventually become something else.

Among other things, a successful career progression program requires the following:

1. recognition that opportunity can mean moving *laterally* in the organization in pursuit of broader experience as well as upward
2. a genuine commitment to employee education and training
3. understanding that individuals must be dealt with as individuals
4. first-rate supervisors

Concerning the latter point, supervisors play a crucial role because they are in a position initially to encourage promising individuals, because they likely will have access to more complete information about career progression opportunities, and because they are in a position to make some career progression developments occur.[27]

The career progression program at Marriott illustrates the intricacies (and the potential for economic and human benefit) associated with successful career pathing.

The Marriott program, originally designed for minority-group employees, focuses on advancing hourly employees up through positions of increasing skill, responsibility and pay, including management-level positions. Employees must request consideration for the career progression program with acceptance contingent upon existing job performance, desire, and aptitude. The employee must say, in effect, "I want to get ahead. I'm ready to work harder, do more, study, and prepare myself for promotion." Adult education courses at local schools are sometimes used to improve skills in reading, personal communications, and mathematics. Customized, step-by-step programs are developed by personnel specialists for each employee in the program. Participants learn new job skills by training at least one hour a day beyond the regular employment time for forty days. When a vacancy occurs, the participant then trains an additional four weeks to become proficient in the job. This step requires full-time, forty to forty eight hour weeks. Successful on-the-job training then leads to promotion, full responsibility for a new job, higher wages, and the opportunity to again pursue advancement. Program participants making too little progress due to lack of effort are dropped from the program. [28]

COMPENSATION

Although evidence indicates that today's employee requires more than just money from his or her work, this evidence should not be interpreted to mean that today's employee is uninterested in money. Unfortunately, the writings of such noted behavioral scientists as Herzberg and Maslow have inadvertently persuaded many executives that pay is not very important and that it can only be a source of dissatisfaction. Arthur Whitehill, Jr. writes:

> Almost twenty years ago, Frederick Herzberg and his associates gave top-level executives a bias from which they have never recovered. Separating mere 'maintenance factors' from true 'motivators,' these researchers identified the latter as the real superstars of motivation theory . . . There is a good chance that managers have been talked into serving champagne and caviar

while ignoring the muffled pleas of workers for more meat and potatoes.[29]

Whitehill is not arguing that Herzberg's "motivation" factors (for example, task variety, independence, responsibility) are unimportant, but rather, that "maintenance" factors (for example, good working conditions, convenient work hours, pay and benefits) are important too. Whitehill, in short, is arguing for balance between the two dimensions. He is saying, in effect, that you should ask the employees before deciding that maintenance factors are unimportant to them.

Edward Lawler writes:

... when executives seek ways to increase motivation and productivity, they tend to forget about pay-system changes, concentrating instead on approaches such as job enrichment, team building, and management training. But research on pay does not support this view ... Pay seems to have a strong impact on satisfaction and consequently on absenteeism and turnover. Further, when pay is tied to performance, evidence has shown that it also contributes to motivation.[30]

Simply put, the compensation package offered the employee in exchange for his time and energy is important to him. In spite of this, it is still common practice in banks and thrifts to pay relatively low wages to all but the upper echelons of personnel. We would submit that the importance of compensation to people who work and the importance of having good people suggests that the time is at hand for management to question an industry tradition of paying with titles instead of cash.

The evolution towards more intense competition with more competitors, the phenomenon of electronic banking, the explicit and inexplicit costs of fifty percent annual turnover rates among tellers, the growing insistence of the "new worker" for fair treatment, the rising tide of consumerism in banking that is in part due to inexcusably poor service rendered to consumers—these and other influences support the idea that financial institutions should both pay more and pay more intelligently to attract, keep, and motivate the best people available.

Importantly, paying more than the industry norm does not necessarily mean making lower profits. Delta Airlines enjoys the reputation among insiders in the airline industry of paying unusually high wages and yet Delta consistently shines among industry peers when it comes to profitability. That Delta has managed to stay nonunionized and year after year records one of the lowest personnel turnover rates in the entire industry undoubtedly contributes to its exemplary profit history.

A 1977 *American Banker* feature story extolling the three year earnings performance of new management at Rainier National Bank (Seattle) indicates that one of the things new management did was to improve compensation levels. Robert Truex, the CEO, is quoted as follows:

> We weren't spending enough on personnel. Now we are paying most people a lot more and we've greatly expanded our benefits programs. In 1975 we spent less than $500,000 on medical and dental benefits. Last year, with fewer people, we spent $1.6 million.[31]

Generally, organizations should attempt to design compensation programs that encourage job performance in concert with its long-term objectives. More specifically, compensation programs should ideally minimize arbitrariness, be nondiscriminatory, (equal pay for equal work regardless of sex or race), reward good performance, be perceived as adequate and fair, and recognize that individuals are people, not numbers.

This discussion on compensation does not fly in the face of industry programs to reduce total people costs. The design is to improve *individual* productivity. Such programs evaluate compensation not in terms of individual pay scales but rather in terms of total compensation dollars spent to accomplish a particular task or function. How much does the new account function, credit analysis, or budgeting process cost? By analyzing these costs, in total or by component parts, more efficient methods of conducting various activities can be identified and implemented.[32]

Looked at differently, the real costs of poor compensation packages could be to induce the expense of unionization and the loss of market share by substandard, uncaring employee performance.

We now turn to a discussion of several compensation concepts that we expect will attract the attention of a growing number of banks and thrifts.

Merit Pay

Paying well to attract and retain quality personnel is one thing. Paying more to those who work hard and effectively than to those who don't is an additional important consideration. Pay systems that assume that each employee in a given job classification is the same, except for years of service, fail to recognize the inherent individuality of people. Individuals differ from one another in many ways, including job performance. To compensate identically a group of people who perform nonidentically on the job tends to be counterproductive in terms of encouraging improved job performance when it is weak and sustaining job performance when it is strong.

Traditionally, banks have been far more inclined to pay on the basis of merit at the middle and higher levels than at the lower levels. We would argue that there is reason to extend the merit philosophy throughout the organization although, to be sure, effectively implementing a merit program at the lower levels is not a simple matter. The concept is, after all, a responsibility decentralizing concept and required are a good performance appraisal system and good supervisors. Indeed, merit pay plans are still another reason why supervisory excellence at the lower levels is no less important than supervisory excellence at the higher levels.

Skill-Evaluation Pay

Consistent with the philosophy of paying individuals, not groups who happen to share the same job classification, is the concept of skill-evaluation pay. The pay systems of many organizations, including banks and thrifts, are designed on the basis of classifying given jobs and then paying the "going rate" for the job.

Among the weaknesses of this approach are its failure to reward individuals for all the job-relevant skills they have and its failure to encourage individuals to learn new job-relevant skills. In short, employees are treated as job-holders rather than as individuals, which is an approach of growing disadvantage in banking's changing environment.[33]

The philosophy of skill-evaluation pay is to recognize through compensation the number of jobs an individual can perform. Skill-evaluation pay plans, although by no means easy to implement, do offer the advantages at the lower levels of reinforcing a career pathing program, of providing personnel a broader perspective of how the organization functions, of cross-utilizing personnel in those functions having uneven staffing requirements (e.g., using some lock box personnel in the branches on Friday),[34] and, as already noted, of providing incentive for self-improvement.

Fringe Benefits Cafeteria-Style

Traditionally, the most common type of fringe benefit program in industry have been those providing equal amounts of benefits (for example, life insurance or vacation days) to all members of the organization at similar levels. While this approach commonly recognizes differences among levels in an organization (e.g., senior management receives a different package than salaried middle management), it does not recognize the differences that exist among people at the same organizational level. However, existing research clearly indicates that what is a valued benefit to one employee is not necessarily a valued benefit to another employee.

When researchers ask employees to allocate a hypothetical raise among various benefits, factors such as age, marital status, and family size influence the selection made. Whereas younger, unmarried men tend to prefer more vacation time, young married men tend to prefer higher pay. Whereas older employees want improved retirement benefits, younger employees want more cash now.[35]

One response to the reality that people are different is the concept of "cafeteria-style" fringe benefits. As the term "cafeteria" suggests, the idea is that, within certain boundaries, employees spend as they wish the total fringe benefit sum available to them. Employees cut the "pie" for themselves rather than the bank doing it for them.

Not unlike other innovations, the cafeteria approach to benefits creates certain practical problems. For example, accurately costing certain benefits in advance can be difficult and the bookkeeping aspects of administering the compensation program become more complex. Nevertheless, the advantages seem to outweigh the disadvantages. In considering the advantages, Lawler writes:

> The choice brings home to employees rather clearly just how much the organization is spending to compensate them and ensures that the money will be spent only on the fringe benefits they want. Thus it can increase employee perceptions of the value of their pay package and also increase their pay satisfaction, improving organizational effectiveness by decreasing absenteeism and turnover and generally allowing the organization to attract a more competent workforce.[36]

According to a 1975 Chamber of Commerce survey, the overall average costs for fringe benefits in banks and other financial institutions amounted to 37.5 percent of the total payroll as compared to the figure of 35.4 percent for industry in general. In terms of actual dollars, the average fringe benefits cost for banks was $1.86 an hour and $3,745 per year.[37] We would suggest that if banks are going to invest this heavily in fringe benefits, then there is even more reason to give people what they specifically want.

Looked at differently, this is the same strategy advanced for dealing with commercial and retail customer markets—the notion of customer segmentation and personalized, tailored packages of financial services.

Flexible Working Hours

Still another action strategy that recognizes the "individuality" of employees is that of flexible working hours (hereafter referred to as flexitime). Although not strictly a compensation matter, attractive working hour arrangements can be thought of as a fringe benefit, hence the flexitime concept is presented in this section.

As its name suggests, flexitime provides employees with greater freedom in selecting work hours than is customary in the eight to five type of workday. Although still working the normal number of hours in a given week, employees on flexitime may vary starting and finishing times within certain prescribed boundaries. Typical flexitime systems in America involve "core time" (when all employees must be present) and "flexible time" (when work schedules are discretionary). Core time generally corresponds with peak work load patterns.

In Germany, where flexitime got its start, a quarter of the workforce was on flexitime by early 1977. At this writing, over 3,200 American companies are engaging in flexitime to one degree or another and some, like Metropolitan Life, have totally converted to this new system. [38]

One bank that has experimented with flexitime is State Street Bank of Boston. The State Street program is fairly typical in the sense that it has involved only selected departments during its early stages (for example, Trust Operations and Corporate Accounting) and revolves around the use of "time bank" equipment for recording actual time worked by each flexitime employee. Each arrival and departure, including lunch, is recorded on the equipment. Employees are expected to conduct personal business (for example, a doctor's appointment) on their own time. Representative of the flexitime schedules that have been used at State Street is core time of 11:00 a.m. to 2:00 p.m. and flexible times of 7:30 a.m. and 2:00 p.m. to 5:30 p.m.

The State Street experience with flexitime suggests many of the reasons behind the growing popularity of this concept in the United States. Both the Bank and its employees seem to have benefited. Among the benefits reported for the Bank are increased job satisfaction, the elimination of punctuality as an issue, less personal business conducted on company time, a dramatic decline in overtime pay, reduced personnel turnover, additional recruiting leverage, and expanded cross-training activity.

Among the benefits reported for the employee are increased job satisfaction, shorter commuting times, more time for leisure or family activities, and added cross-training opportunity. Following State Street's initial trial period for flexitime, participating employees voted 119 to 3 for its continuance.[39]

To be sure, flexitime is a concept that is still essentially unpolished, that flies in the face of tradition, that is not without pitfalls (for example, the unavailability of key people when they are unexpectedly needed); and that may well prove unworkable for certain types of banking jobs. Nevertheless, the thought here is that flexitime will attract considerable attention within banks and thrifts in the years immediately ahead. Flexitime is, after all, a means for more precisely tailoring the job to fit the specific needs of the individual holding it (for example, a working mother). It is also a means to help "professionalize" the job, to treat people as professionals and to then expect professional performance from them. Flexitime is, in the words of one consultant who has worked with the concept, ". . . a giant step towards personal autonomy."[40]

CONCLUSION

A primary purpose of this Chapter is to suggest that a financial institution competes with banks and nonbanks in the people resources market just as it does in the retail and commercial customer markets. Since banking is a service business (which means that much of what customers buy from banks is labor, human acts, and performances), the attraction of the best people resources, and the retention and motivation of them, becomes crucial indeed.

What is required is good marketing or, more specifically, good *internal marketing.* Internal marketing concerns thinking of employees as internal customers, thinking of jobs as internal products, and, just as with external marketing, seeking to design these internal products to meet the needs of these internal customers while satisfying the objectives of the organization. The rationale for internal marketing is the same as that for external marketing: The probabilities of attracting, retaining, and motivating the best possible customers (internal/external) are greater if need-meeting products are offered to them in exchange for their resources (labor/money).

The first third of the Chapter briefly reviewed a number of challenges associated with the people resources market that, in a collective sense, enlarge the importance of good internal marketing. Discussed were the changing values of the American labor force, the pressures and intricacies of affirmative action, the soon-to-intensify competition with thrift institutions for banking personnel, the increasing proportion of "nonbanker" specialists employed by banks, the need to foster more and better personal selling in banking, the growing size and complexity of banking institutions, and the threat of unionization.

Most of the remainder of the Chapter was devoted to a discussion of some of the strategies and implementation programs that could be (and we believe, increasingly will be) used to improve and to enhance the internal products (jobs) that financial institutions sell. The discussion focused on specific programs in the areas of organizational communications, career development and growth, and compensation. Repeatedly stressed throughout this discussion was the need to recognize and act upon the inherent uniqueness of the individual. One commonality surfacing in the discussions of such diverse concepts as feedback, career pathing, and cafeteria benefits was the idea that *market segmentation* (recognizing that people are different and tailoring offerings for their specific needs) is no less relevant to internal marketing than to external marketing.

With this analysis of the people resources market now behind us, we turn in the next chapter to a discussion of still another of banking's important markets—the investors market.

FOOTNOTES

1. Studs Terkel, *Working* (New York: Pantheon, 1974).
2. Leonard L. Berry, "People Want a Bank That Cares," *American Banker*, September 22, 1976, p. 4.
3. Anthony J. D'Ermes, "Revolution and Social Change," *Bank Administration*, Volume 48, January 1972, p. 28.
4. See "Discrimination Cases Still on the Rise," *Banking*, September 1976, p. 14.

5. See Marylin Mathis and David H. Jones, "Finding More Women and Minorities for Management-Level Jobs," *Banking*, March 1974, pp. 94–100.

6. Frederick Deane, Jr., "The Woman as Banker: A Viewpoint," remarks made before the National Conference of the National Association of Bank Women, September 23, 1974, Orlando, FL, p. 12.

7. S. Wayne Bazzle, "Banks and Their People in the World of Tomorrow," remarks made before the National Personnel Conference of the American Bankers Association, September 18, 1974, Minneapolis, MN, p. 16.

8. Leonard L. Berry and James H. Donnelly, Jr., *Marketing for Bankers* (Washington, DC: American Bankers Association and American Institute of Banking, 1975), pp. 158–9.

9. Bazzle, p. 5.

10. Berry and Donnelly, p. 161.

11. See, for example, Wayne K. Kirchner and Marvin D. Dunnette, "The Successful Salesman—As He Sees Himself," *Personnel*, November-December 1958, pp. 67–70; Thomas R. Wotruba, "An Analysis of the Salesman Selection Process," *Southern Journal of Business*, January 1970, pp. 41–51; William D. Litzinger, "Interpersonal Values and Leadership Attitudes of Bank Branch Managers," *Personnel Psychology*, Summer 1965, pp. 193–198; and Robert W. Haas, "The Missing Link in Bank Marketing," *Atlanta Economic Review*, January–February 1974, pp. 35–39.

12. David Mayer and Herbert M. Greenberg, "What Makes a Good Salesman," *Harvard Business Review*, July-August 1964, pp. 119–125.

13. "New Study: Whither Bank Unionization?" *Banking*, December 1975, p. 8.

14. "Tomorrow's Banker," *United States Investor/Eastern Banker*, February 23, 1976, p. 6.

15. W. Earl Sasser and Stephen P. Arbeit, "Selling Jobs in the Service Sector," *Business Horizons*, June 1976, p. 64.

16. D'Ermes, p. 28.

17. Norwood W. Pope, "Motivating Personnel in the Multi-Bank Holding Company," *Bank Marketing*, February 1974, p. 15.

18. As presented in John Zenger, "Increasing Productivity: How Behavioral Scientists Can Help," *Personnel Journal*, October 1976, p. 514.

19. As quoted in Herbert E. Meyer, "How the Boss Stays in Touch With the Troops," *Fortune*, June 1975, p. 153.

20. G. M. Hostage, "Quality Control in a Service Business," *Harvard Business Review*, July-August 1975, p. 104.

21. "Visible Management at United Airlines," an interview with Edward E. Carlson, *Harvard Business Review*, July-August 1975, p. 92.

22. Zenger, p. 514.

23. See J. Richard Hackman, Greg Oldham, Robert Janson, and Kenneth Purdy, "A New Strategy for Job Enrichment," *California Management Review*, Summer 1975, pp. 57–71.

24. D'Ermes, p. 30.
25. Jeffrey Weersing, "Preparing Today's Banker for Tomorrow," *Bank Marketing*, October 1976, pp. 59–61.
26. Paul L. Matson, "Bank's Criteria Could Be Met Only by a Tailor-made Affirmative Action Program," *Banking*, November 1976, pp. 46–47.
27. Richard B. Frantzreb, "Staff Planning and Development: Improving Skills for Motivating," *Bank Administration*, December 1975, p. 27.
28. Hostage, pp. 103–104.
29. Arthur M. Whitehill, Jr., "Maintenance Factors: The Neglected Side of Worker Motivation," *Personnel Journal*, October 1976, p. 516.
30. Edward E. Lawler III, "New Approaches to Pay: Innovations That Work," *Personnel*, December–October 1976, pp. 11–12.
31. Geoff Brouillette, "Truex, an Outsider, Used Inside Talent in Speeding Rainier Turnaround," *American Banker*, January 27, 1977, p. 10.
32. For more discussion of this topic, see Dr. R. Pierce Lumpkin, "Cost Management," *United States Banker*, August 1977, pp. 6–9.
33. Lawler, p. 14.
34. See, for example, William D. McCluskey, "Cross-Utilization of Clerical Personnel," *Bank Administration*, April 1974, pp. 18–22.
35. Lawler, p. 12.
36. McCluskey, p. 13.
37. "Fringe-Benefit Costs Rise Sharply," *Banking*, January 1977, p. 21.
38. Robert Stuart Nathan, "The Scheme That's Killing the Rat-Race Blues," *New York*, July 18, 1977, pp. 36–37.
39. The last several paragraphs have been based on Warren Magoon and Larry Schnicker, "Flexible Hours at State Street Bank of Boston: A Case Study," *The Personnel Administrator*, October 1977, pp. 34–37.
40. Nathan, p. 36.

13 ACTION STRATEGIES: INVESTORS MARKET

INTRODUCTION

The investors market that provides financial capital in the form of debt and equity is proposed as the final principal market. In combination with the two customer markets—commercial and retail—the people-resources market, and the delivery system, the market in which banks and other financial institutions acquire growth and expansion funds constitutes an effective planning framework.

An additional source of funds remains that has some of the characteristics of deposits as well as some of the characteristics of financial capital. Purchased funds (e.g., Federal funds, large certificates of deposits) may be acquired from customers (like deposits) or from investors (like capital). In contrast to capital funds, they are used for operating purposes, much like short-term liabilities of nonfinancial corporations. Purchased funds typically are short-term and even when acquired from customers are only a tangential part of the relationship. Thus, stategies for procuring purchased funds will be discussed in conjunction with strategies for procuring capital funds.

The results of even a casual environmental analysis indicate a rising need for capital and operating funds to finance the expansion necessary to meet the credit needs of a growing economy. For example, the development of new energy sources and the optimal utilization of existing resources will require massive outlays of investment dollars by the private sector. Much of this investment will be in the form of bank borrowings; in turn, banks will require adequate levels of capital to support these borrowings.

Banks and other financial institutions also will require larger amounts of capital to facilitate internal growth programs, particularly for those many needs associated with a transition to an electronic environment or to "department stores of finance" operating on a regional or trade area basis.

Accordingly, a careful examination of the sources of capital and operating funds in terms of a market in which financial institutions must perform is critical. In this chapter, we will address the functions of capital, projected capital needs and availability, and then target a series of strategies that apply marketing principles to the management and acquisition of capital from investor markets. We also will address the expanding role of operating funds and appropriate strategies for acquiring such funds.

PURPOSE AND FUNCTIONS OF CAPITAL

The use of capital in commercial banks and other financial institutions tends to be more complicated than in other types of business organizations because of the unique depositor relationship. Investors in a bank's (or other corporation's) debt and equity securities explicitly acknowledge the risk that earnings performance may not be adequate enough to support interest or dividend payments; possibly (though in practice, very rarely), principal may not be returned. However, depositors expect that their arrangement with a financial institution will be virtually risk-free. A bank or savings and loan association, after all, is *safekeeping* their funds.

Depositor confidence is based on an assumed conservatism in a bank's activities that reflects a combination of managerial prudence and governmental deposit insurance and regulation. For more than forty years, this confidence has been warranted, since no fully insured depositor has ever suffered a loss. The same cannot be said for creditors and stockholders.

In contrast with industrial organizations that obtain the bulk of their operating and capital resources from creditors and stockholders, banks and thrift institutions acquire most of their funds from depositors. Among commercial banks, the typical equity to total assets ratio ranges from six to nine percent. Only among aggressive holding companies is debt a sizeable contributor to total funds.

It is apparent, therefore, that financial institutions are able to stretch a limited capital base further than industrial organizations. Because of public concern for depositor safety, this greater degree of leverage makes it even more important that banks and thrift institutions be assisted and supervised by governmental authorities. In addition to Federal deposit insurance (more than ninety-five percent of all banks and thrifts have individual accounts insured to $40,000), one or more Federal and state regulatory agencies are involved in the chartering, supervision, and examination of these institutions (see Chart 8.1). Examination and supervision serve a variety of functions but one of the most important is a continuing evaluation of the adequacy of equity capital. Unless capital is adequate in a regulator's judgment, affiliate acquisition or branching applications will be denied. If it is inadequate or impaired, loans may have to be reduced or, at the very least, growth will be halted.

There is no need to review the many technical aspects of this issue. The point is that commercial banks and other shareholder-owned financial institutions must consider not only the attitudes of the investor markets in developing capital management and acquisition strategies, but also the attitudes of the regulatory authorities, equally with respect to total capital, the composition of the capital base, and the use of purchased funds.

Emerging Issues

The entire area of depositor confidence and protection, financial institution regulation, and capital adequacy pose several critical issues that were being widely debated at the time of this writing; these should be considered in formulating strategies.

Before discussing these issues, an explanatory note is necessary. All commercial banks, of course, are owned by shareholders. Among thrift institutions, savings banks and credit unions are organized as *mutuals*; that is, they are owned by depositors, and their capital takes the form of retained earnings or surplus. They do not seek equity capital from investor markets. The nation's savings and loan industry is comprised of both mutual and stock associations. Legislation before Congress in the 1960s and 1970s would have permitted relatively easy conversion from mutual to stock charters, and, if enacted, the prevailing view was that large numbers of mutual institutions would elect this option. That they might bears on the following discussion in the sense that the prospect of mutual institutions converting to stock charter must eventuate in more competition in the investor markets—that is, more organizations seeking growth and expansion funds, thereby affecting projections regarding the availability and price of captial.

Emerging issues to be considered in formulating capital strategies include the following:

1. As banks have experienced rapid growth, equity capital to asset ratios have declined. How much further can they be permitted to decline? How much further can they be permitted to decline without impairing depositor confidence and safety? A related issue is the sizeable discrepancy from one financial institution to another in equity capital to asset ratios. For example, some banks maintain ratios as high as nine to ten percent, while ratios in other banks, particularly the larger money center banks, might be half as high or less. How will regulators view such discrepancies in light of the heightened public policy concerns arising from the economic and financial debacle of 1973–1975?

2. A number of different forms of debt capital such as long-term debentures and subordinated notes (usually with five to seven year maturities) have been appearing more frequently on bank and bank holding company balance sheets. Clearly secondary in claim to depositors and, of course, not covered by deposit insurance, how should they be viewed in testing for capital adequacy? Also at issue is the appropriate degree

of nondeposit leverage, and thus the magnitude of debt to equity ratios.

3. Since the early 1960s, banks have become more and more aggressive in acquiring purchased funds. Also, bank holding companies have sold commercial paper in substantial quantities to provide funds to operate bank-related affiliates. To what extent are these activities prudent? How do they affect the need for capital, especially equity capital?

4. Capital supports a bank's assets, some of which tend to be more liquid than others, with the least liquid being loans generally as contrasted with cash assets and short-term government securities. In this respect, high and/or rising loan to deposit ratios become a capital adequacy issue. How high was one hotly contested argument. What mix was another.

5. Traditionally, banks have followed conservative lending practices compared to other types of lenders. The expansion of bank holding companies into bank-related fields such as leasing, factoring, and construction lending during an era of rapid and inflated economic activity, however, contributed to more aggressive lending policies. A greater element of risk was inevitable. To be sure, many holding companies enjoyed improved earnings performances as a result; some did not; and a number of them encountered serious reverses in such areas as real estate lending as the 1973–1975 recession deepened. This is history. Nonetheless, an issue for the future is how the degree of risk in the asset creation process should be managed. More precisely, what is the proper role of the regulatory authorities in controlling the degrees of risk inherent in various lending activities?

6. Currently, depositors are protected in a general way by deposit insurance and supervisory procedures. Federal insurance, however, directly covers only a *portion* of total deposits—most, but not all. Is there a better approach to depositor protection, particularly one-hundred percent insurance? Are there others? Will they be forthcoming? Although supervisory procedures are similar, they are not necessarily standard for all banks, as evidenced by the dif-

ference in permissible maximum loans to single borrowers among national banks and state banks, or the difference in member bank and nonmember reserve requirements. Is the trend toward standardization, perhaps through a Federal Banking Commission? Is the prospect of compulsory membership in the Federal Reserve System, at least with respect to reserve requirements for banks and other institutions engaged in funds transfers, likely, possible, or improbable?

It is uncertain how these and a number of related issues will be resolved in the years ahead. Nonetheless, an awareness of each must be reflected in a bank's formulation of capital management and acquisition strategies.

PROJECTED CAPITAL NEEDS

In evaluating capital needs, financial institutions must consider requirements imposed by the regulatory authorities, expected asset growth, projections of investment in people and equipment, investor and investment analyst attitudes, and economic conditions.

As we have seen, the requirements of the respective regulatory authorities have become difficult to determine precisely; they are changing, evolving, taking new shape and direction. Very much at issue is the very broad question of capital adequacy and what constitutes capital adequacy; moreover, the various regulators have different views in this controversial issue. Where all reach agreement, however, is in their concern for a bank's historical performance and future plans. Adequacy and thus need is determined by a bank's track record over a number of years and by its evaluation of growth and expansion plans—not visions and "guesstimates," but well-reasoned projections documented by hard facts.

Strength, Growth, and Investment Needs

Most long-range projections of economic activity assume the continued existence of a fluctuating business cycle. They assume that *volatility* rather than *stability* will prove the norm during the foreseeable future. Whereas in the 1960s the New Frontier economists contended that proper use of monetary and fiscal policies could smooth the business cycle substantially, it since has become apparent that such an accomplishment is beyond the scope of existing policy tools. Moreover, the high priority national economic goals of full employment and rapid growth, as pursued with macroeconomic policies, are likely to push the economy up to and even beyond capacity again and again, thereby fueling the fires of inflation. This process occurred three times between 1965 and 1975; the common view is that it appears likely to continue, with the net effect of sharply exacerbating business cycle fluctuations.

Strength

Substantial shifts in the demand for goods and services, the rate of unemployment, the rate of inflation, the availability of credit, and levels of interest rates that result from this *politicization* of economic policy making lead banking (and other businesses) to become that much riskier. Loans that appear perfectly sound during a period of economic expansion can become major problems during a downturn. Sources of funds, especially purchased funds, that are highly reliable during periods of easy money can dry up quickly in a credit crunch, and then reappear with surprising speed as recovery sets in. Although managing assets and liabilities in the expectation of more volatile economic conditions is the most important ingredient for avoiding excessive losses, greater capital strength also is desirable. In addition to the attention that this issue receives from regulators, investors likewise are aware of the need for capital strength as a means of demonstrating an ability to withstand losses. To maintain the lowest overall cost of capital, a bank must manage the various components of its balance sheet so as to control overall risk exposure. In this sense, the cost and probably the availability of capital are not separate from but interrelated to *risk management*.

Growth

As the total assets of a financial institution grow due to economic expansion and aggressive management policies, operating and capital funds must grow commensurately. Depending on the dividend pay-out ratio, a large measure of capital growth will come from retained earnings. The remainder must be procured in the capital markets.

In the 1960s and early 1970s, the tendency among banking organizations (and nonfinancial corporations as well) was to fund most of their external capital needs with debt rather than equity. An atmosphere of rapid and sustained economic growth supported this approach, allowing leverage to contribute to earnings. When economic conditions subsequently deteriorated, the interest cost of the debt became burdensome and investors regarded leverage less favorably. Banking organizations placed greater emphasis on acquiring equity; however, the widespread weakness in common stock values, which persisted well into the ensuing economic recovery, limited their ability to procure capital. In particular, the problems encountered by large one-bank and multi-bank holding companies during the 1973–1975 recession had sapped their aura as glamor stocks. Actual and potential earnings performance notwithstanding, Wall Street's interest in these issues dimmed.

Future growth prospects for banks and other financial institutions appear favorable, indicating substantial operating and capital funds needs. Because of the large, total investment requirements of American industry (especially to improve the quality of the environment while developing new sources of energy), the financial sector is expected to play an expanding role in facilitating economic activity. It is also likely that the financing needs of governmental authorities—state, local, and Federal—will continue to expand in response to public policy imperatives. Therefore, either directly or indirectly, banks will be expected to accommodate these needs.

Then, too, many observers contend that as the massive financing requirements of the economy become more widely apparent to legislators and regulators, banks will be permitted to operate interstate and to acquire additional bank-related institutions. If so, the funds needs of aggressive banks and holding companies will expand even more rapidly. In fact, estimates of bank capital needs, when separated into amounts acquired internally versus externally, indicate that these organizations will be making larger (that is, seeking more dollars than in the past) and more frequent trips to investor markets, especially equity markets.[1]

This contention and its implications will be treated elsewhere in this chapter, along with a discussion of proposed solutions. First, however, another dimension of banking's funds needs requires attention.

Investment

While American industry is engaging in an extensive investment in plant and equipment, banks and other financial institutions also will be making substantial fixed asset investments of their own. It is not overly dramatic, for example, to suggest that the cost of financing the transition to an electronic banking environment will be enormous. Thus, at least for a while, any given growth rate of loans and deposits will require increasing amounts of capital to support an expansion of fixed assets in the form of electronic equipment and support systems. Moreover, as discussed in Chapter 12, as the nature of the banking business becomes more complex and customers demand higher quality service, education and training programs will be expanded materially to prepare employees not to mention customer groups.

These programs are costly and will bite into earnings, although over the long term probably will contribute to their improvement. More important, however, lower earnings levels mean diminished *internal* sources of capital (earning retention) and a greater reliance on *external* investor markets as a source of capital.

In summary, the projected capital and operating funds needs of banks and other financial institutions will be considerable. This will be due to various factors such as:

- the on-going concern of the regulatory authorities with the capital adequacy issue
- the need to bolster the equity base following a period of extensive debt financing and weak common stock prices

- the expected role of the financial sector in facilitating the growing investment needs of industry and government
- the fixed asset investments required of financial institutions to enter successfully into the world of electronic banking

THE MARKETPLACE

There are many buyers in the marketplace for bank debt and equity, and they possess different degrees of sophistication, different levels of purchasing power, and certainly different attitudes and perceptions. These differences will be recognized in subsequent discussions of capital management and capital acquisition strategies. It will become apparent that banks are competing in a very broad marketplace and must employ effective segmentation techniques if they are to perform satisfactorily.

Until the mid-1970s, banks and holding companies depended almost entirely on the traditional financial markets. They went to Wall Street and other financial centers to sell debt and equity and to market commercial paper and large-denomination certificates of deposit.

This audience was a sophisticated one; chiefly, it was the institutional investor and the perceptive, market-wise individual. The marketplace was the pension trust, the investment banker, a commercial bank trust department, the private speculator, and the mutual fund manager. Each of these target segments was backed by the raw size of its purchasing power, the wisdom of analysts, data available from increasingly detailed bank annual report and quarterly statements, and the data required to satisfy the Securities and Exchange Commision's disclosure requirements. It was, on balance, a *professional marketplace.*

It can be fairly said that this marketplace turned cautious with respect to bank offerings during the 1973–1975 recession and its aftermath. As already explained, bank equities no longer were among Wall Street's glamor issues. Debt, even at a competitive price, was less easy to sell; its sale was even more of a problem if a banking organization tended to be of a relatively small size, highly leveraged, or located in a region considered economically depressed or overstrained by recessionary developments. Even the acquisition of very short-term funds, including Federal funds, became more difficult.

Accordingly, a growing number of banking organizations began turning inward, away from traditional money centers toward their own geographic markets. Cheif executives and finance officers, for example, began "telling and selling" brokers and leadership groups in countryside communities. Employee stock purchase plans and dividend reinvestment programs became more commonplace and more intensely marketed. Newspaper advertisements and savings account statement stuffers called attention to subordinated debt issues offered directly by the company at competitive rates (sometimes one-third higher than savings account rates) and available in denominations as low as $500 with maturities ranging between five and seven years.

In effect, a "new" marketplace was being identified and structured—i.e., the bank employee and the bank customer. *Banking began retailing debt and equity.* Most important, levels of investor purchasing power and knowledge, and, we would add, performance expectations tended to differ from the needs and capacities of institutional investors and the professional marketplace.

One critical difference illustrates this point. The institutional investor by its nature is not inherently loyal. It tends generally to move in and out of the marketplace in search of high performance, with evident impacts on price structures in the relatively "thin" market for bank stocks.

By way of contrast, the employee or local customer evidences great loyalty as an equityholder. This investor will stick with a banking organization in good times as well as bad times. In this respect, bank managements proved delighted in the postrecession period when, commonly, numbers of shareholders increased without a comparative rise in either stock prices or number of shares outstanding. That more loyal, more stable "little man" had distinctively, individually become part of the marketplace for bank equity.

The same proved true with respect to debt instruments. Commercial paper sales, while nearly impossible in national markets by all but the largest holding companies, flourished in local markets. This investor evidenced interest in accepting longer maturities and a willingness to purchase refinancings.

Admittedly, these contrasts are generalizations. However, they serve an important purpose in depicting the wider scope of the marketplace for bank debt and equity and its implicit differences with respect to felt needs and wants.

PROJECTED CAPITAL AVAILABILITY

The ability of the American economy to generate the level of financing and investment necessary to ensure an ever-rising standard of living was widely debated in the years following the 1973–1975 recession.[2]   An optimistic assessment of this debate might be that although a rising standard of living is not in serious jeopardy, the investors market will not soon provide funds as readily at attractive rates as during much of the postwar era. The reasons for this assessment are detailed and complex; therefore, the following discussion is limited to a review of the major considerations likely to affect a bank's capital management and acquisition strategies.

Major Considerations

Two factors appear to be at the heart of the concern over future investment sector performance and capital availability. First, during the 1973–1975 recession, investment activity deteriorated substantially.   Gross private domestic investment, including expenditures by business for plant, equipment, and inventories and by consumers for housing, fell precipitously in real terms. Even after a recovery in consumer spending was well under way, the investment sector was slow to respond. Many observers were certain that something was fundamentally wrong with the investment sector. One result has been forecasts of long-term inadequate investment and sluggish economic activity; said differently, discussion focused on "a matured economy" and lower levels of real growth. Second, there was concern about the overall capability of the economy and the financial sector to generate sufficient funds. At issue here are a variety of considerations:

- the general bias of tax policies and other governmental policies in favor of consumption as opposed to saving and investment, which in part explains banking's continuing dialogue over Regulation Q ceilings
- the inability of capital consumption allowances (depreciation) to keep pace with replacement costs in an inflationary environment
- the rapid growth of government spending, much of which comes from nontax sources, thus competing with private borrowers for necessarily limited supplies of credit
- the resulting continual stimulative effect of fiscal policy, which requires major reliance on monetary policy through intervention in the financial markets to achieve economic stabilization

None of these considerations is readily quantifiable, but they are very real; for the planner, they indeed are pervasive and should not be taken lighly. On balance, this appraisal of first, demand for capital, and then supply, indicates clearly that for banks and other financial institutions, performance in the investor markets during the years ahead will require the same kind of high quality and marketing-based strategies employed in the two customer and people-resources markets.

STRATEGIES FOR PERFORMING IN THE INVESTORS MARKET

The issue of bank capital management has been stated succinctly by former First Deputy Comptroller of the Currency Justin T. Watson:

. . . there is no amount of capital that will salvage a bank that is grossly mismanaged. Conversely, a strong, well-managed bank can operate on a very thin capital base.[3]

Overall management quality and management of existing capital thus are important determinants of both the need for capital *and* the ability to generate it.

Funds Management Strategies

During the past quarter-century, bank management strategies have shifted in emphasis from asset management (the 1950s), to liability management (the mid to later 1960s), to asset-liability management (the early 1970s), and finally to capital management (the mid-1970s). What this really suggests is that banks have discovered that all balance sheet components are mutually interdependent and that only total balance sheet management can produce the earnings performance necessary to maintain depositor confidence and attract new capital.

Total balance sheet management recognizes the relationship between the retail customer as net supplier of funds and the commercial customer as net user of funds. Thus, despite the more competitive nature of retail banking expected in the future, for all but the largest banking organizations, a balanced approach to these different types of customers will be necessary. Retail customers will be sought largely for deposits and commercial customers chiefly for loans. But even within these catagories a balanced approach must be taken. After all, consumers want loans as well as financial assets and business likewise needs both. The resulting balance, and how it is created and administered, emerges as the true test of managerial skill.

Total balance sheet management also focuses attention on the relationship between risk management and capital strength; particularly in the asset creation process, risk must be managed carefully so that unavoidable errors in judgment are not so great as to threaten capital unduly. Recognition of the degree of risk that is appropriate for varying quantities of capital and the composition of the capital structure is important.

Total balance sheet management recognizes the role of purchased funds in terms of such considerations as liquidity, overall risk, and cyclical fluctuations in economic activity. This contrasts to the outdated concept of liability management, which viewed purchased funds almost in isolation.

These realities are the preconditions for appropriate funds management strategies; their emphasis is on making the most of existing operating and capital funds. At the same time, however, they position a banking organization to achieve readier access to the investors market.

Funds Acquisition Strategies

To perform successfully in the investors market (that is, to obtain sufficient *quantities* and *kinds* of funds at *acceptable costs* or price) banks must apply basic marketing concepts systematically. Satisfactory performance, simply enough, requires both knowing the customers' needs and wants and then satisfying them. *Securities are a product; just like a deposit, they must be marketed.* The product and selling techniques must be researched, packaged, priced, costed, and promoted—i.e., *marketed.* This is the essence of modern funds acquisition strategies; banks are offering a product in a marketplace, just as they do with commercial and retail customers and in acquiring, training, and maintaining skilled people resources.

Researching Investor Needs

As noted by officials of two large money center banks, ". . . it is important to understand the objectives of the investment community and to adapt company policies to satisfy those objectives."[4]   Most important are investor perceptions of their own investment objectives and of a bank's performance. In the 1960s and early 1970s, institutional investors and other professional investors generally were looking for growth stocks; at the same time, they began to perceive that banks and bank holding companies met these criteria. It has been explained that the recession experience caused a shift in investor objectives to a more conservative posture, one that led these investors to demand earnings *stability* from banking organizations. However, their perceptions of banks as stable earners appeared slow to materialize, as evidenced by the relatively depressed prices of bank stocks well into the middle stages of the postrecession recovery. To some extent their reluctance was attributed to the shock waves caused by the failure of such large organizations as Franklin National of New York and banking's heady involvement in REITs. Perceptions notwithstanding, the fact is that bank earnings during this period were quite stable.

Nonetheless, this brief summary illustrates the highly volatile nature of investor wants, needs, and perceptions. They cannot be taken for granted. On a continuing and structured basis, they must be identified through such skillful and systematic research procedures as on-going working relationships with professional investors and analysts, or shareholder and debt-holder surveys. In effect, an on-going environmental analysis is required.

Although straightforward and perhaps simplistic on the surface, knowing and evaluating investor needs requires more than the part-time, cursory attention of a low-ranking staff officer or supervisor. This vital task is best assigned to a bank's corporate treasurer, who presumably is competent in financial analysis and comprehends well the workings of financial markets. In many instances, investment bankers, brokers, and analysts will be contacted at both regional and national levels. To be fruitful, interaction with these buyers and opinion-makers should be frequent and active, not passive. The objectives of the corporate treasurer are first to solicit information about the marketplace and then to provide the marketplace with up-to-date, totally honest information about the organization's performance. In a very real sense, the bank's treasurer must function as a "calling officer." He or she is selling; the difference is that the treasurer is borrowing (selling securities) rather than lending funds. The same disciplines and hard work are required as in making a good loan and keeping it that way.

Earnings Emphasis

First and foremost, professional investors (even less sophisticated ones!) want the highest possible rate of return for a given degree of risk. The ultimate source of that return is the earnings performance of the bank or other financial organization. Serious, permanent investors rarely purchase an institution's securities based on this quarter's or next quarter's earnings. Rather, they seek expectations of strong and stable future earnings as evidenced by historical performance, management quality, market position, and, frankly, the influence of various external forces such as bank image.   In this respect, the Franklin National debacle had far-ranging implications. For example, although no seller of Federal funds experienced any losses on such transactions during the last credit crunch, by 1977 it had become common practice for borrowers of Federal funds to acquire a formal, approved line with potential sellers.

Capital Planning and Marketplace Timing

A systematic and well-researched analysis of future capital needs raises the likelihood of dealing with the investment community under the most favorable circumstances. Expansion plans, investment needs, debt refinancings, and new equity financings generally can be anticipated well in advance. They can be described, documented, and explained; they can be understood; they can be made attractive or inducive. Since the cost and availability of capital funds is likely to fluctuate considerably during the future business cycles, it appears advantageous to strike hard at the right time— to concentrate financings when the funds are most plentiful and least costly, *even if the capital may not be required immediately*. The trick is having it when you need it; if it already is there, so much the better, particularly for planning purposes.

Disclosure and Financial Analyst Relations

Traditionally, banks and other financial institutions have disclosed detailed financial information only through examination reports, which are not available to depositors and investors. This began changing in the 1960s as banking organizations became more frequent visitors to the capital markets. In time, and with considerable pressure from the SEC, banks began disclosing far more financial data than ever before, including detailed explanations of loan losses, nonaccruing asset schedules, and investment portfolio holdings.

The literature on this subject, especially how much disclosure is appropriate, is extensive. In brief, increased meaningful disclosure has become necessary in establishing productive relationships with the investment community and the regulatory authorities. The same, incidentally, applies to relationships with the media and other opinion-makers. Good reporters and financial writers, it is said, can read a balance sheet; whether a truism or a myth, a banking organization cannot afford to be indifferent to the implications of media interpretations, especially where it is dependent on local investor markets.

Many bank holding companies began making annual presentations to security analysts in financial centers (New York, Chicago, Boston, San Francisco, and the hometown was a common circuit) in the late 1960s and thereafter. Initially, and perhaps unfortunately, many of these excursions were designed to impress rather than inform. One inevitable consequence was a building of expectations among investors, professional and otherwise, that proved nearly impossible for individual organizations to satisfy over any extended period of time.

A review of the literature combined with the authors' "on-line" experience in either developing or observing analyst presentations suggests these fundamental guidelines:

- keep presentations short and to the point
- be candid—you're dealing with professionals
- in talking of the future, identify weaknesses as well as strengths
- offer an accurate, dispassionate portrayal of management's business philosophy, policies, attitudes, and perspectives
- avoid "iffy" estimates; document accomplishments and projections and avoid glib generalities

Moreover, the actual presentation is only one portion of a total, on-going relationship with financial analysts; they require a continuous, regular flow of information regardless of the state of the economy, the banking industry, or the individual banking organization. They want to know how well the bank is performing as well as what it is planning to do; they want to know what senior management is thinking, saying, and doing; they want, in sum, communications that earn a reputation for being complete, timely, and accurate.

Finally, it has become apparent that financial institutions must make a special effort in dealing with nonprofessional investors. This is because so few of them really understand how banks operate, how they generate earnings, and why they need capital. These investors are particularly important to regional bank holding companies selling commercial paper directly to individuals in their trade area. The onus is not on the marketplace—the buyer—but rather the seller.

Innovative Approaches

Given a projected heavy demand for funds in the face of limited availability, different approaches for appealing to specific segments of the investors market undoubtedly will be necessary.

Both before and after the recession of the early 1970s, a number of regional holding companies began selling small denomination debt instruments to current security holders, customers, and bank employees. Many of these issues, as previously explained, earned interest well above Regulation Q ceilings and tended to have intermediate-term maturities. Usually, these issues were purchased at a discount for resale by regional brokerage firms; some holding companies, however, sold their note issues directly.

Other such innovative approaches included the following:

- dividend reinvestment by existing shareholders
- employee stock purchase plans at discounted prices
- bank debt and equity instruments offered to customers through the investment division of money desk operations along with other securities and deposit-type accounts
- the addition of equity "sweeteners" to individual retirement accounts (IRAs) or Keogh Plan programs

In the mid-1970s, some banks were considering the legal problems that might arise from the selling of low-denomination forward contracts to consumer-investors on an instalment plan; these contracts ultimately could be converted into either preferred or common stock. Still another approach being considered was the payment of interest in the form of bank debt or equity on consumer certificates. Lest this idea be scoffed at, it will be recalled that some banks in the 1970s actually were paying interest in advance on large deposit accounts in the form of color TVs. What really is the difference between a consumer appliance and a consumer investment; what really is the difference except what each means to the consumer?

A different notion entirely was the idea that a form of equity kicker to be offered to commercial customers as an alternative to a prescribed level of compensating balances. Still another notion taken rather seriously was a so-called "Invest in Your Community" mutual fund, whereby a banking organization and a group of regional industrial and service organizations would join together in marketing a package of diversified equity shares.

Why not? *Indeed, why not is exactly the point.* The chairman and president of Bank of Virginia Company, Frederick Deane, Jr., in an address before the 26th Assembly for Bank Directors offered this critical perspective:

> Today and as a rapidly changing, increasingly competitive financial environment unfolds, our capital planning activities must emphasize
> - innovation . . . looking beyond customary ways of acquiring debt and equity;
> - less dependence on traditional markets for our funds;
> - a willingness to disclose more about our operations in order to satisfy prospective investors as well as regulators;
> - and, as an industry, we must take an active role in pushing for legislative and regulatory changes facilitating innovation and experimentation in the area of capital acquisition.[5]

Deane's comments and the innovative approaches discussed in this section are not advocacy positions favoring violation or circumvention of existing law. They do recognize, however, an awareness that few laws are engraved in stone, unalterable for all times. They recognize the natural link between innovation and progress. Above all, they suggest that if the present mechanisms for acquiring capital appear too limited, then part of any realistic answer involves contemplating change or modification.

In certain instances, we would add, it is apparent that existing laws born of another time and place and pertaining to the past should be changed. The Glass-Steagall Act of 1933 that still prohibits commercial banks from engaging in investment banking (and, as a result, prevents bank affiliates from selling parent holding company securities) is regarded by many as an anachronism. "Why not seek a change," we submit, is the frame of mind that should be adopted by bank managers and planners.

Capital Acquisition Techniques for Smaller Banks

Although the foregoing discussion of bank capital acquisition strategies has had special applicability to larger banks and holding companies, the need is by no means exclusive to this group. In the years ahead, community banks and smaller stock-owned thrifts will be confronted with rising capital needs, principally in the form of equity. One concern to be faced by smaller institutions is the prospect of more liberal branching. An effective competitive response may be branches of their own; however, building branches and obtaining regulatory approval requires additional capital. Because the capital markets traditionally have not been oriented toward smaller organizations, their problems in acquiring capital probably will be more acute than those experienced by larger institutions. This dilemma, moreover, could be compounded as larger institutions intensity efforts to raise capital in local as well as money center markets.

In any event, the need for innovative approaches to capital acquisition will exist among smaller banks. Moreover, it will be necessary to identify and to actively cultivate desirable segments of the investors market. Once this is done, the next task will be to package and promote satisfactory debt and equity programs, particularly among potential investors deemed most familiar with the organization. Many of the approaches applicable to larger banks such as the sale and/or self-sale of subordinated debt could prove effective. Others simply will not, largely because of size differences and locational restrictions. Then, too, smaller institutions often hesitate to sell equity, as doing so could work to dilute control or at least move portions of the ownership base outside local communities.

A vehicle that has become increasingly attractive because of favorable tax legislation is the employee stock ownership trust (ESOT). This program typically is used as a profit sharing mechanism, but the funds are invested in the institution's own common stock. The real benefit of the ESOT is that funds may be borrowed to purchase additional stock, thus increasing equity over the short run. Repayment of the loan is made out of future contributions to the plan from pretax earnings. Most important, perhaps, ESOT does not have the effect of diluting community ownership and control.

CONCLUSION

Investor markets are a third principal market, along with customer markets and people resources markets, in which financial institutions must perform. Capital funds provide the base for procuring deposits and making loans. As the needs of the community or communities served by banks and other financial institutions grow, their ability to take deposits and make loans must grow commensurately. Furthermore, the need for substantial investment in delivery systems and people resources will add to future capital requirements. At the same time, the demand for financial capital in general is expected to be enormous.

It is anticipated that the bulk of a banking organization's additional capital will come from retained earnings, a fact which emphasizes the need for strong and consistent earnings performance.

The remainder of operating and capital funds will come from *marketing* various types of securities to investors in an increasingly competitive marketplace. Marketing means just that: The product must be researched, packaged, priced, costed, and promoted. It must be sold. Vision and innovation will prove vital.

The development of successful funds acquisition programs, regardless of bank size and locational characteristics, begins with identifying the marketplace. This involves understanding its requirements (as well as the bank's needs) and matching them, equally in terms of dollar amounts and capital account composition. Finally, the regulatory authorities must be satisfied. Their primary concern is with the adequacy of capital and how it is managed. Management, as we have seen, is not separate from but interrelated with asset and liability management techniques.

FOOTNOTES

1. For example, see "The Challange Ahead for Banking," Revised Edition, Booz, Allen & Hamilton, Inc., Chicago, IL, 1972; Samuel Chase, "Bank Capital Needs," an unpublished paper presented to The American Bankers Association Planning Conference in Denver, CO, Fall, 1974; and "Capital Needs of Virginia Banks," Tayloe Murphy Institute, University of Virginia, 1974.
2. For example, see Barry Bosworth, James S. Duesenberry, and Andrew S. Carron, *Capital Needs in the Seventies* (Washington, DC: Brookings Institute, 1975); Benjamin Franklin "Financing the Next Five Years of Fixed Investment," in *Sloan Management Review*, Spring, 1975; *The Capital Needs and Savings Potential of the U.S. Economy, Projections Through 1985*, The New York Stock Exchange, New York, September, 1974.
3. Justin T. Watson, "A Regulatory View of Capital Adequacy," in *Journal of Bank Research*, Autumn, 1975, p. 171.
4. T. Carter Hagaman and Heibert J. Marks, "Earnings Stability: Key to the Equity Market," in *Journal of Bank Research*, Autumn, 1975, p. 183.
5. Frederick Deane, Jr., "Capital Needs in Banking," an address to the 26th Assembly of Bank Directors, Pinehurst, NC, November 7, 1976.

CONCLUSION

14 MANAGING, MARKETING, AND PLANNING

INTRODUCTION

Managing is planning. It is the systematic utilization of each of the various steps comprising the planning process in order to make informed managerial decisions that optimize performance in an environment likely to be characterized by more rapid change than in the past. Not only will the changes characterizing *Banking Tomorrow* accelerate at an increasingly faster pace, but their impact on operational procedures, customer service, and competitive relationships should prove profound, far-reaching, and often disturbing. Moreover, they certainly should generate as many challenges as opportunities.

The single, inexorable fact about the future is that it will be much different from today. Management recognizes this; managing comprehends the *futurity* of present decisions. This year's financial budget, next year's advertising campaign, current employment and training programs, the determination to install a "next generation" computer system, even shifts in the asset-liability mix or the capital structure—these all represent present decisions that influence if not prefigure performance in tomorrow's marketplace. These decisions possess an explicit futurity. Planning fulfills a critical purpose in this regard. The systematic development and continuing use of the planning process fosters an understanding of tomorrow's emerging, evolving environment; the parameters, at the very least, take on shape and substance. Accordingly, informed decisions can be readily made.

MANAGEMENT PLANS, NOT PLANNERS

The entire management of a banking or financial organization is involved in the planning process. The planning coordinator or planning council can be likened to a helmsman: He or she steers in an ordered direction; watches for storm clouds and shoals, indicates the need to come about as the wind changes, and observes carefully that sails and lines are correctly and systematically rigged. The coordinator is the watchful guide, not the captain or the mate.

Planning is accomplished by line and staff managers. Initially, the process begins at the executive level—i.e., with the commitment and on-going support of the chief executive officer. It then continues at the executive level with the determination of the organizational purpose or mission and the setting of objectives and goals.

Division level—the retail division, the commercial division, the international division—and departmental managers chiefly are concerned with the evolving of coordinated action strategies. At this point, executive management decides where the organization wants to be and should be at some time in the future. Division and department level managers, line and staff executives alike, focus on how the organization fulfills this mission.

The planning process continues down the organizational ladder, ultimately to return nourished with ideas, blueprints, hopes, and expectations i.e., *with plans*. At line and staff unit levels, managers and key officers and supervisors evolve implementation programs or tactics. Here is where strategies are tested, refined, fleshed-out, integrated, given distinctiveness, perhaps even discarded as unworkable or as overly complicated.

At this and all other levels, the components of planning and the decisions it generates, including decisions to do something as well as not act, are monitored. This final step in the planning process too commonly is subordinated, frequently even overlooked. Yet, it is the lifeblood of planning. It assures continuity, adjustment, accommodation, revision, and new vision.

In the end it is planning performed on a continuing basis that transforms individual managerial decisions into a management system. Managing utilizes planning; Planning makes efficient and effective management happen now and during the coming of tomorrow.

Planning offers no certain promise of success for any financial institution. However, it will heighten the prospect of success or, viewed differently, minimize the chance of failure.

Few observers believe that all of today's 14,000 commercial banks and many more thousand thrift institutions and specialized lenders will exist as independent institutions by the middle or end of the next decade. Assume this is valid. What characteristics, then, most likely will condition survival: size, geography, technological capacity, staff expertise and sophistication, quality of performance, the breadth of well-priced products and services, number of branches? Certainly all of these characteristics and probably many others. But few if any criteria will just happen or evolve as time passes; they must be recognized, prepared for, constructed, implemented, worked at continually, coordinated, and revised. They will not just happen; they must be planned to happen.

Planning applies to banks and other financial institutions regardless of size, locational factors, or even type of financial activity presently performed. On one hand, the planning process can be highly sophisticated, multi-disciplined, formally structured, and highly visible as an on-going corporate activity; conversely, planning can be the chief executive of a small bank with a common-sense perception of events and trends, an official who follows and implements month-by-month personalized, goal-oriented growth programs.

It is common in larger banking organizations for planning to be considered as an offensive activity. Planning's focus becomes being bigger, entering new markets, enlarging the product base, and expanding geographically. In a smaller institution, planning frequently acquires defensive overtones; for example, how to protect market share; how to compete with bigness and its presumed technological capacities; and how to avoid an intensification of market penetration and market competition. Either posture, however, indicates and supports the importance of planning. If the future is to be fewer but larger institutions, the common concern that underlies the need for planning is *survival*.

THE VALUE OF PLANNING

Above all, there really is a singularly important reason to bother with planning. It was identified in the opening sentence of this book: *What will tomorrow be like?*

Clearly it will be different from today, possibly much different. Beyond this point, there are few if any certainties.

The detailed environmental analysis comprising the four chapters of Unit Two assesses where we are today and how the present evolved. Given this fundamental understanding, certain speculations about *Banking Tomorrow* were offered. For the most part, these speculations and their predictive implications were conservative in nature.

It is not, however, particularly important that this environmental analysis rates extremely high in terms of probability within three years, five years, or even longer. We believe it is on target, but how precisely is secondary.

More to the point is that the conclusions reached in this environmental analysis are based on discernible, evolving trends that should reach maturity within the planner's accepted time horizon. They are strong probabilities shaping what tomorrow will be like. Being prepared for this future is what counts. Between now and then the wise build knowingly.

The chief concern of disciplined planners is when, in what form, and with what consequences for an organization this future will unfold. It is with the specific steps, if any, that might be taken now, next month, next year, or at some pinpointed moment ahead that will allow a banking organization to cope distinctively with the challenges and opportunities expected to shape an environment characterized at the very least by these factors:

- more competition from more competitors armed with more banklike powers

- the liberalization or easing of constraints (i.e., Regulation Q, Glass-Steagall, branching, etc.) applicable to serving the needs and wants of customers
- the intensification of consumerist concerns and the reality of changing and expanding public policy imperatives (i.e., the revitalization of the inner city and adequate, least costly energy self-sufficiency)
- the emergence of new economic realities, especially slower rates of real growth and sharply fluctuating business cycles
- the transition to an electronic banking era

The value of planning is its fundamental concern with a vision of tomorrow and the process of successful adaptation and performance. It is, once again, understanding the futurity of present decisions.

THE MARKETS APPROACH TO PLANNING

Planning can become all too easily a confused, stumbling, unproductive, wheel-spinning, hodgepodge activity unless there is a single, very basic reference point. There must be a framework that is understood and applicable equally in the lending division, trust, operations, and factoring affiliate, marketing, and personnel. *There must be a unifying element that by its very nature demands that attention continually and systematically be directed toward change.*

It is our contention that such a framework is provided through the markets approach to planning. This thesis forms the title of this book and its concluding chapter. In sum, successful, high performance banking in the world of tomorrow will be achieved by managing markets through the systematic utilization of planning procedures.

This concept is detailed in Chapter Nine. Its axial principle is that the *marketplace* is where change happens. It is where largely uncontrollable external changes occur that affect banking and financial organizations to varying degrees. This concept also summarizes the undeniable reality that "the customer is the business."

The *customer* is a broad range of attitudes and perceptions, hopes, goals, fancies, even illusions; but above all, the customer is wants and needs that demand satisfaction. The business of banking is serving customers at a profit.

If the *customer is the business*, then the idea of customer must be appreciated in its broadest sense. The customer is the consumer (retail), the corporation (commercial), the employee, and the investor. It is individuals and types of business activity as segments of these markets. It is people as individuals and people in their various collective interrelationships. It is people as local, state, and Federal government. It is people as men and women. It is people as the young and the aged. It is, most significantly, people always changing with respect to wants and needs.

We have identified three principal markets for financial institutions. The first is the *customers market*. It is divided along traditional lines as retail and commercial markets or consumer and business markets. Government certainly could be considered another major segment as could upstream and downstream correspondents and other nonbank financial institution customers. It is because they are less significant either in terms of being impacted by change or in terms of overall banking activity that they have been subordinated. But clearly planning applies to them.

Both retail and commercial customer markets are comprised of suppliers (depositors) and users (borrowers) of funds; these basic functions, along with the funds transfer process (checking account activity), induce a dynamic interplay linking these segments as a single marketplace. It need only be recalled that during the postwar era commercial customers have been net users of funds, while consumers have been net suppliers. Funds are banking's *product*, whether viewed as a term loan, a mortgage, or a credit card transaction. Advising customers on how best to use money is a *service* that banks and other financial institutions offer.

The second market is the *people resources market*. This is most readily identified as bank employees, the human resources that provide products and services to customer markets. It is especially appropriate to think of this market as a resource: a treasure to be husbanded, cultivated, cared for, and wisely used. This is precisely the requirement.   Optimal performance in the customers market depends as much as anything on a bank's people: their skill, motivation, training, and customer orientation.

Finally, we have identified the *market for financial resources* or, more exactly, the *investors market*.

Customers provide and use funds, but the extent to which funds expansion is permitted depends on a bank's capital structure.   In general, capital must grow in equal proportion.   There are two sources of capital, retained earnings and entrepreneurship or venture investment.   Our concern chiefly is with the latter source of growth and expansion funds; it is with strategies for acquiring debt and equity investment from institutional and nonprofessional investors.

It is evident that these three markets are interdependent.   Linking each into an effective whole is an organization's *delivery system*. The delivery system *is not* only a banking organization's computer-based technologies—i.e., the ATM, POS terminal, and the countless other bits and pieces associated with an electronic era.   Electronic technology is only one element in a delivery system, albeit an increasingly pervasive one.   Bricks-and-mortar branches, mini-banks, the credit card, the monthly customer statement, loan application forms, drive-in facilities, commercial loan production offices, loan-by-phone solicitations, the computer itself—all are coordinated, meshing, integral parts of the process whereby bank people *deliver* products and services to customers in a manner that satisfies needs and wants at a profit.

Each of these three principal markets has a competitive dimension.   Banks and other financial institutions *compete* (and, we believe, with increasing aggressiveness) for customers, for competent human resources, and for capital.

Each of these markets, we submit, will be where change occurs as the future unfolds.   Since the marketplace is the object of change, then it must be researched, studied, evaluated, and understood. This requirement explains the need for conducting an environmental analysis and assessing an institution's internal strengths and weaknesses.   What is learned from these critical beginning steps in the planning process becomes the basis for evolving a sense of purpose, and then formulating objectives, action strategies, and implementation procedures.

The markets approach to planning serves chiefly as a unifying element that channels decision making in a coordinated manner toward critical focal points. In this sense, planning becomes the disciplined allocation of *human* and *financial resources* through compatible manned and machine *delivery systems* in a manner that satisfies *customer* needs and wants at a profit.

People deliver financial services and products. Their capacity to perform—for example, to accept more deposits or make more loans—is determined by a bank's ability to increase capital, either through retained earnings or debt and equity acquisition programs. Serving customers more satisfactorily than the competition becomes the object of this activity, with performance generating profits. The idea of allocating resources implies decision making or continuing action within this framework. What emerges is a systematic or disciplined approach for coping with competition and change. What also takes clear shape is the need for *marketing to markets*.

MARKETS, MARKETING, AND THE MARKETING DEPARTMENT

Marketing is not the narrow idea of a marketing department in a financial organization that administers advertising, public relations, and market research programs. Rather, marketing is a philosophy of doing business, an activist philosophy that is customer-oriented. Each bank employee, though admittedly in differing ways, is a marketing person. He or she is involved in the process of delivering services and products to customers. The telephone operator is marketing when he or she helps a customer complete a car loan inquiries. The chief executive officer is marketing when he or she addresses a group of bank stock analysts. The branch manager is marketing when she or he helps a customer complete a car loan application. The operations officer is marketing when he or she devises loan or new account forms. The officer or staff member of a bank is marketing each time a direct or indirect customer interface occurs. *Marketing recognizes that the customer is the business*.

Marketing should also be understood as *selling*. Financial industry traditions have impeded acceptance of this understanding. Selling commonly connotes overly aggressive, pushy, hassling policies that conflict with such desired imagery as discretion, trust, dignity, and safety. But if the word is a negative, the concept, particularly for planning purposes, is not.

Selling signifies reaching out to customers, going to them rather than waiting for them to come to the bank. Selling symbolizes an intensification of competition in the marketplace. No less, it recognizes that in the Age of the People, the customer—investor, consumer, employee, corporation, government, etc.—"will be served, not used." Finally, selling defines performance criteria.

Accordingly, customer needs and wants are to be identified, targeted, and segmented; they must be researched before they can be approached. Beyond this, the product of money and financial service must be packaged, priced, costed, advertised, promoted, and then sold by people who comprehend what they are selling, why, and to what purpose. Effective selling means skilled people who are trained to sell. It means preparing the market to understand how the product helps them or in other ways provides satisfaction. It means, finally, the utilization of techniques and technologies that create a *distinctive* interest in one bank's product over another's. Selling is inducing the customer in a buyer's market to do his or her business with you, not your competitor.

SELLING AND PLANNING

The marketplace, that changing, ever more competitive arena of banking activity, is where products and services are sold. It is to whom we sell. The purpose of planning is to assure that a banking organization is selling the right products, at the right time, at the right price, and in the most efficient manner. Marketing, as distinct from selling, coordinates and activates the plan; it is the link between knowing what to sell and when, and then selling; it is a positive attitude necessitating action.

Planning defines and measures performance. It is the act of managing markets in a systematic fashion. Marketing comprehends the diverse, intricate characteristics of the marketplace and the need for distinctive approaches; it is the testing and sensing of the environment in which banks and other financial institutions operate. Acted on, marketing becomes selling.

What will tomorrow be like?

We don't know for sure, of course, but in all probability it will prove most rewarding to banks and other financial institutions that prepare for it—that understand, manage, and distinctively serve the marketplace, *that plan.*

INDEX